CONSPICUOUS
CRITICISM

∎

New Studies in American
Intellectual and Cultural History
THOMAS BENDER, *Series Editor*

■

CONSPICUOUS CRITICISM

∎

Tradition, the Individual, and Culture in American Social Thought, from Veblen to Mills

CHRISTOPHER SHANNON

THE JOHNS HOPKINS UNIVERSITY PRESS
BALTIMORE AND LONDON

This book has been brought to publication
with the generous assistance of the
Karl and Edith Pribram Endowment.

The Johns Hopkins University Press
2715 North Charles Street
Baltimore, Maryland 21218-4319
The Johns Hopkins Press Ltd., London

Library of Congress Cataloging-in-Publication Data
will be found at the end of this book.
A catalog record for this book is available from the British Library.

ISBN 0-8018-5151-3

For my parents

Contents

■

Preface and Acknowledgments

■

HISTORICAL WRITING ON American social science has tended to focus more on politics than on knowledge. American social science in the first half of the twentieth century appears as a story of intellectuals using social science to advance certain political agendas. Historians have figured the political battle lines of this story as humanism versus positivism, advocacy versus objectivity, and, more generally, democracy versus technocracy. These terms have reduced the history of American social science to yet another cycle of reform and reaction: the activism of the Progressive Era versus the scientism of the 1920s, the radicalism of the depression versus the deradicalization brought on by World War II and the cold war. The left-liberal orientation of much of this historical writing has proved incapable of seriously questioning the larger social-scientific project of the rational control of society, and thus incapable of dealing with social science as a historical problem of knowledge.

This book examines the cultural consequences of social science as a structure of thought apart from any specific political practice. It tells a story not of the rise and fall of "humanistic" social science but of the steady expansion of social-scientific rationality in general. Lest it become what it condemns, my argument proceeds via a close reading of a few social-scientific texts. These texts are by no means obscure, yet neither are they "representative" in the sense of having exerted a direct influence on American social science as a whole. The writings of Thorstein Veblen or C. Wright Mills have a centrality to American intellectual life that is inversely proportional to their influence within their specific disciplines. These texts, and those of Robert and Helen Lynd, John Dewey, and Ruth Benedict, achieve "representative" status by virtue of their direct confrontation with the representative problem of twentieth-century social science: the social consequences of historical and cultural consciousness.

THOSE WHO CAN'T PAY their debts acknowledge them. With this in mind, I would like to thank those who have made this book possible.

First of all, I thank the members of my dissertation committee: Jean-Christophe Agnew, Michael Denning, and James T. Fisher. Their patience with often rambling drafts and their tolerance of certain fundamental differences in worldview went above and beyond the call of duty. Special thanks goes to the late Christopher Lasch, who, despite battling with the illness that eventually claimed his life, read an entire draft of my dissertation. I am deeply indebted to him for his criticism and support. Among my graduate student colleagues, I thank Glenn Wallach and David Stowe for their encouragement and careful reading of most of the chapters of my dissertation. Glenn also provided helpful criticisms of a draft of the conclusion for this book, though I absolve him of all responsibility for its final content. Special thanks goes to Daniel Wickberg for many long conversations and for introducing me to John Owen King's *Iron of Melancholy,* without which I would not have been able to write this book. Finally, I thank James Wooten for his exhaustive knowledge of all things having to do with Max Weber.

For intellectual support, thanks to James Gibbin and Donne Masaki, whom I met while an undergraduate at the University of Rochester. They introduced me to intellectual history; through our conversations over the years, they have shaped much of my thinking on the issues addressed in this book.

Intellectual support alone does not a book produce. I also thank the Woodrow Wilson National Fellowship Foundation, whose grant of a Charlotte W. Newcombe Doctoral Dissertation Fellowship financed the final year of writing my dissertation, and the Job Service of Iowa, whose generous benefits helped in part to fund the revision of my dissertation into this book. Also on the funding front, I am grateful to Paul Gotham, Brian Keeler, and Father Thomas Mull of Sacred Heart Cathedral in Rochester, New York, for just enough employment to enable me to finish writing this book. Thanks also go to my sister, Jane Daloia, and her husband, Paul Daloia, for a quiet place to type in a crucial early stage of the revision process. I also thank Len Fetterly for some very economical duplicating of a revised version of the manuscript of this book.

Special thanks to the Dewey Ave. Boys (and Skirts), for everything.

Finally, and most importantly, I thank my parents, Joseph Francis and Ruth Margaret Shannon, for teaching me what books can't.

Introduction

∎

THE ANTHROPOLOGICAL idea of "culture" has provided twentieth-century American intellectuals with an ideology for the relentless textualization of everyday life through social-scientific inquiry. In this book I argue that the rise of "culture" as a mode of critical self-consciousness has fostered a destabilization of received social meanings necessary for the expansion of both consumer capitalism and critical thought itself. Indeed, critical, humanistic social science, so often arrayed against the market, has just as often been at the vanguard of extending the logic of commodification to the most intimate aspects of people's lives.

In one sense I argue that cultural criticism is, as the saying goes, "complicit in capitalism." Such a formulation, however, tends not only to obscure the meaning of capitalism but also to assume that whatever capitalism is, it provides the material "context" necessary for any properly historical account of intellectual "texts." The perceived split between text and context, and the felt need to link the two in some kind of causal sequence, is itself the legacy of the social-scientific worldview I take as my object of study; I cannot offer a conventional, causal-historical account without reproducing that worldview.[1] As an alternative history, I offer not so much a causal account as an account of causality. I argue that the attempt to master the objective laws of history so as to direct the historical process toward desired ends unites capitalism and its social-scientific critique. Capitalist "commodification" and critical "objectification" both demand the suspension of all normative ordering principles as a prelude to the creation of value and meaning by autonomous human subjects.

In this respect, both capitalism and its social-scientific critique must be understood as the legacy of Enlightenment rationalism, which gave birth to the social sciences in the seventeenth and eighteenth centuries. The driving principle of this rationalism—the opposition of reason to tradition—found its clearest formulation in the philosophy of René Descartes. This philosophy marked a decisive break from premodern thought not only because it set as the philosopher's task the search for a foundation on which to ground certain knowledge but also, and more importantly, as Richard Bernstein has emphasized, because it conceived of this search as one based "only upon the authority of reason itself," as opposed to "unfounded opinions, prejudices, tradition, or external authority."[2] Long after modern thought revised or rejected the Cartesian quest for foundational certainty, it retained an insistence on the autonomy of the thinking subject from the distorting particularities of received social and intellectual traditions.

Cartesian subjectivity bequeathed a way of knowing the world and also a way of being in the world. Nature, society, and everything else external to the thinking subject came to embody the same radical "objectivity" as the subject itself. In premodern thought, nature was a normative order; in Cartesian thought, nature appeared as a mere instrumentality—a neutral means with no inherent ends. Freed from preconceptions as to any "natural" order, Cartesian philosophy saw man creating order by analyzing nature into its constituent parts and synthesizing those parts into a causal order capable of being directed toward chosen ends. With nature reduced to the mechanical laws of cause and effect, the limits of the possible stood as the only objective limits on human desire.[3]

This attitude toward nature found its social equivalent in seventeenth-century social contract theory. The writings of Thomas Hobbes and John Locke marked the first time in the history of social thought that society was seen as existing apart from a larger normative context, the product of merely human rather than divine action. The "individual" of social contract theory existed not in a natural order that united man, society, and nature, but in a "state of nature" distinct from and prior to society itself. Violent or relatively benign, the state of nature appeared as a state of anarchy in which individuals worked on their physical environment free from social obligations to other individuals. Driven by egoism (Hobbes) or sympathy (Locke), these individuals agreed to create society in order to further their interaction with nature under more favorable circumstances. In social contract theory, society stood as an instrumental rather than a normative order; society was the neutral context in which one pursued one's desires by working on nature and engaging in relations of equivalence and exchange with other individuals likewise working on nature.[4]

Eighteenth-century "social science" completed the objectification of society initiated by social contract theory. Culminating in the Scottish discipline of political economy, eighteenth-century social science revealed the objective laws of society to be both structurally organic and historically dynamic.[5] The writings of Adam Smith portrayed human history as a succession of distinct stages, each characterized by a specific relation between the individual "human agent" and an "objective structure" figured as the mode of production. Smith declared that this objective structure determined the art, science, law, and government of each historical period, but that the laws of production and exchange were sufficiently dynamic to allow for the exercise of creative human agency. Rejecting the deductive, rationalist hypothesis of the creation of society through the social contract, Smith's inductive, empirical social science nonetheless routinized the principle of contract as the basis for the continual re-creation of society through production and exchange.[6]

As Roberto Unger has written, this social-scientific worldview implied "that nothing in nature is necessarily or morally foreordained," and thus "birth, death, and the physical forms of human life may be changed in conformity to willed objectives."[7] Eighteenth-century American intellectuals shied away from the Faustian implications of this worldview; nevertheless, they drew freely on the new social science in constructing their ideological justifications for the American Revolution.[8] Since the Revolution, however, American intellectuals have struggled with the moral anarchy latent in the social-scientific instrumentalization of all social relations. The strategies adopted since the revolutionary era may be grouped under two broad intellectual orientations. One, a strategy of segregation, has tried to exempt certain aspects of life, particularly the family, from the instrumental logic of the market. The other, a strategy of integration, has tried to see the dynamic instrumentalization of values as itself a value capable of promoting social order if properly extended to every aspect of life. The first orientation characterized the mainstream of nineteenth-century American thought as represented by the doctrine of "separate spheres"; the second orientation, I contend, has characterized the mainstream of twentieth-century American thought and is represented by the idea of culture as a whole way of life.

The intellectual contours of this reorientation began to take shape in 1899, with the publication of Thorstein Veblen's *Theory of the Leisure Class*. The historical significance of Veblen's book lies not in its supposed cultural approach to economics but in its economic approach to culture. Veblen debunks cultural activities such as religion, marriage, sports, and leisure for inciting exchange relations of "invidious comparison" and "pecuniary emulation." These relations create value from the "secondary utility" of status, honor, or the "relative ability to pay," which then threatens the primary utility of service to "the fullness of life of the individual, taken in absolute terms." Primary utility does not derive from relations of emulation or comparison between people but from the instrumental, "industrial" relations "between mankind and brute creation." [9] Wherever Veblen looks, relations between people threaten the purity of the more basic relation between people and things. Subsequent critical appropriations of the idea of culture in American social science would take a more sanguine attitude toward relations between people, but only after those relations had proved instrumental to the life of the individual, taken in absolute terms.

Veblen's phrase "conspicuous consumption" served as an indictment of the waste and excess of a particular culture that seemed unable to provide for the fullness of the life of the individual. Ironically, Veblen's attack on consumption inaugurated a critical tradition that has created its own kind of waste, an excess of "culture" that follows from the relentless textualization of everyday life through social-scientific inquiry. This tradition is "conspicuous" not for its failure to achieve the "fullness of the life of the individual" but for its failure to acknowledge or articulate a normative order in which such a goal could have any meaning. The idea of culture as a "pattern of values" emerged as a kind of normative ordering principle, but for this critical tradition, "American culture" remained an objective social whole with no power over the inquiring subject.

This relation between the autonomous subject and the objective social whole has served as a substitute for the constitutive relations of tradition that united subject and object in premodern thought. The "complicity" of the tradition of conspicuous criticism in consumer capitalism does not stem from any failure of critical nerve but from a shared, uncompromising commitment to the critical project of uprooting all received traditions. [10] The negative connotations of the word *consumption* in American culture (and in American historical writing) have obscured the root of the instabilities of consumer capitalism in the very "producer" values so often held up in jeremiads as the solid rock of ages. [11] From the Protestant "work ethic" to the social-scientific notion of "workmanship," productivity has served as a single standard of instrumentality hostile to all normative ordering principles and proximate ends or values. A substitute for the mediating rites and devotional practices of the Catholic Church, the work ethic initially offered Reformation Protestants a way of connecting their lives to God through an abstract, personal discipline that could be cultivated in the everyday world of work and family.[12] American Puritans tolerated God as a legitimate "end" or context for the "means" of this work ethic, but their secular heirs quite sensibly recognized Him as yet another confining tradition, yet another limit to that instrumentalization of the self at the heart of the Puritan tradition of self-scrutiny. The conspicuous criticism of Veblen, Robert and Helen Lynd, John Dewey, Ruth Benedict, and C. Wright Mills draws on both religious and secular languages of work. It offers the scientific reflection on society as a reflection on the self, and it seeks to harmonize self and society through a single standard of dynamic instrumentality that is free from all received traditions.

My antagonism to this tradition and to "critical" thought in general should be clear. That my antagonism issues in a stance of detachment that is nothing if not "critical" should also be clear. This is an inescapable irony of metacriticism, and indeed of any kind of sociology of knowledge. Like all social-historical criticism, my argument debunks; it unmasks interests. Against the demands of criticism, however, I do not claim to stand above all traditions, to debunk in the name of some interest-free objectivity, or to debunk for the ironic sake of debunking; rather, I criticize one tradition from another outside of it. I offer a critique of the Reformation-Enlightenment attack on tradition from the perspective of the Roman Catholic insistence that reason, belief, and even unbelief make sense only in the context of some received tradition of inquiry. From this perspective, meaningful inquiry is never free or open; it always entails personal relations of submission on the part of a community of knowers, and its end is to some degree always present in its beginning.[13]

The "tradition" of conspicuous criticism has been able to escape the personal relations of tradition proper, yet it has been unable to escape the tautological nature of all inquiry. Starting from a perspective of social-scientific detachment, it has constructed a democratic social ideal in which all individuals would be able to participate in this detachment and achieve a social-scientific mastery over their environment. Within the conventions of a history monograph, I cannot hope to offer an argument *against* this tradition, but I feel I can at least offer an argument *about* it. The social-scientific assault on tradition has itself become a tradition, one that, like other traditions, entails a certain conception of freedom as well as a certain conception of necessity. This tradition has held up as freedom "the fullness of the life of the individual, taken in absolute terms," yet it has also demanded as necessity the instrumentalization of all natural and social relations in the service of that freedom. If such "freedom" is to be defended, it must be defended in these terms.

CONSPICUOUS
CRITICISM

.

Chapter 1

■

The Perspective of Workmanship

Placing Veblen

BY ALL ACCOUNTS, Thorstein Veblen is "the only true outsider" in the story of Gilded Age, Progressive Era social science. Seemingly unclassifiable and sui generis, Veblen illuminates by contrast the real story of turn-of-the-century social science, a story of professionalization, institutionalization, and deradicalization. When approached on his own terms, Veblen emerges more as a social stylist than as a social scientist. A moralist, satirist, and rhetorician, he reinvented irony as an approach to social theory and set the standard for a new character type distinct to, if not definitive of, twentieth-century American intellectual life—the academic bohemian. As exemplary life or pathological case study, however, Veblen remains a marginal figure.[1]

Much in Veblen's life and work certainly calls forth such a reading. Still, his marginality extends beyond personal and intellectual idiosyncracies. Whatever his status within the profession of economics, Veblen shared with his fellow social scientists the social marginality that defines professionalism. Professional "objectivity" demands that persons, in their capacity as professionals, separate themselves from the personal social ties that might bind them to the nonprofessionals whom they serve with asocial, technical skill. As such, professionalism stands as the culmination of an ideal of neutral social relations bequeathed by seventeenth-century social contract theory and eighteenth-century social science, an ideal in which presocial or asocial individuals consciously create and recreate society through the exchange of goods and services with other similarly constituted individuals.

Through much of the nineteenth century, the free market served as the locus for this neutrality, and the "character" education of the antebellum college sought to provide young men with the internal discipline necessary to act responsibly in a social sphere in which, theoretically, they could not depend on the personal ties of region, religion, or family.[2] By the late nineteenth century, the idea of "character" itself seemed too mired in moral and religious prejudices to serve as a neutral principle, and the glaring inequities of Gilded Age society cast doubt on the democratic promise of the free market. At the vanguard of the ideal of neutral social relations, character gave way to merit and the invisible hand of the market gave way to the visible hand of bureaucracy. Much of Veblen's conflict with his fellow economists stemmed from his perception of their failure to live up to the ideal of neutrality they professed.

Even Veblen's intellectual iconoclasm appears less idiosyncratic when seen in terms of the intellectual iconoclasm of professional social science as a whole. Mainstream professional social scientists ultimately may have legitimated the new industrial capitalist order in the name of an older ideal of American "exceptionalism," but they legitimated a *new* order. They did so in the name of a "science" that was at odds with what were seen to be the moral and religious prejudices that informed antebellum conceptions of "reason" and "objectivity." The new professional social scientists did not "discover" interdependence or historical and structural organicism; these ideas had become social-scientific conventions by the end of the eighteenth century. The new sciences of evolutionary biology and anthropology simply broadened the ideal of interdependence to encompass areas of life (especially religion and morality) previously exempt from rigorous inquiry by the sentimental conventions of the nineteenth-century doctrine of "separate spheres." The extreme rigor with which Veblen applied these new sciences to the study of American society may have offended some of his colleagues, but his thought can hardly be seen as heretical in relation to a social science that came to legitimate itself in terms of such rigor.[3]

Veblen's concern for the fate of "the instinct of workmanship" illuminates by extremity the broader developments of his time. His writing on the instinct of workmanship can be seen as his contribution to the general middle-class discourse of the "crisis of work" in late-nineteenth-century America. Through much of the nineteenth century, a religious language of the Protestant "work ethic" and a secular language of "republican virtue" so shaped popular understandings of citizenship that "work" came to serve as a central metaphor for expressing the relation between the individual and society in America; the preservation of the republic depended on the cultivation of virtue within each individual through the exercise of free labor.[4] By the late nineteenth century, the apparent degradation of work under industrial capitalism seemed to threaten the ability of work to hold society together. Middle-class intellectuals responded to this perceived crisis by developing new professions that promised to save the work ethic—and thus the republic—by expanding the opportunities for meaningful work.

To the degree that historians have not dismissed Veblen's work as idiosyncratic, they have tended to see it as symptomatic of this middle-class anxiety concerning work. Curiously, for all of the attention given to the attack on "conspicuous consumption" found in *The Theory of the Leisure Class,* little or no attention has been given to the idea of production—of "workmanship"—that informs this critique. Too often Veblen's concern for efficiency has been dismissed as his great weakness: the point at which the "humanist idealist" becomes the "hard-boiled mechanist" and the "radical" becomes the "positivist." As a result, Veblen's praise for "industrial experts" and "skilled technologists" has been taken as an endorsement of technocratic social control.[5]

Veblen cannot be so easily dismissed. If we are to get, in Jackson Lears's phrase, "beyond Veblen," we must go through him.[6] This demands coming to a better understanding of the meaning of production and efficiency in Veblen's writing, which in turn demands that we shift our focus from *The Theory of the Leisure Class* to *The Instinct of Workmanship.* Nothing less than a history of "the growth of culture" from the primitive state of savagery to the modern age of machine industry, *The Instinct of Workmanship* is also, in a sense, a history of Veblen's class.[7] In his scientific study of the development of workmanship through history, Veblen writes the objective social relations of professionalism into the "objective" structures of history. By seeing history in terms of the struggle between a technical "use value" of "workmanship" and a social "exchange value" of "pecuniary interest," Veblen merely reproduces the values of the professional class for whom he so often expresses contempt.[8] If his historical narrative does not culminate in the triumph of doctors, lawyers, and academics per se, it nonetheless looks to the triumph of a class whose claim to universality lies in its distance from market relations and its mastery of certain neutral, technical skills.

Instincts, Agency, and History

Veblen roots the evolution of human culture in the interplay of the "instinctive proclivities" of the human organism. Proceeding on "the materialistic assumptions of modern science," Veblen's opening discussion of the instinctual nature of man owes a great debt to the evolutionary biology of his day; however, Veblen cannot be accused of any simple biological determinism (*IW*, xi). Rooted in human biology, instincts are nonetheless the "root of self-direction," the "prime movers in human behaviour." Unlike the unthinking reflex actions that he labels "tropismatic aptitudes," instincts involve "consciousness and adaptation to an end aimed at" (*IW*, 1, 3). Each instinct represents a "distinguishable propensity" within the human organism, yet all instincts overlap to form "a continuous or ambiguously segmented body of spiritual elements" (*IW*, 3, 8–9, 12).

Veblen's embrace of organicism does not suggest a biological determinism so much as a biological indeterminism, a kind of reduction of man to complexity. Still, he roots this instinctual interdependence in a single instinct, the instinct of workmanship. According to Veblen, "There are few lines of instinctive proclivity that are not crossed and coloured by some ramification of the instinct of workmanship," for workmanship embodies the tendency toward the "efficient use of the means at hand and adequate management of the resources available for the purposes of life" (*IW*, 29, 31–32). Each instinct is directed toward a particular end, yet all require the instrumentality of workmanship to achieve those particular ends. Veblen illustrates the relation between workmanship and other instincts through the example of boxing. The "end" instinct of pugnacity motivates the "agent," the boxer, yet the instinct of workmanship directs and guides pugnacity so that it does not assert itself wildly (*IW*, 32). If an "end" instinct like pugnacity is weak, workmanship will lose interest; if such an instinct is too strong, it will undermine workmanship and cause the agent to lose control (*IW*, 34).

Although workmanship represents a "concurrence of many instinctual aptitudes," it is nonetheless "an object of attention and sentiment in its own right" (*IW*, 27, 31). For Veblen, the interdependent instrumentality embodied in workmanship is an end in itself, the chief end of the human organism. With instincts at the root of human agency, and workmanship at the root of all instincts, human agency lies in the matching of means to ends rather than in the ordering of particular ends in relation to one another.[9] A healthy instinct of workmanship favors no particular end instinct; it requires only "work in hand and more of it in sight" and "circumstances of moderate exigence" under which to grow and develop (*IW*, 34). Suspicious of particular ends, workmanship "is initially a disposition to do the next thing and do it as well as may be" (*IW*, 34). A properly functioning organism allows workmanship the freedom to roam from instinct to instinct so that it does not develop any particular instinct to a point at which it could pose a threat to workmanship itself. The constant movement of workmanship maintains the interdependence of the organism and ensures that this interdependence will be balanced and harmonious.

After this initial biological account of ideal instinctual harmony, Veblen devotes most of *The Instinct of Workmanship* to a historical account of real instinctual conflict. He presents history as the story of the periodic repression and liberation of the instinct of workmanship, dividing it into those periods dominated by the instinct of workmanship and those dominated by any instinct other than workmanship. Veblen sees in human history not the conflict between competing instinctual ends so much as the conflict between the "means" of workmanship and the "ends" of all other instinctual activities. All instincts rise and fall in relation to the instinct of workmanship. Indeed, workmanship provides Veblen with the content and the form of history. Like the modern conception of history itself, workmanship consists of both a dynamic principle of ceaseless change ("a disposition to do the next thing") and a rational principle of orderly development ("under circumstances of moderate exigence"). Ultimately, Veblen offers not so much a history *of* the instinct of workmanship but rather history *as* the instinct of workmanship.

As if unwilling to concede the integrity of any instinct other than workmanship, Veblen roots the means/ends conflict of history in a conflict within the instinct of workmanship itself. According to Veblen, "the workmanlike apprehension of . . . the nature of things is twofold: (a) what can be done with them as raw materials for use under the creative hand of the workman who makes things, and (b) what they will do as entities acting in their own right and working out their own ends. The former is matter of fact, the latter matter of imputation" (*IW*, 55). Veblen sees in (a) the true manifestation of workmanship, while in (b) a mere distortion of it. He refers to this distortion of workmanship variously as imputation, anthropomorphism, or authentication. Through the process of anthropomorphism, "conduct more or less fully after the human fashion of conduct, is imputed to external objects" (*IW*, 52).

Ironically, as workmanship develops itself by building up various "end" instincts, "men and things come to be rated in terms of what they (putatively) are—their intrinsic character—rather than in terms of what they (empirically) will do" (*IW*, 179). As certain instinctual activities become authenticated within a culture, they threaten "the free unfolding of workmanship by enjoining a cumbersome routine of ritual" on workmanship itself (*IW*, 122). The magical and religious superstitions that grow out of the authentication of instincts foster an ideal of legitimate secrecy that enables the practitioners of various "end" instinctual activities to "warn the technologist off forbidden ground" (*IW*, 122). With the rise of such taboo areas, "an abiding sense of authenticity comes to pervade the routine of daily life, such as effectually to obstruct all innovations, whether in the ways and means of work or in the conduct of life more at large" (*IW*, 48). Authentication fosters the "irresponsible force" of "personal subservience and personal authority" (*IW*, 168). Soon, "the prerogatives of the ruling class and the principles of authentic usage become canons of truth and right living and presently take precedence of workmanlike efficiency and the fulness of the life of the group" (*IW*, 47). The rise of personal authority at the expense of workmanship leads to a "marked abatement of initiative throughout the community," which threatens the very growth of culture itself (*IW*, 42).

In historical epochs dominated by the instinct of workmanship, interaction between cultures neutralizes the threat of anthropomorphic stagnation within particular cultures. Veblen calls this process of cultural interaction "hybridization." According to Veblen:

> When any given technological or decorative element crosses the frontier between one culture and another, in the course of borrowing, it is likely to happen that it will come into the new culture stripped of most or all of its anthropomorphic or spiritual virtues and limitations, more particularly, of course, if the cultural frontier in question is at the same time a linguistic frontier; since the borrowing is likely to be made from motives of workmanlike expediency, and the putative spiritual attributes of the facts involved are not obvious to men who have not been trained to impute them. (*IW*, 136)

This hybridization fosters a process of change that does not simply develop the instinct of workmanship but itself manifests that instinct. Cultural change *is* work, as borrowed cultural elements "fall into the scheme of things as mere matter-of-fact, to be handled with the same freedom and unhindered sagacity with which a workman makes use of his own hands, and, [can] without reservation, be turned to any use for which they [are] mechanically suited" (*IW*, 137).

Thus, according to Veblen's historical narrative, when the instinct of workmanship chafes under the restrictions and taboos of a particular culture, it looks to the margins of its own culture, even to other cultures, in order to develop itself free from the encumbrances of anthropomorphic rituals. As the instinct of workmanship develops marginal and borrowed elements, they become incorporated into the mainstream of the culture and thus become subject to the taboos of that culture. The instinct of workmanship then again turns to the margins and boundaries of the culture in which it is situated to seek new outlets for its energies. This ebb and flow of workmanlike advances and anthropomorphic retrenchments ultimately serves the growth of culture. The more foreign elements a culture incorporates into itself, the more hybridized it becomes. Anthropomorphism succumbs to matter of fact, which, for Veblen, constitutes evolutionary progress.

Veblen's account of instinctual conflict and cultural change structures history in terms of the rather stark alternatives of workmanlike innovation and anthropomorphic stagnation. Either workmanship has free reign over all the instinctual activities of a culture, or other instincts impose stagnation on every aspect of that culture. All those aspects of the "whole way of life" of man addressed by Veblen's anthropological approach to economics appear, in his account of human history, as epiphenomenal to a more basic reality of workmanship conceived as pure technique. In his "institutional" approach, institutions such as the family, religion, and custom—no less than private property—stand as waste, a drag on workmanship. Veblen's account of history needs no phrase like "cultural lag," for throughout it culture *is* lag. Presented as a study of the growth of culture, *The Instinct of Workmanship* actually presents human history as the growth from culture.

The Era of Savagery

Veblen begins his historical study with an account of the first heroic period of workmanship, the prehistoric era of savagery. John Patrick Diggins has rightly dubbed Veblen the "bard of savagery," for savagery appears in Veblen's work as a kind of golden age from which man has

fallen.[10] Like a Victorian anthropologist "gone native," Veblen cele-
brates the primal vitality of the savage era. Still, he roots this vitality in
the savage privileging of the rational and the technological, not in any
supposed savage distance from modern technology. Veblen's era of savagery appears as a nineteenth-century utopia of production. Not tradition, custom, or ritual, but "the recognized elements of technological
proficiency" are what bind together cultures and communities in the savage era (IW, 146). Each individual workman has equal access to a common fund of technical knowledge; the free flow of information spurs
productivity, which in turn creates the simple abundance in which the
community shares (IW, 144). As with most primitivisms, Veblen's account of savagery privileges a kind of free-floating, polymorphous perversity; however, Veblen's savagery is a polymorphous perversity of instrumental rationality. His account of savage "culture" reveals no dense
web of relations between men, but a pure state of technical interaction
between men and things.[11]

Of course, the strength of workmanship proves to be its downfall.
During the savage era, workmanship realizes its full potential as an interdependent instinct; it comes to define all other instinctual activities. Everyone in the savage era engages in workmanlike activity, thus "the logic
of workmanship becomes the logic of events" (IW, 54). As a result,
workmanlike qualities come to be imputed to other instincts, which then
come to stand as ends in themselves. The technological orientation of the
savage era spares workmanship the taboos of religion and magic, but it
results in an increase in wealth that fosters the development of the instinct of ownership (IW, 156). According to Veblen, the free flow of
workmanship during the savage era develops the "material equipment of
appliances" to a point that brings the "roundabout process of industry
to a more or less determinate place and routine such as to make surveillance and control possible" (IW, 150). Increased control leads to technological advances that make it "worthwhile to own the material means of
industry, and ownership of the material means in such a situation carries
with it the usufruct of the community's immaterial equipment of technological proficiency" (IW, 150–51). Eventually, the "authentication of
ownership" legitimates the authority of property over workmanship,
allowing pecuniary elites to monopolize the technical knowledge right-
fully open to all (IW, 182). After exhausting the safety valve of hybridization, the workmanlike culture of savagery descends into the pecuniary
culture of barbarism.

For Veblen, barbarism represents a fall from savage grace. Like the expulsion from Eden, however, barbarism is a fortunate fall *(felix culpa)*, one that makes possible the salvation of mankind. The shift to pecuniary control is central to the "growth of culture." According to Veblen, "In the economic respect, it appears to have been the most universal and most radical mutation which human culture has undergone in its advance from savagery to civilization" (*IW*, 147). To argue for the positive role of pecuniary culture in human history, Veblen distinguishes between a warlike and a peaceful phase of barbarism. The "predatory" phase of "lower barbarism" in the West extended from the time of ancient Rome, through the barbarian invasions that followed the collapse of the Roman Empire, to the reign of the Catholic Church in the Dark Ages. Since the end of the Dark Ages, however, the West has been engaged in the "pertinacious pursuit of the arts of peace" (*IW*, 171). As the predatory phase of pecuniary culture has given way to "a progressively more covert regime of self-aggrandisement and differential gain, the instinct of workmanship has progressively found freer range and readier access to its raw material" (*IW*, 183). War is as bad for business as it is for the instinct of workmanship, and peace fosters the spread of workmanship as well as the spread of the market.

Thus, for Veblen the growth of culture proceeds dialectically. Peace fosters war, which in turn produces peace; workmanship fosters ownership, which in turn fosters workmanship. Historians often interpret Veblen as simply opposing production to exchange, but *The Instinct of Workmanship* suggests a subtler relation between these aspects of political economy within Veblen's thought. Veblen insists that at heart the market rests on the subjective, individualistic principle of "emulous rivalry," but he praises the market for its objective, impersonal way of assessing brute fact (*IW*, 199–200). This mode of perception embodies the attitude of workmanship, thus the expansion of the market helps spread the instinct of workmanship. For the market to have this liberating effect, it must pass from the predatory to the peaceful stage of pecuniary culture. This transformation takes place during the second major workmanlike era in human history, the era of handicraft.

The Era of Handicraft

For Veblen, the modern era begins with the rise of handicraft in the seventeenth century. The handicraft era develops out of the guild system of the Middle Ages. As with his analysis of savagery, Veblen divides the handicraft era into two aspects: the technical/factual/objective and the pecuniary/authentic/subjective (*IW,* 210). He sees the guilds as economic organizations designed to gain an advantage in the marketplace; indeed, modern "business principles" have their root in the "insistent, pervasive, and minutely concrete discipline in the practice and logic of pecuniary detail" fostered by the guilds (*IW,* 212). Despite these pecuniary concerns, however, guilds leave the technical aspects of workmanship relatively autonomous: "The control which the gilds were initially designed to exercise was a control that should leave the gildsmen free in the pursuit of their work, subject only to a salutary surveillance and standardization of their output, such as would maintain the prestige of their workmanship and facilitate the disposal of the goods produced" (*IW,* 289). The relative autonomy of the instinct of workmanship under the guild system allows for the growth of technology. At the dawn of the modern period, the invisible hand of technological growth leads to an increase in wealth, which in turn leads to an expansion of the market at the expense of the "just-price" system that supported the guilds. The breakup of the guild system, and the hierarchical work relations of that system, results in the rise of a species of "masterless men," the individual, independent workmen who make up the "central fact" of the era of handicraft (*IW,* 234).

Veblen's account of the worker in the handicraft era provides some of the most striking passages in *The Instinct of Workmanship.* Although Veblen ultimately judges the period to be too individualistic, his description of the social world of the handicraftsman finds him lapsing into lyricism. Veblen's sympathy for the handicraftsman provides him with the opportunity to suspend his critical detachment in order to wax poetic about an ideal. In his historical narrative, the era of handicraft stands as the key point of transition in that it looks back to the social ideals of savagery as well as forward to the reinstitutionalization of these ideals on the higher plane of the modern machine process.

The society of the handicraft era is organized around the craftsman, "the individual workman as a creative agent standing on his own bottom, and as an ultimate, irreducible factor in the community's make-up" (*IW,* 234–35). Veblen's willingness to speak in terms of irreducible elements suggests a kind of suspension of analytic rigor. The workman is not simply *an* irreducible social factor, he is *the* basis of all social relations: "In that era industry is conceived in terms of the skill, initiative and application of the trained individual, and human relations outside of the workshop tend also by force of habit to be conceived in similar terms

of self-sufficient individuals, each working out his own ends in sever-
ality" (*IW*, 234). Thus, just as Veblen conceives of history diachronically,
in terms of the development of the instinct of workmanship and the advance of technology, so he conceives of society synchronically, in terms
of relations between individual, technical workers. Again, it is not that
Veblen presents an analysis *of* economics so much as he presents analysis
as economics. History and society do not have economic aspects; they
have their root and essence in economics itself.

This essentialized economics may be divided into two components:
production and exchange or, in Veblen's terms, workmanship and pecuniary control. His account of the relation between these two components
is more complex than one of absolute opposition. To understand precisely what this relation is requires a close examination of one of Veblen's
lyrical reveries on the handicraftsman:

> He draws on the resources of his own person alone; neither his ances-
> try nor the favour of his neighbours have visibly yielded him anything
> beyond an equivalent for work done; he owes nothing to inherited
> wealth or prerogative, and he is bound in no relation of landlord or
> tenant to the soil. With his slight outfit of tools he is ready and compe-
> tent of his own motion to do the work that lies before him, and he asks
> nothing but an even chance to do what he is fit to do. Even the training
> which has given him his finished skill he has come by through no spe-
> cial favour or advantage, having given an equivalent for it all the work
> done during his apprenticeship and so having to all appearance ac-
> quired it by his own force and diligence. The common stock of techno-
> logical knowledge underlying all special training was at that time still
> a sufficiently simple and obvious matter, so that it was readily acquired
> in the routine of work, without formal application to the learning of
> it; and any indebtedness to the community at large or to past genera-
> tions for such common stock of information would therefore not be
> sufficiently apparent to admit of its disturbing the craftsman's naive
> appraisal of his productive capacity in the simple and complacent
> terms of his own person. (*IW*, 235)

Here, in a nutshell, is the classic bourgeois view of society, one that begins and ends with the individual and sees society as merely an aggregate
of such individuals. Though somewhat muted by Veblen's insistence on
the "communal" nature of savage and handicraft society, this social ideal
runs through his account of each heroic period of workmanship.

The ideal of workmanlike individuality assumes an individual's freedom from all past personal relations—"ancestry"—and all present personal relations—"neighbors." For such an individual, freedom is economic freedom, illustrated by temporal detachment from "inherited wealth" and spatial detachment from all "relation . . . to the soil." Veblen locates the individual as craftsman in society but conceives of society in terms of relations of equivalence and exchange. The free-market conception of knowledge latent in Veblen's account of savagery—the notion of knowledge as a resource open to be developed by individual workers—becomes manifest in his account of the era of handicraft. The fruits of this savage society are never shared so much as collected, never held in common so much as redistributed. Veblen never makes clear the reasons for the obligation of the savage workers to their community, and the notion of obligation itself easily falls away in his analysis of the era of handicraft. Equivalence, rather than obligation, constitutes the social bond of the era of handicraft. The craftsman learns a skill and gives as "an equivalent for it all the work done during his apprenticeship." This exchange effectively frees the worker from all personal obligation, allowing him to pursue unfettered his true activity, which is to draw on "the resources of his own person alone," an activity for which the worker stands "ready and competent of his own motion." Thus, the notion of the person as producer, as in effect motion that develops resources, is inextricably bound to social relations of equivalence and exchange.

Veblen presents the flowering of the instinct of workmanship in the era of handicraft as not a narrowly technical phenomenon but a social transformation that reaches into all aspects of daily life. The rise of the "masterless men" of the handicraft era signals the end of the guild system and the whole medieval order of faith, authority, and coercion (IW, 254). In the era of handicraft,

> Creative workmanship, fortified in ever-growing measure by the conception of serviceability to human use, works its way gradually into the central place in the theoretical speculations of the time so that by the close of the era it dominates all intellectual enterprise in the thoughtful portions of Christendom. Hence it becomes not only the instrument of inquiry in the sciences, but a major premise in all works of innovation and reconstruction of the scheme of institutions. In that extensive revision of the institutional framework that characterises modern times it is the life of the common people, their rights and obligations, that is forever in view, and their life conceived in terms of craftsmanlike industry and the petty trade. (IW, 285–86)

"Petty trade" is the social relation that flows naturally from "crafts-manlike industry." As the medieval emphasis on personal and class distinctions tended to minimize the importance of workmanship, so the handicraft era's emphasis on workmanship eliminates personal distinctions, leaving trade as the only meaningful relation between people.

No mere unfortunate by-product of craftsmanlike industry, petty trade actually helps to develop workmanlike attitudes in people. Trade fosters the "impersonal logic," the "statistical habit of mind," that is at the heart of the instinct of workmanship (*IW*, 244–45). For Veblen, "Accountancy is the beginning of statistics, and the price concept is a type of the objective impersonal, quantitative apprehension of things" (*IW*, 245). Within the logic of the price system, all that cannot be assessed in quantifiable terms is unreal or of a lower order of reality (*IW*, 245). In this respect, trade is actually superior to the productive aspect of handicraft. During the handicraft era, the actual working with physical materials still carries with it some of the anthropomorphism of primitive crafts. Even as the spirit of handicraft gives birth to Enlightenment philosophy, it maintains the metaphysical (that is, not observable) postulate of Nature as cause and effect, conceived anthropomorphically in terms of manual labor, rather than as workmanship in general (*IW*, 260–62). The pecuniary component of handicraft escapes this anthropomorphism: "The itinerant merchant's huckstering, as well as the buying and selling in which all members of the community were concerned, would doubtless throw the personal strain into the foreground and would act to keep the self-regarding sentiments alert and active and accentuate an individualistic appreciation of men and things" (*IW*, 244). As a community becomes caught up in buying and selling, "huckstering" becomes the normal way people relate to each other. The deceptions and fabrications of huckstering highlight the malleability, the fluidity of the "personal strain"; they help to discredit metaphysical notions such as "human nature." Trade serves as a logic of persons; but it is an impersonal logic because it calls for the assessment of how individual persons act in particular situations, not how they are supposed to act according to abstract principles. Through trade, people become "facts."

Trade is an epistemologically progressive force in Veblen's account of the growth of human culture. The expansion of trade does, however, lead to an increase in wealth, which in turn fosters a resurgence of the instinct of ownership. Handicraft's anthropomorphization of Nature as work combines with the revived instinct of ownership to provide the basis for a philosophy of natural rights and the authentication of private property. Natural rights philosophy sees property as the fruit of one's labor, but the expansion of the price system enables the fruits to grow so large as to overshadow labor. Workmanship comes to be viewed in terms of salesmanship, and it is corrupted by the ideals of self-aggrandizement (*IW*, 213, 217). The individualism of the handicraft ethic plays into the self-help principles of the price system and prevents the handicraftsmen from banding together to overthrow the price system (*IW*, 269). Ultimately, the expansion of the price system, the increasing specialization of tasks, the expansion of communications, and the increasing diversification of populations combine to bring an end to the handicraft system (*IW*, 313). Born in a burst of technical exuberance fostered by opposition to a decaying feudal system, the experience of work as direct manual labor, and a generally equitable distribution of wealth, the era of handicraft bequeathed the pecuniary legacy of a philosophy of natural rights that would persist despite the passing of the conditions under which that philosophy originally made sense (*IW*, 298).

Veblen refers to the pecuniary legacy of the handicraft era as the "higher barbarism" of modern "business enterprise." The account of the place of modern business in the development of the instinct of workmanship restates the argument of his earlier work, *The Theory of Business Enterprise.*[12] Veblen sees in modern business both a widening gap between finance and production and an increasing corruption of production by finance. Business has developed all its worst tendencies to their (il)logical extremes, and it has left behind all its tendencies toward the matter-of-fact apprehension of men and things. Although business has always engaged in speculative buying and selling in its capacity as a go-between for producers and consumers, in modern times business invests in the industrial process itself. This has brought the speculative process to a qualitatively higher level of abstraction, so business no longer makes money from investments in particular goods or resources but from "the conjunctures arising from the interplay of the industrial processes" (*TBE*, 23). In such a situation, "financiering strategists" can actually make make money through the collapse of certain industries (*TBE*, 28).

For Veblen, that financial gain can result from productive loss is not an "irony" of modern business; it is its motor principle. Financiers have a stake in disrupting all the traditional relations that contributed to the simple equation of financial gain with productive gain: "Broadly, this class of business men, in so far as they have no ulterior strategic ends to serve, have an interest in making the disturbances of the system large and frequent, since it is in the conjunctures of change that their gain emerges" (*TBE*, 29). This situation is so pervasive that it closes off the possibility of any simple retreat into the security of notions like "hard" currency or "solid" capital. The machinations of the stock market are so deeply imbedded in modern finance that distinctions between the tangible and the intangible no longer hold up (*IW*, 155). A credit economy has so completely replaced the older money economy that the line between credit and capital, between debt and property, is no longer clear. Credit and capital both depend on a stock market concerned mainly with appearances; both "capital and credit, therefore, vary from hour to hour and, within narrow limits, from place to place" (*TBE*, 131). For Veblen, "All capital which is put on the market is in this way subjected to an interminable process of valuation and revaluation—i.e. a capitalization and recapitalization—on the basis of its presumptive earning capacity, whereby it all assumes more or less of a character of intangibility" (*TBE*, 154). This process of valuation and revaluation culminates in the capitalization of "good will," which is intangible from start to finish (*TBE*, 154). Among businessmen, even the personal relations that might have given some kind of anchor to this impersonal, abstract financial process succumb to its logic. The "chronic perturbation" of modern business enterprise has become so much a part of the daily lives of all members of modern civilization that people accept it as the normal state of affairs (*TBE*, 34–35).

By Veblen's account of modern business enterprise, the price system has lost all ties to the matter-of-fact kind of thinking that once linked the pecuniary and the productive in a positive way. At the same time, however, by this account of modern industry, workmanship has lost all ties to the anthropomorphic ways of thinking that once linked the productive and the pecuniary in a negative way. Pecuniary control of industry has become so extensive that a financial failing could cripple the productive capacity of modern industry, but these two components of the economy operate on such different principles as to be relatively independent of each other. Thus, the "magnitude and fluctuations of business capital . . . stand in no hard and fast relation to the material magnitude of the industrial equipment" (*TBE*, 131–32). Here, production is "material," solid, tangible, and finance is "fluctuations," fluid, intangible. The "industrial system" provides the "material framework of modern civilization," yet

at present "business enterprise" serves as "the directing force which ani-
mates this framework" (*TBE*, 1). With these stark oppositions, Veblen
presents a picture of modernity as a kind of final showdown between the
two motor forces of history: production and exchange. If modernity may
be seen as the era of business, it may also be seen as the era of the machine process.

The Machine Process

Despite the pervasiveness of the price system, Veblen sees in modern civilization "a qualified or mitigated (sophisticated) return to the spirit of
savagery, or at least a spiritual reversion looking in that direction" (*IW*,
204). In modern civilization, "workmanship rather than prowess again
becomes the chief or primary norm of habituation, and therefore of the
growth of institutions" (*IW*, 204). Although the rise of pecuniary concerns has given salesmanship inordinate control over workmanship, the
modern business class values work as no ruling class before it ever has.
"This high tension of work is felt to be very meritorious in all modern
communities, somewhat in proportion as they are modern" (*IW*, 227).
Even though the work of this business class is emulative in nature rather
than truly workmanlike, it has laid the basis for the fullest possible expression of the instinct of workmanship: the modern machine process.
For Veblen, the machine process, rather than the factory system, large-
scale industry, capitalism, free competition, or the credit economy, is the
distinctive characteristic of modern industry.

The machine process marks a qualitative leap from handicraft because
it combines technical knowledge with science and roots out all the resid-
ual anthropomorphism of handicraft production (*IW*, 303). The shift in
terminology from handicraft to machine, from workmanship to science,
suggests an upping of the rhetorical ante consistent with Veblen's moder-
nity-as-final-showdown scenario. In one sense, science and the machine
would seem to represent a solid, rational alternative to the irrational fluidity of the price system; however, the distinctions between the solid and
the fluid, the tangible and the intangible, break down in Veblen's account
of the modern machine process just as they do in his account of the modern price system.

In Veblen's work, production comes to mirror exchange particularly
with respect to the place of causality in the modern machine process. For

Veblen, the older handicraft conception of causality is too rooted in notions of direct cause and effect and direct material contact to stand as science (*IW*, 330, 325). Handicraft's anthropomorphic "preconception that action can take place only by contact" flies in the face of recent scientific discoveries concerning light, heat, and electricity (*IW*, 330). Modern science offers a much more abstract conception of causality; it gives "an account of an unfolding process rather than a checking up of individual effects against individual causes"; in the modern world, "interest and attention come progressively to centre on this process of cumulative causation" (*IW*, 326). This new conception of causality admits no distinction between quantitative and qualitative notions of cause and effect (*TBE*, 370). Modern science offers not so much a process of causality as an idea of causality as pure process: "The process is always complex; always a delicately balanced interplay of forces that work blindly, insensibly, heedlessly; in which any appreciable deviation may forthwith count in a cumulative manner, the further consequences of which stand in no organic relation to the purpose for which the process has been set going" (*TBE*, 368). Here Veblen praises the same blind complexity that he damns in the price system. The conception of causality at the heart of the machine process shares so much with the anarchic fluidity of the price system that it is hard to imagine how it could produce anything in the conventional sense of industrial production.

Indeed, Veblen takes pains to distinguish the machine process from mere industry. He never addresses the production of particular things; at one point, he even dismisses "practical" efficiency as merely "the ability to turn fact to account for the purposes of the accepted conventions, to give a large effect to the situation in terms of the pecuniary conventions in force" (*TBE*, 320). As "something more comprehensive and less external than a mere aggregate of mechanical appliances for the mediation of human labor," the machine process is in a sense more process than machine (*TBE*, 5). The discipline of the machine is above all "a discipline of the habits of thought" (*TBE*, 312). This discipline

> presumes a certain intellectual or spiritual attitude on the part of the workman, such an attitude and an animus as will readily apprehend and appreciate matter of fact and will guard against the suffusion of this knowledge with putative animistic or anthropomorphic subtleties, quasi-personal interpretation of the observed phenomena and of their relations to one another. (*IW*, 310)

Ultimately,

> Wherever manual dexterity, the rule of thumb, and the fortuitous con-
> junctures of the seasons have been supplanted by a reasoned procedure
> on the basis of a systematic knowledge of the forces employed, there
> the mechanical industry is to be found, even in the absence of intricate
> mechanical contrivances. It is a question of the character of the process
> rather than a question of the complexity of the contrivances employed.
> (*TBE*, 6)

Passages such as these are crucial for understanding what Veblen
means by the discipline of the machine. Historians have tended to view
Veblen as a producerist critic of a pecuniary ethic of conspicuous consumption; they praise his heroic affirmation of producer values, yet they
tend to criticize his unqualified enthusiasm for the machine as playing
into the "cultural logic" of Taylorism and Fordism. By this account, Veblen would consign workers to the role of mere cogs in the machine.[13]
Such an interpretation misses the point of the machine as metaphor in
Veblen's writing, but my point is not to rescue Veblen from such a "vulgar" interpretation, or to show how his conception of the machine is
broader and more humanistic than Taylor's or Ford's, or even to show
that Veblen's theory of the machine was distorted by capitalist use of
the machine. Veblen's notion that the machine embodies critical thought
should lead us not to question his status as a critic so much as to rethink
what it means for thought to be "critical," in Veblen's time as well as in
our own.

For Veblen, the "spiritual concomitant" of the machine is the general
attitude of "workday ideals and scepticism of what is only conventionally valid" (*TBE*, 323). In provocative language reminiscent of Marx's
"all-that-is-solid-melts-into-air" passage from *The Communist Manifesto*, Veblen asserts that the "machine is a leveller, a vulgarizer, whose
end seems to be the extirpation of all that is respectable, noble, and digni-
fied in human intercourse and ideals" (*TBE*, 358). That Veblen sees this
aspect of the machine as decidedly progressive cannot be localized as an
embarassing, now-dated instance of modernist technological hubris, to
be discarded while retaining the truly critical core insights of Veblen's
thought, for the machine *is* the core of his thought. The machine is glori-
fied not so much as the culmination of history but rather as the embodiment of the historical process itself. History is change, and whether this

change comes through cultural hybridization, the growth of technology, or even the expansion of the price system, it involves the progressive uprooting of all animistic, anthropomorphic, personal, or rule-of-thumb elements from a culture. It is with this conception of the machine in mind that we must view Veblen's account of the place of the worker in the machine process.

Veblen's writing contains many incriminating passages that would seem to support the interpretation of his work as advocating some form of technocracy. In *The Instinct of Workmanship,* Veblen baldly asserts that workers do not make use of the machine process, but that, "on the contrary, the machine process makes use of the workman" (*IW,* 306). People often prove refractory to this process, so Veblen even imagines an ideal machine, which is completely automatic and free from human error (*IW,* 307). Still, Veblen sees the heart of the machine process is the interaction between the apparatus and the materials: "It is not simply that the apparatus reshapes the materials; the materials reshape themselves by the help of the apparatus" (*TBE,* 6). The "materials" are human beings (Veblen often refers to culture as "the human material"), thus Veblen sees the machine process as an opportunity for self-creation on the part of the worker (*TBE,* 306). "The working population is required to be standardized, movable, and interchangeable in much the same impersonal manner as the raw or half-wrought materials of industry" (*TBE,* 326). The fluidity of the worker under the machine is a positive advance; it constitutes "the moral effect of machine technology" (*TBE,* 326). This mobility requires of the worker more general technical knowledge than possessed by workers of the handicraft era, and this move toward general skills undermines the instinct of ownership by breaking down the boundaries between specialized skills that were monopolized previously by private groups.

The conception of the "interchangeable" worker with generalized skills must be understood in the context of Veblen's larger view of history and culture. Specialization suggests a kind of taboo, a forbidden ground, a secret kept from those who do not possess specialized skills; when any aspect of culture becomes marked off from others, be it religious practices or technical skills, it degenerates into anthropomorphic stagnation. High points in the history of workmanship see the cultivation of a general body of workmanlike knowledge open to all equally; low points see the monopolization of knowledge by various private groups. As the restrictions set up by handicraft specialization fall away in the modern world, the generalized skills of the machine process spread to all occupations. The general mechanical knowledge of modern workers allows them to move in and out of a variety of occupations, thus opening their minds to new experiences. This constant movement, this crossing of boundaries between different occupations, keeps the matter-of-fact aspects of a particular task foremost in the minds of the workers. This occupational boundary crossing thus serves the same end of uprooting anthropomorphism as the cultural boundary crossing of hybridization. If a worker were limited to one job, there would soon grow up around that job certain idiosyncratic habits, customs, and rule-of-thumb variations on official procedures, all of which would get in the way of the matter-of-fact apprehension of the task.

For Veblen, interchangeability ensures a heightened state of consciousness on the part of the worker. A standardized work force is a work force not of drones but of "creative agents" who share "iconoclastic habits of thought" and a matter-of-fact apprehension of men and things (TBE, 351). Once again, the discipline of the machine is "a discipline of the habits of thought," and these habits "have such a value, therefore, somewhat in proportion as they tax the mental faculties of those employed" (TBE, 312). The machine process weeds out for its purposes those who possess such habits of thought and leaves behind those who do not (TBE, 352). This process is progressive, for those who are able to adapt to the machine are the more intelligent (nonanthropomorphic) members of the society, and their continued participation in the machine process only furthers their intelligence (nonanthropomorphism).

The following passage helps to clarify this understanding of the worker's place in the machine process even as it seems to justify the charge of technocracy:

> It remains true, of course, as it always has been true, that he [the worker] is the intelligent agent concerned in the process, while the machine, furnace, roadway, or retort are inanimate structures devised by man and subject to the workman's supervision. But the process comprises him and his intelligent motions, and it is by virtue of his necessarily taking an intelligent part in what is going forward that the mechanical process has its chief effect upon him. The process standardizes his supervision and guidance of the machine. Mechanically speaking, the machine is not his to do with it [sic] as his fancy may suggest. His place is to take thought of the machine and its work in terms given him

by the process that is going forward. His thinking in the premises is reduced to standardized units of gauge and grade. If he fails of the precise measure, by more or less, the exigencies of the process check the aberration and drive home the absolute need of conformity. (*TBE*, 307–8).

A passage like this, taken on its own, cannot fail to conjure up images of Charlie Chaplin locked into the feeding machine in *Modern Times*. The oversized cogs and wheels that grind up human beings in Chaplin's movie may be what we tend to think of as "the machine," but again it is important to realize that, for Veblen, the machine is above all a habit of mind independent of any particular mechanical apparatus. Indeed, "this routine and its discipline extend beyond the mechanical occupations as such, so as in great part to determine the habits of all members of the modern community" (*IW*, 311).

This equation of the machine process with the whole way of life of the modern community—with, in effect, the culture of the modern community—sheds light on the passage cited above. A rewriting of this passage in terms of "culture" reads as follows:

the process comprises him and his intelligent motions, and it is by virtue of his necessarily taking an intelligent part in what is going forward that the cultural process has its chief effect upon him. The process standardizes his supervision and guidance of the culture. Culturally speaking, the culture is not his to do with as his fancy may suggest. His place is to take thought of the culture and its work in terms given him by the process that is going forward.

Softened in this manner (though later in the century, culture itself would come to be seen as a "machine"), Veblen's insistence on conformity to the machine process seems in line with the classic sentiment of Enlightenment humanism, perhaps best expressed in Marx's dictum that man makes his own history, but not under conditions of his own making. The antinomies of Veblen's thought—intelligent agent versus the machine process—are a particular instance of the antinomies of bourgeois thought in general, liberal or Marxist. For classical liberals, one must discern the universal laws of the market and then act as free economic agents within those laws; for Marxists, one must discern the universal laws of history and then act as historical agents so as to bring about the fulfillment of history in revolution. For Veblen, one must discern the universal laws of the machine process and act as a creative agent so as to develop those potentialities that are consistent with the principles of the machine. Once again, those potentialities are the iconoclastic habit of mind and the matter-of-fact apprehension of men and things.

Such a reading of Veblen helps to make sense of a recurring theme in Progressive social thought, that is, the need to give the worker a sense of his place in the whole work process. This theme is particularly strong in the work of Jane Addams and John Dewey and has led their work to be interpreted as everything from a democratic advocacy of fulfilling, meaningful work to a technocratic imposition of a therapeutic, industrial psychology in the (witting or unwitting) service of capitalism. Both interpretations assume that thinkers like Addams and Dewey are, or should be, talking about actual jobs. This seems to miss the point, a point that Veblen's abstractions make clear. Work for these thinkers is not a particular task or a particular job, but a process, or more precisely, a perception of process. The importance of Jane Addams's workers' museum does not lie in its supposed legitimation or therapeutic evasion of the increasing degradation of work by a Taylorized industrial capitalism but in the way that it teaches people to see work as a process that has a history, that has developed over time, and that has certain distinct stages. In short, people must see work as a museum curator (or a social scientist) would see it.[14] The vision of the whole which a museum gives retrospectively, of the past, social science gives perspectively, in the present.

This vision is as embodied in Jane Addams's Hull House as it is in her *Twenty Years at Hull House*. Thus, to understand the emancipatory ideal of Veblen's vision of machine culture, one need not scour his writings for references to Ford or Taylor, or to particular machines, or to would-be model factories. *The Instinct of Workmanship* does not have to point to any supposedly pure embodiment of the machine process, for it is itself such an embodiment. Its iconoclastic and matter-of-fact apprehension of men and things itself embodies the habit of thought Veblen sees spreading through modern civilization by the extension of the machine process. Veblen sees this iconoclasm as a universal standard that unites productive workers of all classes. As the industrial worker develops this iconoclasm by working in a factory, so the critical social scientist develops it by working on—that is, by studying—the iconoclastic worker. Veblen himself submits to the discipline of the machine in the act of writing about the machine; were his writing to fail "of the precise measure by more or less, the exigencies of the process [would] check the aberration and drive home the absolute need of conformity" (*TBE*, 308). The interdependence fostered by the modern machine process binds workers and intellectuals together not by allowing for the technocratic manipulation of workers by intellectuals but by spreading the single standard of critical thinking to every social class (*TBE*, 7, 17, 323–24).

Knowledge as Estrangement

Whether industrial workers actually experienced the liberation Veblen ascribes to them is a question for social history. Why every social institution in the modern world must be judged in terms of its ability to liberate the individual is a question for intellectual history. Veblen's rather sanguine view of the machine process is best explained not by his distance from the actual experience of industrial workers but by his proximity to a social-scientific structure of perception that filters all experience through the antinomies of liberation versus repression, or reason versus tradition. Within this structure of thought, every social activity, from working in a factory to writing social science, becomes an occasion for liberating one's mind from repressive traditions. Ultimately, worker and social scientist alike appear as variations on a more basic character type: the iconoclastic individual who has served as the hero of most of modern literature.

Postromantic writing often presents the liberation of the individual as both a blessing and a curse. Having heroically pulled themselves out of all traditions, individuals find themselves alienated from all traditions, indeed, from social life in general. Veblen slights this side of iconoclasm in his account of the individual-as-worker, yet he addresses it directly in his account of the individual-as-intellectual. The key work here is Veblen's essay "The Intellectual Pre-Eminence of Jews in Modern Europe." What is striking about this piece is not the characterization of the Jewish intellectual as a rootless, alienated cosmopolitan; there is certainly a long literary tradition for Veblen to have drawn on for that stereotype. What is striking is that Veblen's characterization of what it means to be a rootless, alienated cosmopolitan shares so much with his characterization of the savage workman, the early-modern handicraftsman, and the modern interchangeable worker. For Veblen, Jews are first of all a "hybrid" people.[15] The hybrid status of Jews, rather than any particular Jewish trait, is responsible for their intellectual preeminence ("IPJE," 223). Veblen characterizes this hybrid status in the following manner:

> It appears to be only when the gifted Jew escapes from the cultural environment created and fed by the particular genius of his own people, only when he falls into an alien line of gentile inquiry and becomes a naturalised, though hyphenate, citizen in the gentile republic of learning, that he comes into his own as a creative leader in the world's intellectual enterprise. It is by loss of allegiance, or at best by force of a divided allegiance to the people of his origin, that he finds himself in the vanguard of modern inquiry. ("IPJE," 225–26)

For Veblen, since Jewish intellectuals have to break from their own traditions in order to enter gentile intellectual life, they are in a better position to break down gentile traditions. Once again, boundary crossing carries with it the skeptical frame of mind that is essential to modern science and scholarship ("IPJE," 226–28). In this liminal, boundary position, the Jewish intellectual accepts neither the Jewish nor the gentile world: "By consequence he is in a peculiar degree exposed to the unmediated facts of the current situation: and in a peculiar degree, therefore, he takes his orientation from the run of the facts as he finds them, rather than from the traditional interpretation of analogous facts in the past. In short, he is a skeptic by force of circumstances over which he has no control" ("IPJE," 229). Crossing the boundary between two cultures gives the intellectual, much like the hybrid savage, a relatively unmediated, matter-of-fact perspective on men and things. Jewish intellectual "renegades" possess the "free-swung skeptical initiative" that allows them to see each tradition for what it really is, "only an ephemeral web of habits of thought" ("IPJE," 228).

Such an understanding of the world, however, issues in alienation from the world. The outsider/intellectual "becomes a disturber of the intellectual peace, but only at the cost of becoming an intellectual wayfaring man, a wanderer in the intellectual no-man's-land, seeking another place to rest, farther along the road, somewhere over the horizon. They are neither a complaisant nor a contented lot, these aliens of the uneasy feet; but that is, after all, not the point in question" ("IPJE," 227). What is the point in question? Simply the constant intellectual wandering that is criticism. Criticism may liberate, or it may alienate, but it must be free to wander, and in that wandering be free to uproot any tradition it may find. With criticism, as with capitalism, all that is solid melts into air.

The Jewish intellectual stands as representative of the modern, cosmopolitan, humanistic scholar of any ethnic background. In *The Higher Learning in America,* Veblen addresses the problem of modern humanistic scholarship in the broadest possible terms. Unlike natural scientists, social scientists take as their object of study "matters which intimately touch the community's accepted scheme of life."[16] Social scientists

> are occupied with inquiry into the nature of the conventions under which men live, the institutions of society—customs, usages, traditions, convention, canons of conduct, standards of life, of taste, of morality and religion, law and order. No faithful inquiry into these matters can avoid an air of scepticism as to the stability or finality of someone or other among the received articles of institutional furniture. (*HL,* 180–81)

The "jealous orthodoxy" of backward masses and conservative scholars alike seeks to limit social-scientific inquiry in order to preserve "the articles of the current social creed" (*HL,* 181). Social-scientific criticism requires detachment from the traditions of all classes, a detachment which often issues in the suspicion or hostility of all classes, which then issues in the kind of alienation associated with the Jewish intellectual.

Veblen's account of the embattled, alienated scholar seems at odds with his account of the heroic march of the modern machine process. Ideally, the machine process should leave no established social practice exempt from its discipline; alas, although it "touches wider and wider circles of the population, and touches them in an increasingly intimate and coercive manner," not all areas of life have succumbed to its discipline (*TBE,* 372–73). The traditions of the past, particularly religion and the price system, linger on. Ultimately, Veblen sees his age as one of "transition," in which the "discipline of the machine process has not yet had time, nor has it had a clear field," to realize its full potential as a principle of interdependence (*IW,* 322).

Critical social scientists writing in Veblen's wake would devote themselves to clearing the field for the expansion, if not the final triumph, of the machine process. This field clearing would have as its goal not the end of transition but the liberation of the dynamic principle of transition embodied in a machine process unfettered by received traditions. The first step in clearing the field would be fieldwork itself. Veblen's anthropological approach to economics appeared as a "realistic" alternative to the hopelessly abstract, deductive theories of the orthodox economic thought of his time. However, by the 1920s, the empirical rigor of the rising discipline of sociology made even Veblen's work seem little more than an armchair analysis of American life. After all, Veblen did no fieldwork. Still, with the principle of transition at its very core, Veblen's thought invites the kind of revision that can only reproduce what it seeks to move beyond. To understand this dialectical process of revision, we must turn to Robert and Helen Lynd's *Middletown,* which, through its critical use of the anthropological concept of culture, represents both the most significant attack on armchair social science in the wake of Veblen and an even more relentless writing of the instinct of workmanship into the flux of experience.

Chapter 2

■

Middletown as Transition

Why "Middletown"?

ROBERT LYND AND Helen Merrell first met each other while hiking on Mount Washington in the summer of 1921. As the two struck up a conversation, Helen mentioned that she had been reading Thorstein Veblen's *Theory of the Leisure Class*. This seemed to forge a bond between the young, socially conscious seminary student and the recent graduate of Wellesley College. The two soon married, and within three years found themselves united by a social-science book of their own, a community study of Muncie, Indiana, that would become the most influential work of its kind in the history of American social science.[1] A study of the effects of industrialization on a small Midwestern town between 1890 and 1920, *Middletown* stands in the Veblenian tradition of social science not only in its concern for debunking popular prejudices but also, and more importantly, in the way in which it takes "work" as the organizing principle of its narrative.[2] Through their appropriation of the anthropological notion of culture as a whole way of life, the Lynds invest Veblen's instinct of workmanship with an empirical intensity beyond anything approached by Veblen himself, and they effectively write the demands of workmanship into every aspect of human life.

Like Veblen, the Lynds were both representative and marginal figures in the social science of their day. They aspired to the empirical and analytic rigor of the scientism that dominated sociology during the 1920s, but they both lacked formal training in sociology. The success of *Middletown* brought the Lynds professional acceptance, but the study itself took shape outside of the institutional channels of mainstream, academic social science, in the Institute for Social and Religious Research, a nonprofit organization funded by John D. Rockefeller Jr. The institute's choice of a community-study project followed the sociological conventions of the times, but the choice of a homogeneous, Midwestern small town contrasted sharply with the emphasis that leading sociologists such as W. I. Thomas and Robert Park placed on the study of the diverse racial and ethnic communities of major urban areas.[3]

Unlike Veblen, the Lynds explicitly address the problems of placement, marginality, and representativeness. *Middletown* opens by addressing not the problems facing the people of Middletown but the problem of studying those problems. Despite its narrative, almost novelistic tone, *Middletown* opens with an unprecedented reflection on methodology in its foreword, by the anthropologist Clark Wissler.[4] Defending the Lynds' anthropological approach, Wissler writes:

> What is not realized is that anthropology deals with the communities of mankind, takes the community, or tribe, as the biological and social unit, and in its studies seeks to arrive at a perspective of society by comparing and contrasting these communities; and whatever may be the deficiencies of anthropology, it achieves a large measure of objectivity, because anthropologists are by the nature of the case "outsiders." To study ourselves as through the eye of an outsider is the basic difficulty in social science, and may be insurmountable, but the authors of this volume have made a serious attempt by approaching an American community as an anthropologist does a primitive tribe. It is in this that the contribution lies, an experiment not only in method, but in a new field, the social anthropology of contemporary life.[5]

Even as Wissler's foreword functions as an authenticating device for *Middletown* as a work of science, it presents *Middletown* as a work that challenges accepted scientific conventions. The Lynds draw on the methods of an established discipline such as anthropology, but they direct these methods from the conventional study of "savage" peoples to the unconventional study of "civilized" peoples. *Middletown* stands outside not only the mainstream of society by virtue of its status as an "objective" social science but also the mainstream of sociology by virtue of its innovative methodology.

Ironically, the Lynds' very detachment serves as a measure of their engagement with reality. Even as their objectivity pulls them outside of their object of study, it also draws them deeper into that object. According to Wissler, *Middletown*'s methodological stance embodies the recent "realization that we must deal directly with life itself, that the realities of social science are what people do" (v). Wissler writes, "True, many attempts have been made to find the basic factors in society, but these factors have been sought, for the most part, in the laboratories of biology and psychology, which is not unlike groping behind the scenes and digging under the stage, disregarding the comedies, tragedies, and dramas in plain sight" (v). Wissler's use of artistic metaphors suggests affinities between social anthropology and drama criticism, yet he sees the Lynds' brand of drama criticism as tougher, more exacting, more strenuous, and more accurate than a hard physical science like biology could be in dealing with society. Scientists who have broken free from the laboratory, the Lynds are not so much outsiders as outsiders looking in: detached enough to capture the social whole, yet engaged enough to see that whole in all its particularity.

The Lynds' placement as social scientists parallels the placement of the people of Middletown as objects of social-scientific inquiry. Wissler criticizes previous studies for their tendency to focus either too narrowly on the level of individuals or too broadly on the level of statistical abstractions. Then he praises the Lynds for navigating between these extremes: "There remains, however, the obvious condition that the masses of individuals concerned live and function in communities, and that picture will not be complete until these communities also are made objects of study" (vi). "Community" here serves as a middle ground, a Middletown, between abstract social forces and isolated individuals. As the Lynds take a detached-yet-engaged approach to the people of Middletown, so those people live as individuals-in-communities. An attempt to combine analytic rigor and synthetic wholeness, this formulation of middleness sees understanding as lying in the shifting of perspectives back and forth between the particular and the general, the individual and the community. No golden mean or stable point of synthesis, this social-scientific middle is a dynamic point of synthesizing and resynthesizing the individual and the community. Wissler's foreword makes no strong claims for the specific findings of *Middletown,* and the Lynds themselves constantly hedge, qualify, and apologize for the crudeness and incompleteness of their data. What Wissler, and *Middletown* as a book, argue for is "the manner of social anthropology," the perspective of inquiring middleness, the idea of culture as a relation rather than a substance. In short, *Middletown* makes an argument about form, not content, and it takes as its task the writing of this form into the objective structures of society.

The instability of this form becomes apparent in the opening attempt to sketch out what is "middle" about Middletown. The Lynds see Middletown as representative of America as a whole, or at least of the process of industrialization within America. That this representativeness should be figured as middleness suggests both the subjective middleness of the sociological perspective laid out by Wissler and the objective middleness of a statistical average, the middle point between two extremes. Any sympathetic reading of chapter 1, titled "Nature of the Investigation," will have to concede that the Lynds go to great lengths to address the problem of their own subjective preconceptions and the objective bias of the particular characteristics of Middletown. The Lynds concede that there is no real "typical city," but they maintain that "the city studied was selected as having many features common to a wide group of communities" (3). What are these features? Middletown has a temperate climate; it has recently experienced rapid demographic growth; it has industry based on modern, high-speed technology, yet it is not a one-industry town; it has a local, nonuniversity art life to "balance" this industry; it has no "outstanding peculiarities which would mark it off from the mid channel sort of American community"; and it is in "that common-denominator of America, the Middle West," which served as the historic meeting point of colonists from New England, New York, and the South. True to its history, Middletown has maintained a homogeneous, native-born population, with few blacks or immigrants. With its population between twenty-five and fifty thousand people, Middletown is "large enough to have put on long trousers and to take itself seriously, and yet small enough to be studied from many aspects as a unit." Taken together, these traits show Middletown to be self-contained, yet not isolated, to exist apart from, yet still communicate with, the outside world of America at large (7–8).

The Lynds list these characteristics in order to establish the "middle-of-the-road quality about Middletown" (9). This in-betweeness seems to grow out of the landscape itself, as the Lynds quote an Isaak Walton League characterization of the Midwest: "This Corn Belt . . . is not a land to thrill one who loves hills, wild landscape, mountain panorama, waterfalls, babbling brooks, and nature undisturbed. In this flat land of food crops and murky streams rich with silt, man must find thrills in other things, perhaps in travel, print, radio, or movie" (225). This passage brings out two important aspects of the middleness at work in *Middletown*. The middle is on the one hand boring; it is flat, with no peaks or valleys. Aesthetically, it is practically barren; nature exists simply for use. The Midwest's streams are filled with silt, and its produce—"food crops"—suggests not a satisfying bounty but a nasty and brutish subsistence. Paradoxically, the very barrenness of this middle flatland inspires an assertion of human powers through travel or man-made thrills such as print, radio, and movies. One gets the impression that a more seductive landscape would have sapped Midwesterners of the sturdy self-reliance that is their trademark.

Deprived of the peaks and valleys of nature, midwesterners have had to make their own peaks and valleys. In arguing this point, the Lynds quote a John Dewey essay titled "The American Intellectual Frontier": "The 'Middle-West,' the prairie country, has been the center of active philanthropies and political progressivism. It has formed the solid element in our diffuse national life and heterogeneous populations. . . . It has been the middle in every sense of the word and in every movement. Like every mean, it has held things together and given unity and stability of movement" (8). Relegated to a rather inconspicuous footnote early on in the book, this passage nonetheless embodies values concerning cultural change that are essential to understanding *Middletown*. According to this passage, the "solid element" of American life is also the most fluid and dynamic one—that element concerned with the philanthropic and politically progressive remaking of the world. For the Lynds, stability must always be seen in relation to flux. Simply to speak of a solid element itself conjures up notions of stagnation and isolation, however, a solid element takes on great value if placed in the context of a "diffuse national life and heterogeneous populations." The values of the Midwest, and the "middle" in general, are not so much "unity and stability" as "unity and stability *of movement*" (emphasis added). In the world of *Middletown*, every "solid element" needs a fluidity that it can bring order to as a discipline against stagnation, just as dynamic change needs a solid element to prevent it from degenerating into aimless flux.

The dynamic nature of the middle speaks to the primary concern of *Middletown*, the study of cultural change. The Lynds define the cultural change they present in their account as "the interplay of a relatively constant native American stock and its changing environment" (8). The establishment of this notion of cultural change as the central problem of *Middletown* constitutes the ideological work of the opening profile of Middletown. It is not, however, because of the way this notion substitutes the Midwestern W.A.S.P. for the diverse peoples of race, ethnicity, and region that make up America as a whole but because of the way that this definition gives the man-nature, or man-thing, relation priority over relations between men. The homogeneous population of Middletown serves as the individual writ large, and for all of its "cultural" analysis, *Middletown* basically offers a study of how this individual interacts with its material world. This definition pairs a "constant" or solid element located in a human subjectivity, the "native American stock," with a "changing" or fluid element located in an objective social/material world, an "environment." At times, the changing environment itself will appear more solid than the human subjectivity so often drifting aimlessly within it, but the ideal of some productive union of solid and fluid elements drives the Lynds' line of inquiry.

Work as Culture

As soon as the Lynds establish Middletown as a solid element through which to study cultural change, they break down this solid element into its constituent parts. The Lynds divide Middletown life into six categories: 1. getting a living, 2. making a home, 3. training the young, 4. using leisure, 5. engaging in religious practices, and 6. engaging in community activities (4). As soon as they establish these divisions, they apologize for reducing the complexity of Middletown life to six broad, rather abstract categories. They excuse this seeming reduction as a "methodological expedient" intended to lift their study to an "impersonal plane"; however, they offer no excuse for their assertion of "The Dominance of Getting a Living" (4, 21). In the Lynds' study, work serves unequivocally as the reference point for all the varied activities of Middletown life. "As in trying to discover the underlying meaning to Middletown of its getting-a-living activities" appears as an obligatory introduction to the Lynds' account of the underlying meaning of activities ranging from going to church to listening to the radio to preparing meals (402). The primacy given to work establishes *Middletown* as not only a study of *modern American culture* (which is, in some sense, dominated by work) but more importantly as a *modern study* of American culture in that it takes work as naturally prior to all other cultural activities. As the descriptive becomes the normative in the Lynds' account, the problem of work in *Middletown* comes to lie not in the dominance of getting a living so much as in the failure of getting a living to be meaningful and fulfilling.

The solid root of Middletown culture, work must nonetheless be broken up into its constituent parts. From the outset, the Lynds establish work as a mysterious reality that needs to be penetrated, deciphered, and decoded by social science: "At first glance it is difficult to see any semblance of pattern in the workaday life of a community exhibiting a crazy-quilt array of nearly four hundred ways of getting its living. . . . On closer scrutiny, however, this welter may be resolved into two kinds of activities. The people who engage in them will be referred to throughout the report as the Working Class and the Business Class" (22). For the Lynds, this distinction between the working class and the business class "is the most significant single cultural factor tending to influence what one does all day long throughout one's life." From it flow distinctions such as Holy Roller/Presbyterian, Ford/Buick, Sew We Do Club/Art Students League, and Odd Fellows/Masonic Shrine (24).

Ironically, even as the Lynds argue for the centrality of the working class/business class distinction, they practically qualify it out of existence:

No such classification is entirely satisfactory. The aerial photographer inevitably sacrifices minor contours as he ascends high enough to view a total terrain. Within these two major groups there is an infinite number of gradations. . . . There is naturally, too, a twilight belt in which some members of the two groups overlap or merge.

Were a minute structural diagram the aim of this study, it would be necessary to decipher in much greater detail the multitude of overlapping groupings observable in Middletown. Since what is sought, however, is an understanding of the major functional characteristics of this changing culture, it is important that significant outlines be not lost in detail and the groups in the city which exhibit the dominant characteristics most clearly must, therefore, form the foci of the report. (23)

These passages do not suggest confusion on the part of the Lynds so much as the aporia of analysis and synthesis that characterizes modern social-scientific thought as a whole.[6] The attempt to synthesize the varied activities of Middletown life according to a "single cultural factor" threatens to simplify the complexity of Middletown as a whole, yet the "closer scrutiny" intended as an antidote to oversimplification threatens to analyze the class structure of Middletown into "an infinite number of gradations" that would seem to render all synthetic statements suspect. Indeed, the Lynds themselves explicitly voice such suspicions: "Wherever throughout the report either Middletown or any group within the city is referred to as a unit, such a mode of expression must be regarded as simply a short hand symbol. Any discussion of characteristics of groups are of necessity approximations only and the fact that the behavior of individuals is the basis of social behavior must never be lost sight of" (24). Unable to and seemingly unconcerned with resolving this methodological dilemma, the Lynds simply concede the limitations of their study and the necessity of a social-scientific division of labor: aerial photographers on a cultural reconaissance mission, they invite the microscopic follow-up of "a minute structural diagram." If the Lynds' rather perfunctory qualifications point to any resolution at all, it seems to lie in favor of the "multitude of overlapping groupings" that problematize conventional understandings of both group and individual behavior. Even as the Lynds claim to forsake "detail" for "significant outlines," their study focuses on a "twilight belt" of experience that transcends the working class/business class division.

In shuttling back and forth between the synthetic and the analytic, between outlines and details, the Lynds initially stress the absolute difference between the working class and the business class: "Members of the first group, by and large, address their activities in getting their living primarily to *things*, utilizing material tools in the making of things and the performance of services, while the members of the second group address their activities predominantly to *people* in the selling or promotion of things, services, and ideas" (22). The Lynds figure this basic opposition of things versus people also as one of hands versus tongues, making versus selling, tools versus institutional devices, and perhaps most importantly, the material versus the nonmaterial (22). These distinctions are at once descriptive and normative, on the surface as a pattern of culture yet implying a deep essence that is somehow being repressed by that culture. Part of the Lynds' sociological "shorthand," these distinctions imply a normative hierarchy of experience in which things are somehow more real than people. In setting up a distinction in terms of material tools versus nonmaterial institutional devices (as opposed to, say, institutional devices versus noninstitutional material tools), the Lynds privilege the material and make it the reference point by which to discuss the distinction; the material precedes the nonmaterial, making precedes selling. In the Lynds' account of Middletown life, the earlier rising hours of the working class seem to speak for the primacy of "making," a technical relation between man and thing, to "selling," an exchange relation between men (53).

These distinctions are, of course, the tropes of Veblen's instinct of workmanship. Like Veblen, the Lynds make these distinctions only to undermine them. These distinctions provide the Lynds with a vocabulary with which to approach a "twilight belt" between making and selling, the instrumental and the institutional, or the material and the nonmaterial. They approach this twilight belt not in terms of an objective occupational structure but in terms of a subjective quality of experience that would seem to defy simple class analysis. The "solid" encounter with things by the working class and the "fluid" encounter with people by the business class both fall short of a kind of solid fluidity that serves as the critical standard by which the Lynds assess Middletown life.

Middletown has been seen as a critique of the debilitating effects of the money medium of exchange on the life of Middletown. On closer examination, the book seems to locate the problem, of which the cash nexus is only one manifestation, at a still deeper level. The relative distance of the working class from exchange relations provides no privileged position from which to interact with the environment of Middletown as a whole. According to the Lynds, the working class and the business class of Middletown have both "forsaken the less vicarious life of the farm or village" (44). For the working class, this vicariousness is a function of "industrial tools [that] have become increasingly elaborated"; for the business class, it is a function of their role in the "noticeable swelling in the number and complexity of the institutional rituals by which the specialized products of the individual worker are converted into the biological and social essentials of living" (44). To see the problem of Middletown as one of vicariousness suggests that the people of Middletown experience life secondhand, yet at this point in the analysis it is not clear what firsthand experience would be, since it seems to reside in neither "things" nor "people."

The Lynds locate the vicarious quality of Middletown life in the "gap between the things people do to get a living and the actual needs of living" (39). The business class would seem to be more removed from these actual needs than the working class; in their role as intermediaries, they operate the "devices for converting the actual products of labor into the necessities and satisfactions of life . . . the exchanging or arranging for exchange of money for usable things in stores, banks, and offices" (45). The use of the metaphor of "devices," however, points to certain tensions and contradictions in the way the Lynds frame the problem of vicarious experience throughout *Middletown*. On the one hand, "device" is a technological term; the development of technology has produced many new devices to expand human powers, to build bridges wherever perceived gaps exist, and thus, in a sense, to overcome distance. On the other hand, a device can be a kind of trick, a gimmick, a rigging of reality. The Lynds suggest this second sense of "device" by referring to the mediating activities of the business class as a "set of rituals." Rituals, as in Veblen, are always suspect as distortions of reality (45).

The working class's seemingly direct, technical encounter with things cannot overcome the vicariousness of Middletown life in general. Even a quintessentially technical, thing-oriented activity such as construction must be "extensively financed by the banker" (46). This characterization suggests a corrupting influence external to the technical process of construction itself, but financial distortions such as "discounting second mortgage notes" are themselves described in conventionally technical metaphors such as "machinery" (46–47). This conflation of the technical and the financial suggests not only the corruption of pure construction by credit but also the "mechanical" nature of business-class work itself: "under the rules prescribed by 'business,' he [the business man] seems subject to almost as many restrictions as the machine dictates to the worker who manipulates its levers" (45). Thus, this vicariousness results not from one class (business) imposing its experience (the money medium of exchange) on another but from the interaction of two similar yet distinct kinds of lived experience.

Whatever this vicariousness is, it would seem to have something to do with the cluster of meanings surrounding the metaphor of the machine. Yet what is the "machine" if it can be used to describe both business-class paperwork and working-class industrial labor? For the Lynds, the metaphor of the machine seems to express best the alienation experienced in modern work in which jobs, figured as "routinized activities," have little relation to "the food, sex, and shelter needs of human beings" (39). But what is "work" that it should ideally be connected in some immediate way to human "needs"? What is immediate or direct experience if even the hard materiality of industrial labor appears vicarious because it does not result in the direct production of food, clothing, and shelter "needs"? To answer these questions in the context of *Middletown*, we must turn to the central question posed by the Lynds in light of the dominance of getting a living in the lives of the people of Middletown: Why do they work so hard?

This question serves as the title for the final chapter in the Lynds' section on "Getting a Living." The question suggests concern for the subjective meaning of work in the lives of workers; the Lynds primarily address the "why," not the "what" or "how," of work. This turn to the psychology of work, however innovative for its time, in many ways marks a return to the classical economics of seventeenth- and eighteenth-century social science. Classical economic thought rejected traditional understandings of human nature in order to examine the "true" motivations that lie behind human actions; economics has to a large degree been psychology right from the start, and classical economists themselves felt that they had uncovered what the Lynds refer to as "the most powerful impulses of human beings" when they developed their notion of rational self-interest (73). In the perpetual revolt against formalism that is social-scientific revision, each generation of social science exposes the shallowness of the previous generation's conception of human motivation, and then proceeds to offer a deeper account of that motivation. The specific content of this human depth varies from generation to generation, but the move to depth perpetuates a social-scientific structure of thought in which true, deep, essential human needs stand opposed to, or repressed by, false, superficial, socially constructed human wants.

The Lynds' critique of the degradation of work under industrial capitalism follows the logic of this social-scientific revision. Industrialism itself grew out of a certain social-scientific attitude toward work, and the Lynds' social-scientific critique of industrialism only reproduces that attitude at a deeper level. Consider, for example, the opening passage of chapter 8, "Why Do They Work So Hard?":

One emerges from the offices, stores, and factories of Middletown in some bewilderment why all the able-bodied men and many of the women devote their best energies for long hours day after day to this driving activity, seemingly so foreign to many of the most powerful impulses of human beings. Is all this expenditure of energy necessary to secure food, clothing, shelter, and other things essential to existence? If not, precisely what over and beyond these subsistence necessaries is Middletown getting out of its work? (73)

From this passage, it would seem as if the Lynds see work as essentially an "expenditure of energy" in which man engages to secure "subsistence necessaries" such as "food, clothing, shelter, and other things essential to existence"; however, although the passage clearly criticizes the general experience of work in Middletown, its very abstraction of a variety of occupations into a general category of work, conceived of as a certain reserve of energy which may be properly or improperly expended, only reproduces the dominant conception of labor under industrial capitalism. One need not equate the Lynds with a Taylor or a Gilbreth to see them as operating within the same conceptual (and class) world that defines work in terms of energy. Like modern efficiency experts, the Lynds fear the "best energies" of people are somehow being misspent.

Within this conceptual world there are distinctions, and these distinctions tend to get ordered in a variety of highbrow/lowbrow, depth/surface oppositions. Middle-class humanists tend to see the Lynds' ideal of work as the deep or highbrow one, with Taylor and Gilbreth's conception merely a superficial, lowbrow vulgarization of this ideal; middle-class businessmen tend to see things somewhat the opposite. Alas, on the slaughter bench of social-scientific revision, yesterday's humanist becomes, in a sense, today's businessman, and yesterday's essence becomes today's social construction.

The idea of essence as "depth" is inherently unstable, for it admits of no context in terms of which to be evaluated. In moving away from surface, depth moves away from all normative ordering contexts. Consider the following passage: "Thus this crucial activity of spending one's best energies year in and year out in doing things remote from the immediate concerns of living eventuates apparently in the ability to buy somewhat more than formerly, but both business men and working men seem to be running for dear life in this business of making the money they earn keep pace with the even more rapid growth of their subjective wants" (87). Here, in Veblenian fashion, the Lynds contrast a use value of human needs—"the immediate concerns of living"—to a morally and intellectually inferior exchange value of "subjective wants." They clearly see the problem of work in Middletown in terms of the battle of needs versus wants over possession of the "best energies" of men, but the language that structures their account renders the distinction between needs and wants terminally moot.

Consider the Lynds' characterization of work in terms of "subsistence necessaries" (73). On one level, the philosophers and practitioners of the most brutal forms of industrial capitalism would have no argument with this characterization of work; however, one could argue that capitalists are not concerned with "real" subsistence, only a self-serving vulgarization of "true" subsistence. The Lynds would then represent the highbrow critique that conceives of subsistence as not those nasty and brutish essentials that keep a person working despite grinding poverty but the simple bounty that satisfies true needs as opposed to the superfluous wants "over and beyond" those needs. Such a simple bounty is, however, not so simple. The Lynds never really define particular needs, and their critique in no way implies any proper ordering of human needs in a relation that would suggest some notion of a simple bounty. In avoiding one kind of essentialism, the Lynds fall into another; rather than judging Middletown by some substantive conception of human nature, the Lynds judge it by a procedural one. In the Lynds' account, the failure of Middletown lies not in its failure to bring about a proper ordering of particular human needs but in its failure to liberate a general category of human needs from an equally general category of human wants. No substance in its own right, "human needs" appears merely as a residue of debunked human wants. Ultimately, this debunking itself emerges as the essential human activity.

In their discussion of industrial work, the Lynds abstract particular human needs into a general category of needs that they label "personality." According to the Lynds, modern work in Middletown "demands little of a worker's personality save rapid, habitual reactions and an ability to submerge himself in the performance of a few routinized easily learned movements"; consequently, "the amount of robust satisfaction ... [people] derive from the actual performance of their specific jobs seems, at best, to be slight" (75–76, 73). That the Lynds should tie work so closely to something called "personality" speaks of the post-Protestant, modernist cultural milieu in which they wrote, but *Middletown* makes claims for this understanding of work that extend far beyond this rather limited milieu. In the Lynds' historical narrative, the Middletown of 1890 serves as a preindustrial, almost premodern past against which to assess the modern, industrial Middletown of the 1920s. To charge that modern work lacks "the satisfactions that *formerly* accompanied the job" suggests not only that the people of 1890 were satisfied with their work but also that the work of that time was organized to ensure the satisfaction of the human personality (76; emphasis added). Medieval craftsmen certainly did not make this connection between work and personality.[7] The culturally Protestant workers of the Middletown of the 1890s may indeed have made this connection, but in having a thirty-year period in the history of a small Midwestern town stand for the epochal shift from preindustrial to industrial, from premodern to modern, *Mid-*

dletown essentializes a basically Protestant, modernist psychology that sees work as an occasion for the development of personality.

Just what is "personality" that work should demand so much of it? Consider the following passage in which the Lynds describe the craft of glassblowing as practiced in the 1890s: "It is important to note that the speed and rhythm of the work were set by the human organism, not by a machine. And with all the repetition of movement involved, the remark of an old glass-blower should be borne in mind, that 'you never learn all there is to glass-blowing, as there's always some new twist occuring to you' " (41). Here we have work in the state of nature. The "rhythm of the work" is set not by the thick social relations of a craft guild, or any social relations for that matter, but by "the human organism"—a biological unit which, in this characterization, seems to have no social ties. The Lynds here abstract the "pure" technical aspect of craft from all social relations and naturalize this technical aspect so that it becomes the solid core upon which external social forces such as the machine act. Once the Lynds do this, the dynamic or novel aspects of work come to stand as the defining characteristics of work as a whole; the robust satisfaction of preindustrial work appears tied primarily to there always being "some new twist" in the work process. This imperative of perpetual novelty in work reflects the Lynds' conception of personality. In a sense, to have a personality is to develop a personality, and the self-development that the Lynds see in craft work serves as a microcosm of the developmental frame of *Middletown* as a whole.

Even when the Lynds do address the social relations of preindustrial work, they do so in a way that makes those relations appear as little more than personality writ large. They describe the shift from craft to industrial work as a "shift from a system in which length of service, craftsmanship, and authority in the shop and social prestige among one's peers tended to go together to one which, in the main, demands little of a worker's personality" (75). The craft values of this passage—length of service, shop authority, social prestige—certainly suggest social relations of some kind; but when they can be compared, or even contrasted, to the demands that industrial machinery makes on the "worker's personality," they become secondary to, or a function of, the more basic phenomenon of personality. This passage suggests a transhistorical nexus of personality as the basis for comparing craft and industry. The organic unity of length of service, craftsmanship, shop authority, and social prestige has value because it seems to demand much of, and thus help develop, the worker's personality. By rooting the problem of industrial work in the "decrease in psychological satisfactions derived from the sense of craftsmanship and in group solidarity," the Lynds imply that the organization of preindustrial work was somehow a projection of the basic needs of the human personality.

From this psychological base, the Lynds subsume all particular crafts under the general category of a "sense" of craftsmanship, a feeling of being craftsmanlike. By positing an actual historical decline in something called a sense of craftsmanship, the Lynds effectively read a bourgeois Protestant work ethic into a basically prebourgeois form of organizing work. The medieval guilds that bequeathed craft techniques to the preindustrial phase of the bourgeois era did not organize crafts to ensure the fulfillment of the individual; indeed, they did not see in the craftsmen who made up their ranks "individuals" in the modern sense of that term. Guild restrictions on output and control of prices would prove to be anathema to the bourgeois work ethic, with its emphasis on individual independence and the development of the technical aspects of work figured objectively as the forces of production. The key point of contrast between craft and industrial work lies not in psychological satisfaction or technical proficiency but in their respective attitudes toward the social and natural world. Craft represents an ideal of work geared toward security and stability, not risk and development. Particular crafts, in some sense incommensurable with each other, take on meaning not from a shared technical instrumentality but from their particular places within a larger natural and social order that, while not necessarily static, has a constancy that must somehow be respected. There may always be new twists in the technical aspect of a craft, but craft organization still assumes that in the end, there is nothing new under the sun; any changes in the work process must be held accountable to an order larger than work, an order that contains work.

In contrast to craft, the modern work ethic equates work with the social order itself. Everything in society outside of work proper must conform to its demands. Far from lacking "new twists," the modern work ethic, especially as embodied in industrialism, makes novelty central to the work process; moreover, the imperative of constant improvement makes the old ways of work obsolete. The modern work ethic approaches nature and society not as a normative order to be respected but as a set of neutral, objective laws to be directed and redirected toward man's desired ends. The constant improvement of the work process issues in the constant revision of the social order. In this process of revision, the order one respects and holds oneself accountable to is not nature or society, but the process of instrumental reasoning itself, whose seat is the individual consciousness.

The Lynds' account of the relation between work and the social order draws on all of the individualizing and psychologizing tropes of the modern work ethic. As they see craft in terms of a "sense of craftsmanship," so they see social life in terms of group "solidarity," that feeling of belonging, that psychological substitute for constitutive social bonds that has plagued bourgeois thought since the rise of sociology in the nineteenth century.[8] By rooting the social bond in a feeling located in the psychological makeup of individuals, the most enlightened sociologists of the nineteenth century believed they had found an antidote to modern anomie that would nonetheless preserve the freedom and independence associated with modern individuality. True to this tradition, the Lynds root craft solidarity in an even more basic craft independence, and they identify this independence as the primary need of the human personality repressed by the machine.

According to the Lynds, the modern industrial worker is trapped in a "whole complex of doing day after day fortuitously assigned things, chiefly at the behest of other people" (52). Consequently, "The work of a modern machine-tender leaves nothing tangible at the end of the day's work to which he can point with pride and say 'I did that—it is the result of my own skill and my own effort!' " (76). The tangibility lost in modern machine work clearly must mean more than the ability to touch things, for by the Lynds' definition, working-class people work with their *hands* on *things*. Tangibility here seems to refer to a feeling of "pride"; more specifically pride in possession and control, not of things, but of one's "own skill" and "own effort." The Lynds associate the tangibility of preindustrial work with the worker's independence, his lack of indebtedness to his fellow man; appropriately, they link the seeming intangibility of modern work to a situation in which, for the worker, "neither present nor future appears to hold . . . much prospect of dominance on the job or the breaking through to further expansion of personal powers" (80). The Lynds here translate a bourgeois social convention into a deep, ahistorical, psychological need: The human personality requires work by which to achieve dominance and expand personal powers. In this way, they effectively essentialize or naturalize the bourgeois social relation of independence, the very social relation that Veblen's history of culture presents as flourishing in the initial stages of the era of handicraft.

The intangibility of modern work speaks to the vicarious quality of Middletown life as a whole (44). The problem facing Middletown as it engages in the activity of getting a living also faces it as it engages in the other activities that make up the whole way of life of Middletown culture. Wherever the Lynds look, they find a crisis in workmanlike independence. Ironically, the Lynds find a cultural equivalent of the machine in nothing less than Middletown culture as a whole. The various activities that the Lynds examine have not been mechanized per se, but they take on the same mechanical rigidity found in industrial work by virtue of their connection to received customs and traditions.

This concern for Middletown achieving independence from its own traditions parallels the Lynds' concern with their own independence from their own traditions, that is, their own "objectivity" with respect to Middletown. The Lynds' opening remarks make clear that their social-scientific objectivity lies not in their freedom from bias but in their attempt to move beyond bias. Their account of Middletown life posits no stable point of independence from received traditions; rather, it calls attention to the failure of Middletown to engage in the process of pulling itself out of its received traditions. In the intellectual world of *Middletown,* there is no immediacy in itself, simply the move beyond vicariousness; no tangibility, simply the move beyond intangibility; no human needs, simply the move beyond human wants; and no personality, simply the move beyond social conventions. This movement itself constitutes the dominance, the expansion of personal powers that is the essence of workmanlike independence, and this workmanlike independence serves as the single standard that the Lynds' anthropological approach brings to bear on the whole way of life, the culture, of Middletown.

Culture as Work

The Lynds' sympathetic account of craft work should not be mistaken for any simple nostalgia for Middletown's preindustrial past. For the Lynds, the main problem lies not in industrialization itself, but in Middletown's failure to respond intelligently to the changes brought on by industrialization. Just as the issue of psychological satisfaction "must never be lost sight of as we observe Middletown getting its living, making its homes, spending its leisure, and engaging in other vital activities," so, too, the issue of intelligence "should be borne in mind throughout the entire range of earning a living, making a home, leisure time, training the young, religious and community activities" (52, 37). Satisfaction and intelligence serve respectively as the soft, qualitative, and the hard, quantitative, components of the ideal of work through which the Lynds view every aspect of Middletown culture.

The path to psychological satisfaction in work lies in an intelligent encounter with the industrial present. Unfortunately, Middletown has failed to engage in such an encounter. For the Lynds, Middletown's failure of intelligence manifests itself chiefly in the persistence of a "casual" attitude toward the "assignment of life occupations" in the face of widespread psychological dissatisfaction (52). Despite the increasing specialization of modern work, job selection still seems to depend "more upon the work available than upon the subtleties of the individual"; this in turn "tends to fasten upon getting a living an instrumental rather than an inherently satisfying role" (52).

The Lynds concede that Middletown has made some effort to deal intelligently with the problem of work. Middletown has established vocational guidance programs for high school students, complete with intelligence tests through which to discern "the subtleties of the individual" and bring about the "intricate matching of jobs and personalities" (48). Despite these efforts, however, "most of the city's boys and girls 'stumble on' or 'fall into' the particular jobs that become literally their life work" (48). As the Lynds try to explain the persistence of these casual attitudes, they turn to the issue of cultural values: "The pioneer tradition that 'you can't keep a good man down' and the religious tradition of free rational choice in finding one's 'calling' have helped to foster a *laissez-faire* attitude toward matching the individual and the job" (48). This passage would seem to be a clear example of the Lynds' famous "cultural-lag" argument, in which they attribute the troubles of Middletown to the disjunction between old values and new material conditions; according to this argument, new conditions require new values. What exactly, however, is the relation between new values and old values, new conditions and old conditions? Can a "*laissez-faire* attitude toward matching the individual and the job" be equated with casualness and contrasted to rational guidance? The Lynds have been characterized as advocates of some sort of centralized planning as opposed to laissez-faire individualism, but this opposition goes as unexamined in studies of the Lynds as it does in the Lynds' work itself.[9] Put simply, there is nothing "casual" about laissez-faire. It is an economic ideology which assumes that all people are rational individuals with a potentially limitless number of wants. The rationality that constitutes these individuals demands a rigorous examination of self so as to determine which (arbitrary) wants one possesses and how to devise the proper means to attain these wants. Far from rejecting this rationality, centralized planning simply transfers it from the individual to the state, which from its modern inception has been conceived of as a kind of megaindividual, Hobbes's "mortal god," the Leviathan.

The Lynds do not attack the idea that "you can't keep a good man down," simply the "pioneer" version of that maxim. They do not reject "free rational choice in finding one's calling," but a particular "religious" conception of rational choice. According to the Lynds, "traditional social philosophy assumes that each person has a large degree of freedom to climb the ladder to ever wider responsibility, independence, and money income" (65). This characterization of the "traditional social philosophy" would seem to equate the "pioneer," "religious," and *"laissez-faire"* characterizations of the previous passage with a kind of individualism that "assumes that each person has a large degree of freedom." In what sense, however, is vocational guidance a corrective to individualism when it is concerned ideally with uncovering "the subtleties of the individual" so as to implement a more "intricate matching of jobs and personalities"? The individual is clearly still at the center of such a worldview. The Lynds criticize the old social philosophy not for valuing the freedom of the individual to attain "ever wider responsibility, independence and money income" but for failing to perceive the need for new means to achieve those ends.

The rational individual of classical economic thought was never an untutored genius, and advice manuals have been central to the bourgeois world since its inception.[10] Advice manuals must legitimate themselves in two ways: First they must assert their superiority to all previous advice manuals in giving the individual an edge over his competitors; second, they must protest that the only real edge a person can get comes not from trusting any manuals but from trusting oneself. Advice manuals present a kind of authority that always denies its own authority. Vocational guidance and intelligence testing may represent a paradigm shift in this advice-manual tradition because of their social-scientific approach to the individual, but within this paradigm, a similar process of revision goes on. All previous methods for discerning interests and aptitudes have not been scientific enough, and the present method simply offers a more scientific drawing out of the subtleties and complexities that exist objectively in the individual. Vocational guidance presents the individual to himself, and asks the individual to trust himself.

Like advice manuals, vocational guidance represents a simultaneous move from rigidity to flexibility and from flexibility to rigidity. Vocational guidance offers a chance at a better-paying job that would provide one with greater economic freedom, but it also roots out all casualness in arriving at one's life work. Vocational guidance demands that an individual first submit to an examination, and then learn to examine himself, so that he may exercise a responsible and independent *choice* of a vocation. In this way all vocations, all jobs, become first and foremost acts of intellectual labor, born in acts of choice that are the fruit of a rigorous examination of one's self and one's options.

Middletown itself must be seen in this advice-manual tradition. By presenting Middletown to itself, *Middletown* asks Middletown to trust itself—or at least to trust its true self, the rational, objective processes that lie beneath the surface confusion of social life. *Middletown*'s account of vocational guidance must be seen as itself an act of vocational guidance, one directed at Middletown as a whole as it struggles to make choices and deal with change. Broader in scope than conventional vocational guidance, *Middletown* offers Middletown the opportunity to enter the world of intellectual labor, in which self-consciousness makes informed decisions after self-examination. As with all of the organizing concepts of *Middletown,* intellectual labor exists not as a substance in itself but in the movement away from something else, in this case, manual labor. The ideal movement captured by the terms manual and intellectual labor should be seen not as a move from "hands" to "brains," or even from working class to business class, but rather from stasis to change, from stagnation to growth, from conventional to unconventional occupations.

Of course, the existing vocational guidance programs in Middletown have failed to initiate this movement from manual to intellectual labor. This failure cuts across class lines. In the working class, the Lynds see some aspirations to improvement in the tendency of working-class boys to "enter the same line of work as their fathers somewhat less commonly than a generation ago," but they conclude that most "boys naturally tend to gravitate towards the stock occupations understood and recognized by the community" (51). So, too, with business-class children. Students answering vocational guidance surveys often express "uncommon preferences" such as music and architecture, but when existing guidance services attempt to direct students toward the professions, they wind up "unconsciously directing them towards a few lines of work—the traditional professions" (51). Stock occupations and the traditional professions are class variations on the "usual group habits" that prevent Middletown from taking a properly intellectual approach to the problem of work.

This failure of intelligence with respect to vocational guidance serves as a model for the general failure of Middletown culture. The family traditions that interfere with intelligence in the selection of a job appear even more entrenched in the other social activities of Middletown life. Despite the Lynds' suspicions of family ties, they do not simply dismiss these traditions as unworthy of serious consideration. The Lynds are social scientists, and nothing human is foreign to them. Or perhaps because they are social scientists, everything human is foreign to them, and therefore needs to be studied, deciphered, decoded, and explained. Thus, the Lynds on "Making a Home" in Middletown:

> Here, then, in this array of dwellings, ranging from the mean and the cluttered to the spacious and restful, Middletown's most "sacred" institution, the family, works out its destiny. Within the privacy of these shabby or ambitious houses, marriage, birth, child-rearing, death, and the personal immensities of family life go forward. Here, too, as at so many other points, it is not so much these functional urgencies of life that determine how favorable this physical necessity shall be in a given case, but the extraneous detail of how much money the father earns. (102–3)

As in work, the problem cuts across class lines: From "the mean and the cluttered to the spacious and restful," all homes share in the pathology of the "sacred" institution of the family.

Still, the Lynds do not dismiss family life completely. In true Veblenian fashion, the Lynds see that even so traditional and personal a relation as the family has a redeeming use value in its service to "functional urgencies of life" such as "marriage, birth, child-rearing, death." This use value at present needs liberation not only from the familiar "extraneous detail" of finance and exchange but also from the somehow equally extraneous attitudes that the people of Middletown take toward the family. The ironic italics around the word "sacred" question the actual sanctity of family life in the daily practice of Middletown life, yet they also reassert that sanctity in new terms at the level of theory. This passage suggests that Middletown's hands-off, reverential attitude toward the family bears much of the responsibility for the disjunction between the functional necessities of families and the actual homes that at present provide these necessities. The Lynds appear positively indignant that "the personal immensities of family life" be allowed to "go forward" so casually in the "privacy" of Middletown's "shabby or ambitious houses." It is because the family is so important, and because it is in a present state of such disarray, that it can no longer be left to mere chance. In the new social-scientific dispensation, scrutiny itself serves as a measure of sanctity.

The dangers of casualness appear at the very start of family life, the period of courtship and marriage. According to the Lynds, "most of Middletown stumbles upon its partners in marriage guided chiefly by 'romance' " (114–15). If this sounds a bit like the Lynds' characterization of the way people tend to fall into the jobs that become their life's work, it is no coincidence. The Lynds explicitly acknowledge this parallel in a footnote, comparing the ways of courtship in Middletown to "the equally casual method by which Middletown youths stumble upon the kind of work by which they forever after earn their living. The casualness of procedure in both these cases is probably traceable in part to the same inherited conceptions regarding the individual's 'freedom' and 'rationality' " (115).

The Lynds do not reject the freedom and rationality of the individual, simply the "inherited conceptions regarding" that freedom and rationality. Not surprisingly, they locate the root of Middletown's courtship problems in that most traditional of inherited beliefs, religion:

> The close identification of love with the religious life of the group has tended to import into courtship some of the same inscrutibility that envelops the religious life of Middletown. By the same token the religious taboo upon "carnal love" has carried over into the situation so that, although sexual exclusiveness in marriage is demanded both by law and custom, virtually no direct consideration is given prior to marriage to the physical and sexual compatibility of the two contracting parties. (115)

Here we see a logical extension of that close attention to the "subtleties of the individual" at the heart of vocational guidance. The Lynds here suggest that courtship should match particular men to particular women on the basis of certain aptitudes deemed appropriate to marriage. That "physical and sexual compatibility" are viewed as the central aptitude of marriage should not be taken as prurience or a reductive biologism. The Lynds see sex as so important because it is the most inscrutable of all taboos in Middletown; they locate the main problem of courtship and love in this inscrutability itself rather than in any particular sexual beliefs or practices. The recurring problem in *Middletown* lies in Middletown's failure to adopt the irreverent perspective of social-scientific scrutiny toward every aspect of its life.

The imperative of scrutiny is written into the Lynds' very definition of marriage. They see marriage in terms of the very workmanlike relation of intellectual labor leading to psychological satisfaction; they see marriage as the "frank exchange of ideas" between "two contracting parties" that results in a certain "emotional outcome" (144, 115, 120). Middletown has to some degree broken with traditional or "sacred" conceptions of marriage and accepted this "more democratic system of relationships," but it still suffers from a general "lack of frankness between husband and wife, far-reaching in its emotional outcome" (144, 120). Lack of frankness leads to "cruelty," which the Lynds interpret as a euphemism for sex problems: "It is impossible to say to what extent this charge is connected with the sex relation, but it seems probable that, in some cases at least, the connection is close. . . . Time and time again the wife of a working man spoke with obvious emotion of the fact that the responsibility for the prevention of pregnancy was placed upon her by a non-cooperative husband" (123). As the Lynds scrutinize marriage in Middletown, so they hold the husbands and wives of Middletown accountable for their failure to scrutinize each other. In the moral and intellectual world of *Middletown*, marriage depends solely on the communication and cooperation of "two contracting parties." With no place for a "sacred" conception of marriage as a union that transcends the wills of the individuals involved in it, *Middletown* reduces marriage to "the adjustments between a man and his wife" (129). Its meaning exhausted in the negotiations of two independent wills, marriage becomes simply what two people make of it, the sum total of their intellectual frankness and emotional satisfaction.

In the Lynds' social-scientific framework, the "social" meaning of marriage lies in the way in which external social factors impinge on the workmanlike interaction of independent individuals. The Lynds see "cruelty" as the leading cause of divorce in Middletown, but they do not blame the lack of frankness at the heart of cruelty simply on the ignorance of individuals; rather, they insist that the "antecedents of divorce are imbedded in the whole complex of Middletown's culture touching the adjustments between a man and his wife" (129). In their social analysis of the antecedents of "cruelty," the Lynds uncover a class "pyramid" with respect to frankness on issues of birth control: "At the top, among most of the business group, the use of relatively efficacious contraceptive methods appears practically universal, while sloping down from this peak is a mixed array of knowledge and ignorance, until the base of ignorance is reached. Here fear and worry over pregnancy frequently walk hand in hand with discouragement as to the future of the husband's job and the dreaded layoff" (125–26). The Lynds move out from a simple class analysis to place the birth control issue in a "whole complex" of social factors, such as "rapidly changing standards of living, irregular employment, the increasing isolation and mobility of the individual family, growing emphasis upon child-training and upon education and other long-term family plans such as insurance and enforced home ownership on a time payment basis" (125). Still, they present these social factors as external to birth control, a kind of exchange value always influencing, conditioning, or corrupting a more basic technical use value of contraception itself.

This class analysis breaks down in the move from the issue of frankness to that of emotional outcome. Relative economic freedom may help to liberate a use value of intelligence, but this bears little relation to the liberation of the use value of psychological satisfaction. Psychological dissatisfaction cuts across class lines. The Lynds concede that there "are many homes in Middletown among both working and business class families which one cannot enter without being aware of a constant undercurrent of sheer delight, of fresh spontaneous interest between husband and wife," yet they quickly add that "such homes stand out by reason of their relative rarity" (130). Middletown is "tending to demand more of a tolerable marriage," but does not seem to be getting it (128). Most members of both the working class and the business class seem to live lives of quiet desperation, with only the "small duties and automatic responses to the custom of the daily round of living . . . [to] imperceptibly but surely mitigate the tragedies and disappointments of existence" (130). With divorce simply not an option for the many still mired in old traditions, "marriage seems to amble along at a friendly jog-trot marked by sober accommodation of each partner to his share in the joint undertaking of children, paying off the mortgage, and generally 'getting on' " (130). On the emotional as well as intellectual level, the ideal of marriage as individual, conscious, spontaneous intellectual labor faces the constant drag of marriage as traditional, mechanical, automatic manual labor.

This democratization of desperation should not obscure the class values that drive the Lynds' analysis. The business class may not be more satisfied than the working class, but they are more frank. Despite the disjunction between frankness and satisfaction, the business-class value of frankness serves as the single, universal standard by which to assess the various activities of Middletown life. Detached from even so subjective an "end" as psychological satisfaction, frankness becomes an end in itself. The Lynds never argue that business-class frankness leads to fewer divorces and more satisfaction because they see marriage not in terms of union or disunion, satisfaction or dissatisfaction, but in terms of a "frank exchange of ideas" between "two contracting parties" or a "sober accommodation of each partner to his share" (521). Frankness emerges as a procedural norm, a way of assessing how one approaches an activity without actually making substantive judgments about the activity itself. Frankness itself eludes such substantive assessment, for while it is an end in itself, it represents nothing by itself. No stable quantity or quality, frankness exists only in the move from a preconscious "sober accommodation" to a fully conscious "exchange of ideas."

As the Lynds turn to other aspects of family life, the movement within which frankness has meaning reveals itself to be the Veblenian historical narrative of the emergence of matter of fact from rule of thumb. The historical narrative implicit in the Lynds' discussion of the spread of a "more democratic system of relationships" becomes explicit in their discussion of a seemingly less "sacred" aspect of family life: housework. As with work in general, domestic crafts in Middletown have experienced an "overnight" transformation from "primitive hand skills" to "modern machines" (172). Unlike industrialization in general, however, "the increased use of labor-saving devices" by women in the home marks a positive advance in domestic work (172):

Under the old rule-of-thumb, mother-to-daughter method of passing down the traditional domestic economy, when the same family recipe and doctor book—with "Gravy" in its index followed by "Grey hair, how to treat"—was commonly cherished by both mother and daughter, the home tended to resist the intrusion of new habits. (157)

Even as late as 1890, when housework was still a craft passed down from mother to daughter—what Bentham scornfully called "ancestor wisdom"—the Middletown housewife moved in a narrower world of "either-or." "There is a right way and a wrong way to do everything, and you might just as well learn the right way as the wrong way," was the household gospel on which many present-day housewives were brought up. (175)

Today the various alternatives in the performance of her housework combine with the new alternative things to do in her newly-acquired leisure time to turn the either-or world of her mother into an array of multiple choices. (176)

To speak of the "narrower world" of the Middletown of 1890 suggests a certain progressivist arrogance, and, more importantly, it assumes that the Middletown of the 1890s and 1920s may be seen as commensurable, simply broader or narrower versions of each other. Even as the Lynds present a more sanguine view of mechanization than in their account of glassblowing, they reinforce the underlying assumptions that frame their critique of industrialization: the reduction of craft to technique, and the linking of technical skill to the individual human personality apart from relations to other people. This asocial conception of technique—Veblen's matter of fact—then serves as a transhistorical nexus by which to evaluate the change over time of various activities. The above passages concede the personal relations of craft only to debunk them. The Lynds concede that domestic crafts were "passed down from mother and daughter," but they see these personal relations merely as inhibiting "the intrusion of new habits." Ultimately, the Lynds place domestic crafts in a social and historical setting only to dismiss that setting as epiphenomenal to the real story of history, the development of broader techniques.

Increasingly, Middletown itself has come to embody the subordination of the personal to the technical that structures the Lynds' analytic framework. As the heroic development of technology opens the home to "an array of multiple choices," it also breaks up the traditional authority structure of family life: "More than a few of the mothers interviewed said that their daughters, fresh from domestic science in school, ridicule the mothers' inherited rule-of-thumb practices as 'old-fashioned' " (133). The Lynds quote a disgruntled father to the same effect: " 'Why even my youngster in kindergarten is telling us where to get off,' exclaimed one bewildered father. 'He won't eat white bread because he says they tell him at kindergarten that brown is more healthful' " (133).

As the frank exchange of ideas between husband and wife reduces sex primarily to a matter of birth control, so the frank exchange of ideas between parents and children reduces food primarily to a matter of nutrition. Frankness entails the move from rule of thumb to matter of fact, from "the traditional domestic economy" to a "domestic science" detached enough from family life to see it in terms of its "functional urgencies," yet engaged enough to invest children with a technical expertise capable of undermining the traditional authority of parents (103). Ultimately, the Lynds conclude that despite resistance and the common "reassertion of the traditional *noli tangere* attitude toward the 'sacred institution' of the home," these intrusions of expertise are fast becoming the rule, not the exception, of Middletown life (177).

Fragmentation and Integration

Middletown seems to tell two very different stories. In its account of industrial labor, it tells a story of increasing standardization, regimentation, and dependence; in its account of home life, it tells a story of slow but sure diversification, emancipation, and independence. The meaning of *Middletown* does not lie in either of these stories by themselves but in the relation between the two stories in the Lynds' larger narrative of social change. For the Lynds, social change is a dialectical process. Mechanization brings standardization and alienation, yet also diversification and individuation; it threatens fragmentation, yet promises integration on a higher plane of true workmanlike independence. This dialectic of fragmentation and integration militates against any firm conclusions as to the direction of social change in Middletown. The objective dialectic of social change issues in a subjective dialectic of the interpretation of social change. Social-scientific scrutiny must be sensitive to the integration within every apparent fragmentation and the fragmentation within every apparent integration. Ultimately, *Middletown* argues for the acceptance of the constant reinterpretation of social change, not simply acceptance of social change.

The dialectic of fragmentation and integration operates between distinct social activities and within particular activities themselves. The mechanization of housework compares favorably to industrialization in general, but on closer scrutiny, the female world of making a home appears threatened by the same loss of independence experienced in the male world of making a living. The Lynds' assessment of women's magazines places "the intrusion of new habits" and the "array of multiple choices" in a different light: "Through these periodicals, as well as through the daily press, billboards, and other channels, modern advertising pounds away at the habits of the Middletown housewife. Whole industries mobilize to impress a new dietary habit upon her" (158). Given the earlier treatment of the intrusions of domestic science, this passage suggests that the Lynds do not oppose incessant pounding per se, but merely a particular kind of incessant pounding, that is, advertising. Clearly some kind of pounding is necessary to shake people out of their inherited, rule-of-thumb habits. A properly functioning process of social change should not pound less, but pound better.

What does it mean to pound better? The Lynds give some sense of a proper pounding in a rather obscure footnote concerning the spread of home washing machines:

> This is an example of the way in which a useful new invention vigorously pushed on the market by effective advertising may serve to slow up a secular trend. The heavy investment by the individual family in an electric washing machine perpetuates a questionable institutional set-up—whereby many individual homes repeat common tasks day after day in isolated units—by forcing back into the individual home a process that was following belatedly the trend in industry towards centralized operation. The whole procedure follows the customary haphazard practice of social change: the issue is not settled on its merits; each Middletown household stands an isolated unit in the midst of a baffling battery of diffusion from personally interested agencies: the manufacturers of laundry machinery spray the thinking of the housewife through her magazines within a shower of "educational" copy about the mistake of a woman's neglecting her children for mere laundry work, and she lays down her magazine to answer the door-bell and finds there the suave installment payment salesman ready to install a $155 washer on trial to be paid for in weekly installments if satisfactory. The whole question has to be settled in terms of such immediate and often incidental considerations by each isolated family unit. (174–75)

Here we have the whole world of *Middletown* in a nutshell, in a footnote. Every observable activity—and all activities are observable—may be broken down into its use and exchange components; however, this distinction itself requires constant scrutiny, for every seeming use value conceals a dangerous exchange value. Thus, the electric washing machine is "useful" in that it embodies a "secular trend" away from "isolated units" toward "centralized operation," but this usefulness has its dark side in the "rapid and uncontrolled spread of such devices." The Lynds present the development of technology as the progress from "a right way and a wrong way to do everything" to an "array of multiple choices," but this passage suggests that some choices are more free than others, that is, the choice of a centralized laundry service is more free than the choice of a home washing machine. The proper pounding that the Lynds have in mind for Middletown would seem to have something to do with "the trend in industry toward centralized operation," which the Lynds juxtapose to "the customary haphazard practice of social change" that has rendered the families of Middletown "isolated units" trapped in "individual homes." A proper pounding would seem to lie in the trend toward integration, an improper pounding in the trend toward fragmentation.

Still, the dialectic of fragmentation and integration that structures *Middletown* militates against any simple reading of centralization. This passage presents not simply a conflict between centralization and isolation but also between two kinds of centralization: the "trend in industry toward centralized operation" versus the "baffling battery of diffusion," the "spray" and "shower" of information from advertising and women's magazines. These two trends represent the use and the exchange components of centralization in general: technical and industrial centralization reflects the objective "merits" of an "issue," while "market" centralization reflects "immediate and often incidental considerations." The Lynds never make clear what precisely distinguishes use from exchange in the process of centralization; the intrusion of "a useful new invention" such as an electric washing machine would seem to embody the same sort of technical advance over rule-of-thumb habits they accept without question in their account of domestic science and hope for in their account of birth control. What this passage does make clear is that in *Middletown*, use and exchange have no meaning in themselves, but exist only in relation to each other. Use value emerges not simply from the juxtaposition of the technical to the personal but from uncovering the "personally interested" elements lurking beneath the surface of seemingly technical phenomena. A technological change that appears as a principle of order at the microlevel of the individual home may appear as a principle of disorder at the macrolevel of society as a whole. This constant patholo-gizing-by-recontextualizing drives the dialectic of fragmentation and inte-gration and deprives centralization of any stable meaning in *Middletown*.

Ironically, the dialectical structure of the Lynds' own social-scientific study seems to mirror the market instabilities that plague Middletown's struggle toward centralization. *Middletown* itself embodies one kind of centralization in that it attempts to bring every aspect of life under one roof, in one book; however, the catalog of lags, contradictions, and in-consistencies that make up this centralization suggests not a sense of a social whole but a kind of textual anxiety concerning the possibility of a social whole. Indeed, there is an almost comic parallel between the Lynds' own social-scientific project and the "baffling battery of diffusion from personally interested agencies" that they criticize in their work. In the footnote on washing machines, the Lynds attack advertisers for play-ing on maternal fears and insecurities through the "shower of 'educa-tional' copy about the mistake of a woman's neglecting her children for mere laundry work" (How dare people claim to have a family's love and happiness at heart when they really just want to make money!). But that "suave installment payment salesman" who appears at the door of the poor "isolated" Middletown housewife might find that doorway a bit crowded, for chances are the Lynds or a member of their research team would also be there, preparing to pry even more deeply into the fears and insecurities of that same housewife in the name of social-scientific objec-tivity.

Consider one of *Middletown*'s most egregious advertisements for it-self, from the Lynds' discussion of husband-wife relations: "In a number of cases, after the interviewer had succeeded in breaking through an ap-parently impenetrable wall of reserve or of embarrassed fear, the house-wife would say at the close of the talk, 'I wish you could come often. I never have any one to talk to' " (120). A scene straight out of a nine-teenth-century novel or the recent bestseller *The Bridges of Madison County*, here the social scientist stands in for the artist/outsider who brings a few moments of happiness to a doomed housewife trapped in a loveless marriage. In the context of *Middletown* as a whole, such a scene argues for the necessity of social science to break the chains of repression and open up the blocked lines of communication that are at the heart of the malaise of Middletown life. Middletown needs the use value of communication, not the exchange value of mere salesmanship.

Middletown housewives may really want communication. Of course, they may also really want washing machines. To talk about home life in terms of either wants or needs, however, is to individualize what is inescapably a social relation, and this reduction of the social to the individual constitutes the ideological common ground of advertising and social science. Both advertising and social science help to reconstruct the classical liberal worldview that conceives of society as primarily a collection of individuals pursuing their desires; both see relations between people exhausted in the voluntary relations of consent and contract. The Lynds try to distinguish between the true or deep consent of communication and the false or shallow consent of salesmanship, but in doing so they only reinforce the value of individual satisfaction at the heart of both those forms of exchange. The Lynds' account of the "cruelty" of resistance to birth control by Middletown's husbands parallels the washing machine ads that warn "about the mistake of a woman's neglecting her children for mere laundry work." In both cases, the moral imperative to accept technological change stems from the ability of technology to alleviate physical burdens so as to allow people to interact in a deeper, more emotional manner. By reducing family relations to those of communication, *Middletown* and modern advertising deprive those relations of any meaning beyond the conscious interaction and mutual satisfaction of individuals.[11]

As a social ethic, communication demands that relations between people actually foster the independence of individuals. The battle lines in *Middletown* are not social science and the market but dependence and independence. Of course, given the "dialectical" structure of the Lynds' argument, these lines are never clear. The communications revolution embodied in the spread of advertising and mass-market women's magazines fosters both dependence and independence. Witness the Lynds' account of the radio:

The place of the radio in relation to Middletown's other leisure habits is not wholly clear. As it becomes more perfected, cheaper, and a more accepted part of life it may cease to call forth so much active, constructive ingenuity and become one more form of passive enjoyment. Doubtless it will continue to play a mighty role in lifting Middletown out of the humdrum of every day; it is beginning to take over that function of the great political rallies or the trips by the trainload to see a monument dedicated that a generation ago helped to set the average man in a wide place. But it seems not unlikely that, while furnishing a new means of diversified enjoyment, it will at the same time operate, with national advertising, syndicated newspapers, and other means of large-scale diffusion, as yet another means of standardizing many of Middletown's habits. Indeed, at no point is one brought up more sharply against the impossibility of studying Middletown as a self-contained, self-starting community than when one watches these space-binding leisure-time inventions imported from without—automobile, motion picture, and radio—reshaping the city. (270–71)

The dialectical "subtlety" of the Lynds' assessment of the radio cannot hide the hierarchy of values implicit in the social ethic of communication, mass or otherwise. The Lynds pass no final judgment on the radio, but this passage makes clear that the promise of radio (and implicitly, all social change) lies in its potential "to call forth so much active, constructive ingenuity," and its threat lies in its potential to "become one more form of passive enjoyment." The Lynds assess mass communication not in terms of any particular relations between people, or even in terms of any particular content of information communicated, but in a quality of individual experience, that is, active as opposed to passive. The active/ passive dichotomy has its social equivalent in the alternatives of "lifting Middletown out of the humdrum of everyday" versus becoming "a more accepted part of life," and "a new means of diversified enjoyment" versus "another means of standardizing many of Middletown's habits." The constructive potential of radio would seem to lie in its ability to free people from accepted social conventions, to expose them to new and diverse experiences; however, as radio itself becomes an accepted social convention, it may lose its transgressive power and simply foster the established norms it has helped to create. To the degree that radio is new and unconventional, it fosters independence; to the degree that it becomes old and conventional, it fosters dependence.

The objectivity that refuses to pass judgment on the radio nonetheless establishes the tension between dependence and independence as the essential social tension in Middletown life. The Lynds invest this tension with a certain timeless quality as they subsume social activities as different as listening to the radio at home in the twentieth century and attending a public, political rally in the nineteenth century under the ahistorical "function" of "lifting Middletown out of the humdrum of everyday." When this general function operates properly, it sets "the average man in a wide place"; when it works improperly, it proves to be "space-binding." In either case, this functionalism psychologizes the social bond, replacing concrete, substantive relations between people with an abstract, formal relation between the individual and the social whole. This understanding of social life subordinates qualitative distinctions between various kinds of social wholes to the quality of the process of perceiving any social whole. The independence that the Lynds demand of a properly functioning social whole requires not that the individual be free from the social whole but that he be engaged in an active, constructive interaction with it.

Ultimately, the values implicit in the Lynds' objectivity turn out to be the single value of objectivity itself. As readers of Middletown and writers of *Middletown*, the Lynds appropriately enough figure this objectivity in terms of social literacy. Alas, Middletown seems to suffer from an epidemic of social illiteracy:

> The city boasts of the fact that only 2.5 per cent of its population ten years of age or older cannot read and write, and meanwhile the massed weight of advertising and professional publicity are creating, as pointed out above, new forms of social illiteracy, and the invention of the motion picture is introducing the city's population, young and old, week after week, into types of vivid experience which they come to take for granted as parts of their lives yet have no training to handle. (222)

Here again the anxiety in the Lynds' account stems not from any particular social change in itself but from the inability of Middletown to deal actively and constructively with the social changes that confront them. The assumption that ordinary people need "training" to understand movies suggests a certain technocratic agenda lying beneath the Lynds' surface objectivity, but the use of the concept of literacy in *Middletown* suggests the need to reconsider the standard image of technocracy as a social system in which evil (or well-intentioned-but-misguided) experts manipulate the helpless masses. To speak of "reading" a movie does not seem to stretch the notion of literacy too far, but the Lynds also speak of the "stifling of self-appraisal and self-criticism under the heavily diffused habit of local solidarity" as yet "another type of social illiteracy" (222). Here literacy is not simply a reading, but a critical reading—and not simply the critical reading of cultural productions but of social relations as well. Literacy places the individual at odds with others so as to scrutinize relations between people, to distinguish a shallow, false "local boosting" from a deep, true group solidarity. Of course, the distinction between a shallow and deep solidarity lies in the degree to which a solidarity allows for social literacy, which in turn requires the privileging of nothing less than the social scientist's stance of critical detachment.[12]

The Lynds pass no final judgment on the quality of solidarity in Middletown. They simply report "Things Making and Unmaking Group Solidarity" (478). The final judgment they do pass is that Middletown is always reading or not reading, always literate or illiterate. When literate, Middletown displays sensitivity to the "cluster of underlying factors" that contribute to social change; when illiterate, it gives "superficial explanations" for social change (185). Literate Middletown embodies nothing less than the perspective of *Middletown* itself, for the Lynds' notion of reading is inextricably bound to their notion of social-scientific objectivity. If *Middletown* argues anything, it argues that Middletown must pull itself out of its environment so as to examine it critically. In its very production and distribution, *Middletown* acts as a self-fulfilling prophecy of a universal literacy in which all things exist to be read by everyone.

If *Middletown* embodies this ideal of literacy, Middletown, alas, does not. The Lynds judge Middletown to be in, but not of, the process of social change. Aware of certain "discrepancies in its institutional system," Middletown is only "reluctantly conscious" of its problems, and that only "from time to time." Truly in the middle, Middletown appears to have lost its way in the transition from "old categories" to "the new situation" (501). When Middletown seeks a "remedy" to a "problem," it tends to fall back on "traditional verbal and other symbols," or "a stricter enforcement or further elaboration of existing institutional devices," or "an emotional defense of the earlier situation" (501, 502). In effect, Middletown tends to fall back on its culture. Ironically, in its attempt to give an account of the everyday, *Middletown* marginalizes the everyday. The privileged moments in *Middletown* are those in which people transcend the everyday, making the transition from rule of thumb to matter of fact. True to their objectivity, the Lynds do not prescribe any particular new values, but simply the transcending or objectifying of old values. Culture in *Middletown* appears as a lag not on technological change but on cultural consciousness itself. Objectivity in *Middletown* leads nowhere in particular, simply beyond the Middletown of the present. The Lynds present *Middletown* not as a blueprint for social change but simply as a "deeper-cutting procedure" for reexamining the institutions of Middletown than Middletown itself has been able to accomplish on its own (502). Every work of objectivity is, however, also a work of advocacy. *Middletown*'s deeper-cutting reexamination of Middletown's institutions all but demands the restructuring of those institutions to facilitate the transition from rule of thumb to matter of fact. Within a year of its publication, *Middletown* saw its implicit demands made explicit in John Dewey's *Individualism Old and New*.

Chapter 3

■

A New Individualism

A Contradictory Condition

THE PROGRESSIVE THOUGHT OF Veblen and the Lynds turned to the anthropological concept of culture as a tool for analyzing society in terms of a dynamic process that transcends the intentional actions of individuals within it. The account of cultural change in *The Instinct of Workmanship* and *Middletown* nonetheless bequeathed a certain ideal of subjectivity appropriate to a larger objective social process: As objective social forces act on individuals, so subjective individuals may act on social forces. A contemporary of Veblen and a teacher of Robert Lynd, John Dewey would make this implicit subjectivity explicit in his 1930 work *Individualism Old and New*. Although it was written in the early years of the Great Depression, Dewey's work follows all the conventions of the Progressive analysis of the perils of prosperity. By seeing in economic depression a much deeper "Crisis in Culture," *Individualism Old and New* reaffirms the Progressive insistence on the priority of culture to economics.[1] Dewey's work moves beyond Veblen and the Lynds, however, by linking explicitly the crisis in culture to the problem of "The Lost Individual" (51). In doing so, *Individualism Old and New* signals the transformation of the culture concept from a tool of analysis to a resource for individual liberation.

A series of thematic essays rather than a sustained philosophical argument, *Individualism Old and New* opens with a review of *Middletown* titled "The House Divided Against Itself." Following the Lynds, Dewey takes Middletown to stand for America, and he sees America's division as not economic but cultural, not between classes but within America as a whole:

It is becoming a commonplace to say that in thought and feeling, or at least in the language in which they are expressed, we are living in some by gone century, anywhere from the thirteenth to the eighteenth, although physically and externally we belong to the twentieth century. In such a contradictory condition, it is not surprising that a report of American life, such as contained, for example, in "Middletown," should frequently refer to a "bewildered" or "confused" state of mind as characteristic of us. (9)

There is something slightly disingenuous about Dewey's democratic "us." *He* is certainly not caught between thirteenth-century thoughts and feelings and twentieth-century externalities. Still, the tone of this passage suggests a certain genuine confusion: Dewey genuinely cannot understand how people can persist in believing biblical accounts of creation at a time of widespread secondary-school education, or how people can persist in their glorification of the sanctity of the home in a time that has seen a 600 percent increase in divorce within one generation (14–15). Dewey has little patience with those who would attribute this contradictory condition simply to the ignorance of the masses, yet his conclusion that "the rapid industrialization of our civilization took us unawares" would seem only to offer a cross-class or collective ignorance as an alternative explanation (16).

Having confronted America's collective befuddlement, Dewey lays out the path to collective enlightenment. He roots the contradictions of the present in the contradictions of the past; as he looks to the past, he finds that "our tradition, our heritage, is itself double" (17). America's heritage "contains in itself the ideal of equality of opportunity and of freedom for all," yet it carries with it the residue of an "older tradition, that of business conducted for money profit" (17, 18). This doubleness has produced modern industrial America's "pecuniary culture," which Dewey sees as "a novel combination of the machine and money" (18). Like Veblen, Dewey sees in the machine "a significantly new habit of mind and sentiment" that has been "obscured and crowded out" by the dominance of pecuniary interest. Unlike Veblen, Dewey links this habit of mind to a specific set of American cultural values, the "spiritual factor of our tradition, equal opportunity and free association and intercommunication" (18, 124). Dewey presents the machine as not simply a leveler of traditions but as itself a kind of tradition. In this way, Dewey can demand that Americans not accept new values so much as accept old values under new conditions. The machine embodies American culture "in itself," the "essential Americanism" of equality and freedom for all (17, 18). Thus, as Dewey challenges America to accept the machine, he merely challenges America to accept itself, to understand its true nature.

Dewey figures this self-understanding in terms of a certain cultural dialectic. This dialectic operates synchronically in the relation between culture and the individual and diachronically in the relation between past and present. Synchronically, Dewey insists that the "solution of the crisis in culture is identical with the recovery of composed, effective, and creative individuality." The "machine age" must embody the traditional values of equality of opportunity and free association "not merely externally and politically but through personal participation in the development of a shared culture" (142, 124, 33). As the old pecuniary culture repressed individuality, so a "new culture expressing the possibilities immanent in a machine and material civilization" will liberate individuality through the creation of culture itself (143). Diachronically, the imperative of individual participation will transform the random alternation between the "creeds and theories" of the past and the "institutions and practice" of the present into a self-consciousness matching of a particular past (equality of opportunity) to a particular present (the machine) (14).

Dewey's dialectic rehabilitates culture as something more than "lag" and individualism as something more than the pursuit of economic gain. For Dewey, the shift from a pecuniary culture to a machine culture has established social conditions that make possible the development of an "individuality of a new type" (49). As the old individualism developed itself by developing the social whole of the free market, so the new individualism will develop itself by developing the social whole of culture conceived of as "the type of emotion and thought that is characteristic of a people and an epoch as a whole, an organic intellectual and moral quality" (122). Understanding this new individualism requires some understanding of the place of the old economic individualism in American thought.

American Individualism

The term *individualism* grew out of the nineteenth-century European reaction to the French Revolution's attempt to make individual rights the basis of social life. Conservatives looked to an organic ideal of tradition, and radicals looked to a progressive notion of "society," but both could agree that the individualism of mainstream liberal thought was something to avoid at all costs. The American Revolution may have avoided the bloody excesses of its French counterpart, but by the 1830s, it had fostered a combination of capitalist economic relations and liberal democratic social relations that seemed, at least to foreign observers like Alexis de Tocqueville, to offer anarchy as the only alternative to state regimentation. Once again the problem was located in individualism, which Tocqueville defined as "a deliberate and peaceful sentiment which disposes each citizen to isolate himself from the mass of his fellows and to draw apart with his family and friends," thus abandoning "the wider society to itself."[2] Realizing that America lacked both the organic traditions to which European conservatives looked for order and the state structures that European radicals hoped to convert to a principle of order, Tocqueville saw in the humble voluntary association America's best defense against social atomism.

Tocqueville's voluntary association ultimately failed to provide an alternative to individualism as a social relation. Even as it provided psychological security and some kind of social order, it reinforced the primacy of voluntary, consent-based relations to social life. As individualism in one form or another came to set the terms of social life, the idea of the individual underwent a rehabilitation in both Europe and America. By the middle of the nineteenth century, certain French thinkers began to distinguish between individualism, which implied social anarchy, and individuality, which implied independence and self-development. Figured in terms of a move from a quantitative to a qualitative individualism, this new individualism was often tied to artistic movements that sought to forge an aesthetic that would reconcile the individual and society. American Transcendentalism provides an interesting counterpart to the new individualism of Europe, for in it we find an indictment of not only the vulgar individualism that Tocqueville observed but also the voluntary associations and reform movements that Tocqueville saw as the antidote to this vulgar individualism. At its most extreme, Transcendentalism could see any association between individuals, however voluntary, as coercive and restrictive.[3] Still, the Transcendentalists, like their European counterparts, had a social vision of sorts; they, too, sought to bring about a reconciliation of the individual and society through a new individualism based on creativity and self-expression.

Henry David Thoreau's *Walden* offers perhaps the richest account of the Transcendentalist quest for a new individualism. *Walden* certainly provides one of the most strident critiques of "possessive" individualism in nineteenth-century America.[4] The title of the first chapter, however, suggests that Thoreau's experiment in the woods is not simply a retreat from economic life but an attempt to fashion a purer "Economy" than that offered by the world.[5] Thoreau models his ideal economy on the ancient *oikos,* or household economy, rather than the capitalist market; but significantly, Thoreau's household is a household of one. Like Veblen's account of savagery in *The Instinct of Workmanship,* the primary creative experience for Thoreau lies in the encounter between man and nature, with nature always positioned at the border of social life. The social relations of Thoreau's life at Walden manifest themselves in the production of *Walden* as a book. As Veblen's savage workman returns from the border region to develop his culture, so Thoreau must emerge from the woods to develop his culture by sharing with others his primal encounter with nature.

Upon his return, Thoreau comes to terms with the world through the very terms of the world. Thoreau's social vision does not reject economic man and his relations so much as it purifies, reconstitutes, and develops them on a higher level. Thoreau manifests what may be called a kind of this-worldly aestheticism: Even as he calls for society to shift its focus from matters of "trade" to those of "thought," he reconstructs thought in the very image of trade. In a key passage in *Walden,* Thoreau interprets imperial expansion from Columbus to Lewis and Clark as "an indirect recognition of the fact that there are continents and seas in the moral world to which every man is an isthmus or an inlet."[6] Thoreau sees in trade not merely a foreshadowing but also a pale reflection of thought, for "it is easier to sail many thousand miles through cold and storm and cannibals, in a government ship, with five hundred men and boys to assist one, than it is to explore the private sea, the Atlantic and Pacific of one's being alone."[7]

There is a long tradition, going back to the Greeks, of privileging the contemplative life over the life of worldly action; however, in this tradition, the superiority of the contemplative life lies in its distinctiveness, its difference from worldly action. A warrior is not an imperfect philosopher; a knight is not an imperfect priest. Warrior and philosopher, knight and priest, are distinct, hierarchically ordered social roles. Thoreau replaces the vertical social distinctions of hierarchy with the vertical psychological distinctions of depth. He subsumes all social activities under a single continuum of thought, so that global exploration appears not as an abdication of the nobler-yet-distinct calling of the contemplative life but as a neurotic distortion of the more basic activity of thinking. Thoreau's scorn for imperial expeditions stems from his sense of their having failed a test of psychological strenuosity, the single standard by which to judge both his experiment at Walden and such expeditions.

This single standard of rigorous self-scrutiny carries with it a particular social vision. For Thoreau, self-examination serves as a precondition for a proper social existence; it prepares the individual to live in society in such a way as "to maintain himself in whatever attitude he find himself through obedience to the laws of his being, which will never be one of opposition to a just government, if he should chance to meet with such." Ostensibly, Thoreau offers this relation between the individual and society as an alternative to the romantic posture of opposition for its own sake, yet he overcomes this adversarial stance only by equating society with individual conscience. Ideally, Walden as a temporary retreat prepares one simply for reentry into a social world conceived in terms of Walden itself. Thoreau replaces the Delphic command to "Know thyself"—for which self-knowledge is in a large part knowledge of one's own mortality, one's own limitation—with the command to "Explore thyself," with its notion of an ever-expanding internal frontier, whose only limits are those of the will and resolve of the explorer. This expanding frontier encompasses not only one's particular country, but the world in general, enabling the explorer "to speak all tongues and conform to the customs of all nations."[8] Thoreau's vision ultimately renders the individual a kind of nodal point of order capable of synthesizing all the disparate elements of worldly flux through the act of contemplation.

Thoreau's notion of contemplation cannot be equated with economics, but it must be seen as the "depth" to which economics is the "surface." The "laws of being" and self-interest are not the same thing, but both assume a certain quality, be it conscience or desire, that exists prior to society yet finds its fulfillment in a harmonious social whole. The antagonistic coupling of "values" and economics in much of nineteenth-century thought—whether in Thoreau's opposition of thought to trade, or in the larger battle between "culture" and "society"—suggests the power of the belief in some principle, located in the individual, that exists prior to society and to which society must somehow be held accountable.[9] By the late nineteenth century, the move from a quantitative to a qualitative individualism entailed not so much a move from society to culture as an attempt to synthesize these previously antagonistic principles. European social democracy and American Progressivism took shape as movements that sought to expand the freedom and value of the individual not by rejecting the economic edifice of industrial capitalism but by bringing its tremendous productive capabilities under control in the service of the individual.[10]

American Progressivism has rightly been described as a "search for ordered individualism."[11] The Progressive commitment to harnessing large-scale organization in the service of individual liberty—what Herbert Croly calls using "Hamiltonian means" to achieve "Jeffersonian ends"—must be seen as a development in, not a rejection of, American individualism.[12] Some version of this new individualism characterized the mainstream of Progressive thought up through the "association idea" of the last great political Progressive, Herbert Hoover. Hoover's commitment to both "purposeful planning" and private property has led historians to portray him as a transitional figure "torn by conflicting values," able to direct "giant bureaucracies" yet still committed to "the tradition of self-help."[13] Hoover himself, however, saw no conflict between these values, as he makes clear in his 1922 work *American Individualism*, which was written while he was in his political prime as secretary of commerce. In this work, Hoover defends large-scale bureaucracy as simply the most recent organizational form of an older and enduring individualism: "The economic system which is the result of our individualism is not a frozen organism. It moves rapidly in its form of organization under the impulse of initiative of our citizens, of growing science, of larger production, and of constantly cheapening distribution."[14] Here Hoover presents large-scale organization as itself the product of individual initiative. The very novelty of bureaucracy speaks to the persistence of the social fluidity so often associated with the older individualism of the small property owner. Hoover denounces the "demagogues, of both radical and standpat breed, [who] thrive on demands for the destruction of one or another of these organizations as the only solution for their defects." Against these alarmists, Hoover argues that "industry and commerce . . . have erected organisms that each generation has denounced as Frankensteins, yet the succeeding generation proves them to be controllable and useful."[15]

Hoover does not defend bureaucracy per se so much as the fluidity of an individualistic economic system that "moves rapidly in its form of organization under the impulse of initiative of our citizens." He sees large-scale bureaucracies as neither the culmination nor the eclipse of individualism but simply the "organisms" that set the (neutral) conditions for the development of a new individualism. Conditions may change, but "our basic social ideas march through the new things in the end." Ultimately, "progress requires only a guardianship of the vital principles of our individualism with its safeguard of true equality of opportunity."[16]

The vital principles that Hoover would have bureaucracies guard extend beyond mere "legalistic justice based upon contracts, property, and political equality." Under any conditions, the development of American individualism must proceed from an understanding that of "the impulses that carry us forward, none is so potent for progress as the yearning for individual self-expression, the desire for creation of something." America, unlike Europe, is "a society fluid to these human qualities," because lacking "the frozen strata of classes," it allows for the rise of the individual through the exercise of creative impulses. America's creative mobility "aims to provide opportunity for self expression, not merely economically, but spiritually as well"; indeed, "the maintenance of productivity and the advancement of the things of the spirit depend upon the ever-renewed supply from the mass of those who can rise to leadership."[17] In presenting America's fluid social structure as the basis for economic and spiritual creativity, Hoover assumes an ideal of creativity that places a premium on a certain quality of fluidity. As Thoreau cannot conceive of a self-knowledge that is not a self-exploration, a movement across an ever-receding spiritual frontier toward ever-new continents of the self, so Hoover cannot imagine a properly functioning society in which people are not always rising, always developing their talents so as to move from one social/spiritual position to another.

Ultimately, Hoover avoids Thoreau's extreme antinomianism by turning from a social ethic of conscience to one of cooperation. Again, Hoover's social vision should be seen as a development of, rather than an alternative to, nineteenth-century American individualism. Hoover sees in cooperation not a rejection of competition but "the initiative of self-interest blended with a sense of service." This definition suggests the individualistic orientation of both competition and cooperation. If anything, a cooperative social order may be seen as even more individualistic than a competitive one, for it requires an even more strenuous assertion of individual effort—that is, self-interest *plus* service—to ensure social order. Even so critical a commentator on America as Tocqueville sees the anarchy of capitalist competition balanced by service-oriented voluntary associations; Hoover's call for a "sense of service," for an exploration of the "continents of human welfare," must be seen in the context of this

Tocquevillian formulation of the problematic of American individualism.[18] In both Tocqueville and Hoover, the "soft" side of service tempers the "hard" side of self-interest, but both function to build up a social order geared toward the spiritual/material growth of individuals.

Middletown and *Individualism Old and New* both stand as social-scientific rewritings of the kind of Progressive individualism espoused by Hoover. The Lynds may not argue explicitly for a "better, brighter, broader individualism," but their analysis of the shift from rule of thumb to matter of fact exhibits nothing if not what Hoover called "a willingness courageously to test every process of national life upon the touchstone of . . . the intelligence, the initiative, the character, the courage, and the divine touch in the individual."[19] All individualisms assume some context, be it the market or large-scale organization, within which the individual acts. The Lynds' social-scientific version of Hoover's Progressive individualism moves beyond large-scale organization to the much broader notion of culture as a whole way of life as the proper setting in which to understand individualism. Following the Lynds, Dewey sees in "The Crisis in Culture" the problem of "The Lost Individual." Dewey's attempt to formulate a solution to this problem may be seen as a prescriptive articulation of the descriptive account of the cultural individualism found in *Middletown*.

The Lost Individual

Dewey's account of the lost individual proceeds from the classical liberal insistence on the priority of instrumental, man-thing relations to substantive relations between men. For Dewey, the lost individual finds himself not by coming home but by understanding the road he is on. The individual comes to this understanding not by connecting himself to people but by connecting the "inner man" and the "outward scene" (65). Dewey sees the "unrest, impatience, irritation and hurry that are so marked in American life" as symptomatic of "an acute maladjustment between individuals and the social conditions under which they live" (56). Dewey traces this restlessness not to the dislocations of industrialism per se, but to the emergence of a "corporateness [that] has gone so far as to detach individuals from their old local ties and allegiances but not far enough to give them a new center order of life" (61). Dewey's invocation of "local ties," those "loyalties which once held individuals, which gave them support, direction, and unity of outlook in life," suggests something like

Tocqueville's notion of the habits of the heart. However, as Dewey moves from a description of the present to a prescription for the future, he translates the notion of traditional ties between people into a notion of "solid and assured objects of belief and approved ends of action" (52). This formulation might seem merely an awkward or unfortunate choice of words were it not for Dewey's persistent reference to local ties as "objects." Dewey elsewhere asserts that "stability of individuality is dependent upon stable objects to which allegiance firmly attaches itself," and that "human nature is self-possessed only as it has objects to which it can attach itself" (52, 61). Tocqueville sees local ties as capable of providing a stable base for voluntary social relations precisely because such ties were not themselves voluntary, but received, handed-down, preconscious "habits." Dewey's social-scientific rewriting of Tocqueville makes allegiances conscious and voluntary "objects" to be "approved," while it strains to invest these objects with all of the emotional power of preconscious traditions. Ultimately, Tocqueville sees habits possessing individuals, while Dewey would have individuals possess habits, and thereby possess themselves.

Dewey figures this social/self-possession in terms of a "sense of social value" and a "sense of social fulfillment" (54). Social value and fulfillment lie not in direct relations with other people but in a certain relation to objective social conditions. People must forsake the "principles and standards that are merely traditional" and submit to "the realities of the age in which they act" (70). For Dewey, the realities of the age already "work upon us unconsciously but unremittingly," but they currently find their work impeded by the persistence of traditional "opinions that have no living relationship to the situations in which we live." Were people to turn from traditional ties to an objective tie to reality, the realities of the age would be able to "build minds after their own pattern," and "individuals might, in consequence, find themselves in possession of objects to which imagination and emotion would stably attach themselves" (70, 71). Thus, even as Dewey demands that individuals submit to an objective social reality, he characterizes this reality in terms of individuals possessing intellectually and emotionally stimulating objects.

By accepting "reality," individuals simply accept the necessity of their own empowerment:

It is part of wisdom to note the double meaning of such ideas as "acceptance." There is an acceptance that is of the intellect; it signifies facing facts for what they are. There is another acceptance that is of the emotions and will; that involves commitment of desire and effort. So far are the two from being identical that acceptance in the first sense is the precondition of all intelligent refusal of acceptance in the second sense. There is a prophetic aspect to all observation; we can perceive the meaning of what exists only as we forecast the consequences it entails. When a situation is as confused and divided within itself as is the present social estate, choice is implicated in observation. As one perceives different tendencies and different possible consequences, preference inevitably goes out to one or the other. Because acknowledgment in thought brings with it intelligent discrimination and choice, it is the first step out of confusion, the first step in forming those objects of significant allegiances out of which stable and efficacious individuality may grow. (72–73)

For Dewey, social fulfillment lies in social control. In his formulation of social fulfillment, he depicts the "social" as a dynamic causal sequence whose "integrity" lies in a proper match between the "conscious intent" of and the "consequences actually effected" by human action (58). The causal orientation of Dewey's understanding of social life reduces the "prophetic" to the predictive; society can be understood "only as we forecast the consequences it entails." Prediction and control depend on seeing this causal sequence as a formless flux of "different tendencies and different possible consequences" which, while "confused and divided within itself," nonetheless embodies a rational instrumentality capable of being directed toward human preferences. The move from "emotions and will" to "the intellect" depends on seeing in the bewildering variety of the current social situation not simply a threat to cherished traditions but more importantly an opportunity for the exercise of "intelligent discrimination and choice." This act of choice is a creative process, one of "forming those objects of significant allegiance" that Dewey sees as the "possession" of those individuals who accept the realities of their age. As social reality shapes individuals, so individuals shape social reality through the creation of values.

Dewey's social vision emphasizes the directing of an instrumental potentiality over any particular direction taken. Dewey prescribes not particular ends but the general process of individuals creating and choosing ends. This emphasis on process over substance leads him to conceive of social life primarily in terms of social change:

Analysis of even a casual kind discloses that these conditions are not fixed. To accept them intellectually is to perceive that they are in flux.

Their movement is not destined to a single end. Many outcomes may
be projected, and the movement may be directed by many courses to
many chosen goals, once conditions have been recognized for what
they are. By becoming conscious of their movements and by active participation in their currents, we may guide them to some preferred possibility. In this interaction, individuals attain an integrated being. The
individual who intelligently and actively partakes in a perception that
is a first step in conscious choice is never so isolated as to be lost nor
so quiescent as to be suppressed. (148–49)

Here Dewey presents social change as the necessity appropriate to a freedom conceived in terms of the expansion of individual perception and
consciousness. Dynamic, transformative conditions issue in dynamic,
transformative individuals; the principle of transformation thus harmo-
nizes intentions and consequences and overcomes the present split between the inner and the outer world. The individual maintains his integrity within this larger process of social change by taking an "active" role
in this process, and the primacy of the "interaction" between the individual and his conditions in this process ensures that the individual will be
free from the domination of other people.

Relations between people are so peripheral to Dewey's "social" vision
that his "found" individual seems to have not overcome isolation so
much as attained a higher level of isolation. Isolated but not lost, quiescent but not suppressed, this new individual has attained a connection
to reality in general that makes connection to particular people almost
superfluous: "We should not be so averse to solitude if we had, when we
were alone, the companionship of communal thought built into our mental habits. In the absence of this communion, there is the need for rein-
forcement by external contact. Our sociability is largely an effort to find
substitutes for that normal consciousness of connection and union that
proceeds from being sustained and sustaining members of a social
whole" (87–88). "Normal" social life is not companionship, but "the
companionship of communal thought built into our mental habits." Like
the Lynds' account of boosterism, Dewey presents "sociability" as a potentially contaminating "external contact," a physical substitute for what
should be an intellectual matter. In Dewey's social vision, people do not
live with each other so much as they have a "consciousness of connection
and union" with each other.

This ideal of social consciousness need not imply passive contemplation or physical isolation. Dewey clearly sees it as the necessary precondi-

tion for social activism. Still, the key to Dewey's social vision lies not in his commitment to activism but in his conception of companionship as first and foremost a recognition that everyone is part of an objective social process; a companionship that proceeds from any less-than-objective principles such as blood or locality appears as mere sociability, the dreaded conformity. The sense of the "social whole" that Dewey offers as the only solution to the problem of the lost individual thus renders social life as a kind of mental energy loop constituted by "sustained and sustaining members." Individuals sustain a dynamic, changing social whole by creating new values through interaction with their changing environment; in turn, these individuals are themselves sustained by a social whole that impresses upon them the inexorable reality of a social world in which individuals sustain the social whole through their creative activity.

By rooting social life in the consciousness of social life, Dewey suggests that if we knew the "social whole" we would not have to know anyone in it. Even when he tries to locate his rather abstract social vision in some kind of concrete social situation, he turns, like Thoreau before him, to that most asocial of all places, the frontier:

> It is no longer a physical wilderness that has to be wrestled with. Our problems grow out of social conditions: they concern human relations rather than man's direct relationship to physical nature. The adventure of the individual, if there is to be any venturing of individuality and not a relapse into the deadness of complacency or of despairing discontent, is an unsubdued social frontier. The issues cannot be met with ideas improvised for the occasion. The problems to be solved are general, not local. They concern complex forces that are at work throughout the whole country, not those limited to an immediate and almost face-to-face environment. (92–93)

Here, again, is a social world without any people in it. In order for society to be an "adventure" rather than "the deadness of complacency or of despairing discontent," Dewey must depict it in terms of nature or of the environment: Society is a "social frontier." The chief characteristic of this social frontier is its freedom from the particularities of place and time. Spatially, the metaphor of the frontier suggests the "general" as opposed to the "local"; it represents the boundlessness of the "complex forces that are at work throughout the whole country" rather than the limitations of the "immediate and almost face-to-face environment."

Temporally, the metaphor of the frontier suggests a society in the process of being integrated; as the "physical wilderness" of the old frontier stood as a mark of geographical expansion both achieved in the past and yet to come in the future, so the "social conditions" that make up the new frontier of "human relations" point to both problems solved in the past and those to be addressed in the future.

Particularities of place and time seem to suggest limitations on the free "venturing of individuality." Dewey's commitment to the individual manifests itself in his commitment to modernity's eradication of these particularities. His writing takes on a tone of awestruck humility as he catalogs the "impersonal forces" shaping modernity's new "collectivist scheme of interdependence." "Mass production and mass distribution . . . have created a common market . . . held together by intercommunication and interdependence"; this system of "concentrated control" has rendered "distance eliminated and the tempo of action enormously accelerated"; leaving no aspect of life untouched, this new interdependence "finds its way into every cranny of life, personal, intellectual, emotional, affecting leisure as well as work, morals as well as economics" (37, 47). Expressing the fear that accompanies all true awe, Dewey also addresses the dark side of this dynamic interdependence. The apartments and subways of the modern city have led to "the invasion and decline of privacy." In the modern interdependent society, "private 'rights' have almost ceased to have a definable meaning." Modern communications networks have exposed individuals "to the greatest flood of mass suggestion that any people has ever experienced" (42). Collectivism's promise of "united action" and "integrated opinion" carries with it the threat of "organized propaganda and advertising," through which "sentiment can be manufactured by mass methods for almost any person or any cause" (43).

Dewey's sensitivity to the dangers of collectivism in no way undermines his basic commitment to modern interdependence. Dewey's acceptance of modernity serves as a model for the submission to "reality" that he urges on his readers; his "acceptance . . . of the intellect" refuses to "weigh [the] merits and demerits" of modernity in general, but rather looks to discern the merits and demerits within each particular social change (72, 43). Take, for example, the decline of thrift and the rise of consumerism. Dewey expresses some concern for the "increased buying . . . promoted by advertising on a vast scale, by instalment selling, by agents skilled in breaking down sales resistance"; however, he insists that "certain changes do not go backward. Those who have enjoyed high wages and a higher standard of consumption will not be content to return to a lower level" (43, 44, 46). Dewey thus accepts modern consumerism, but accepts it critically, intelligently; he objects not to consumerism per se but to the present lack of "inherent criterion for consumption values." Private enterprise promotes a false consumerism because it has failed to take "the point of view of consumption . . . the standpoint of the user and enjoyer of services and commodities." Dewey objects to the "kind of consumption . . . that leads to private gain" because it favors "exchange or sale values" over the "values in use" of pure consumer satisfaction (135).

This use value serves as an objective criterion by which Dewey and his readers may intelligently accept the realities of the age. The criterion of use transforms mass consumption from an opportunity for economic gain to an opportunity for individual self-creation:

> The multiplication of means and materials is an increase of opportunities and purposes. It marks a release of individuality for affections and deeds more congenial to its own nature. Even the derided bathtub has its individual uses; an individual is not perforce degraded because he has the chance to keep himself clean. The radio will make for standardization and regimentation only as long as individuals refuse to exercise the selective reaction that is theirs. The enemy is not material commodities, but the lack of the will to use them as instruments for achieving preferred possibilities. Imagine a society free from pecuniary domination, and it becomes self-evident that material commodities are invitations to individual taste and choice, and occasions for individual growth. If human beings are not strong and steadfast enough to accept the invitation and take advantage of the proffered occasion, let us put the blame where it belongs. (157–58)

As Dewey divides the commodity form into its exchange and use components, the exchange component of "pecuniary domination" appears as a distortion of a much more basic and essential use component of the "release of individuality." In itself, the commodity form embodies not so much financial exchange as individual choice. The contradiction at the heart of America's pecuniary culture lies in its promotion-yet-restriction of the principle of free individual choice; America has located the "means and materials" of choice in money, yet it has restricted access to this means through the promotion of private gain. Dewey traces the failure of existing consumerism not to the vulgarity or shallowness of consumption as opposed to production but to the limits placed on the former by the unequal distribution of wealth. Indeed, Dewey figures consumption itself as a potentially productive experience, an opportunity for individual growth through the exercise of free choice; figured thus, consumption becomes, in effect, consummation. With consumption rehabilitated as an active, productive experience, the acceptance of reality demands of the new individual the courage to consume, the courage to live the strenuous life of individual growth through mass consumption.

Dewey's social vision does not exhaust itself in the proliferation of material commodities. The lost individual must first find himself by interacting with his environment, but he must then find other people with whom to share the experience of this interaction. With oppressive ties of personal authority broken by the priority of the individual-social whole relation, relations between people may themselves become occasions for individual growth. For Dewey, the individual ethic of growth through consumption has its complement in a social ethic of growth through communication. In proposing relations of communication as a rational alternative to relations of exchange, Dewey shifts the locus of social interaction from the capitalist market to the scientific community.

Culture and Communication

Few aspects of Dewey's thought have been as misunderstood as his conception of the relation of science to social life. Dewey's persistent call for a "collective intelligence" in which "the masses . . . share freely in a life enriched in imagination and aesthetic enjoyment" has been interpreted as everything from a naive democratic utopianism to a sinister technocratic totalitarianism (125).[20] Sympathetic interpretations have stressed Dewey's humanistic "ends," hostile interpretations have stressed the coercive nature of his social-engineering "means," and, recently, more subtle interpretations have tried to reconcile these seemingly contradictory means and ends.[21] These interpretations share Dewey's own inability to transcend classical liberalism's social antinomy of consent versus coercion. The classical liberalism of the seventeenth century rejected the hierarchical power relations of feudal society in the name of supposedly power-free relations of consent and contract; the Progressive liberalism of the twentieth century has sought to expose the power relations latent in contract while salvaging some power-free ideal of pure consent. An analysis of Dewey's conception of science reveals how Progressive liberalism's attempt to formulate relations of pure consent carries with it all the unacknowledged power relations of classical liberalism's conception of freedom of contract.

As a principle of social organization, Dewey's conception of science follows economics most directly by linking the liberation of man to the control of nature. In his account of the rise of the scientific attitude toward nature, Dewey follows classical liberalism's historical narrative of the progress from religious superstition to secular reason:

> That there is much at any time in environing nature which is indifferent and hostile to human values is obvious to any serious mind. When natural knowledge was hardly existent, control of nature was impossible. Without power of control, there was no recourse save to build places of refuge in which man could live in imagination, although not in fact. There is no need to deny the grace and beauty of some of these constructions. But when their imaginary character is once made apparent, it is futile to suppose that men can go on living and sustaining life by them. When they are appealed to for support, the possibilities of the present are not perceived, and its constructive potentialities remain unutilized. (151–52)

This progress from "imagination" to "fact" has transformed nature from "the grim foe of man" to "the friend and ally of man" (151). For Dewey, the "power of control" reconciles man and nature by rendering "nature more amenable to human desire and more contributory to human good" (153).

Control seems like a dubious principle on which to base a friendship, but Dewey's conception of control cannot be equated with simple domination. In making his case for science, Dewey offers a subtle, complex relation of domination between man and nature: The move from "imagination" to "fact" is a move from quantity to quality. Dewey's progressive reading of history plays modern science against not only premodern religion but also early modern science, with its man/nature dualism and mechanical worldview. Modern science offers an organic worldview, one that sees the control of nature as a function not of exploitation, but of understanding: "Science, one may say, is but the extension of our natural organs of approach to nature. And I do not mean merely an extension in quantitative range and penetration, as a microscope multiplies the capacity of the unaided eye, but an extension of insight and understanding through bringing relationships and interactions into view" (97). The control of nature requires sensitivity to the "relationships and interactions" that bind nature together as an organic whole. A properly organic understanding of nature brings with it the realization "that man with his habits, institutions, desires, thoughts, aspirations, ideals and struggles, is within nature, an integral part of it" (153). The idea of man and nature as parts of a single organic whole, however, does not question the place of control as the organizing principle for that whole. Nature controls man through certain objective laws, certain "relationships and interactions" that must be respected; man, in turn, controls nature by understanding these laws, by bringing them "into view" so as to render "nature more amenable to human desire and more contributory to human good." As simultaneously controlled and controlling entities, man and nature both exist as "possibilities," as "constructive potentialities" that must somehow be utilized and developed.

Dewey's conception of rational social relations simply transfers the control relation of natural science from an organic natural whole to an organic social whole. Like Veblen and the Lynds, Dewey figures this control relation in terms of work:

> We are given to thinking in large and vague ways. We should forget "society" and think of law, industry, religion, medicine, politics, art, education, philosophy—and think of them in the plural. For points of contact are not the same for any two persons and hence the questions which the interests and occupations pose are never twice the same. There is no contact so immutable that it will not yield at some point. All these callings and concerns are the avenues through which the world acts upon us and we upon the world. There is no society at large, no business in general. Harmony with conditions is not a single and monotonous uniformity, but a diversified affair requiring individual attack. (166–67)

This passage would seem to contradict Dewey's earlier insistence on the social as a "general" rather than "local" phenomenon. The two passages taken together, however, point to Dewey's concern for conceptualizing a new individualism that can mediate between the particular and the general. Work accomplishes this mediation in actual social practice; it consists of a "variety of callings and concerns" as distinct as "law, industry, religion, medicine," yet it also subsumes these particular occupations under the general function of providing "avenues through which the world acts upon us and we upon the world." Specific occupations do not accomplish specific tasks so much as they provide "points of contact" with one's conditions; however, these contact points "are never twice the same" for "any two people," and every interaction "produces a new perspective that demands a new exercise of preference" (167). The spatial diversity between each occupation complements the temporal diversity within each point of contact. The "selective choice and use of conditions have to be continually made and remade," and there "is no contact so immutable that it will not yield at some point." As natural science demands the control and development of nature, so a social science demands the control and development of society.

The imperative of revision at the heart of Dewey's organicism introduces a tension designed to keep social harmony from lapsing into social stasis. Dewey's scientific organicism offers not a reconciliation of individual and society, but a process of reconciling individual and society that Dewey views in terms of problem solving:

> It is a property of science to find its opportunities in problems, in questions. Since knowing is inquiring, perplexities and difficulties are the meat on which it thrives. The disparities and conflicts that give rise to problems are not something to be dreaded, something to be endured with whatever hardihood one can command; they are things to be grappled with. Each of us experiences these difficulties in the sphere of his personal relations, whether in his more immediate contacts or in the wider associations conventionally called "society." At present, personal frictions are one of the chief causes of suffering. I do not say all suffering would disappear with the incorporation of scientific method into individual disposition; but I do say that it is now immensely increased by our disinclination to threat these frictions as problems to be dealt with intellectually. The distress that comes from being driven in upon ourselves would be largely relieved; it would in part be converted into the enjoyment that attends the free working of mind, if we took them as occasions for the exercise of thought, as problems having an objective direction and outlet. (162–63)

For Dewey, relations between people are "occasions for the exercise of thought," opportunities for "the free working of mind." Since "perplexities and difficulties are the meat on which [knowing] thrives," knowing people and knowing ourselves depends on the problematizing of our relations to others and to ourselves. As the power of control frames man's relations to nature with the either/or of imagination and fact, so the dictum that "knowing is inquiring" frames social life with the either/or of "being driven in upon ourselves" and treating the "frictions" of social life "as problems to be dealt with intellectually." These alternatives imply that all social relations, from the "more immediate contacts" to "the wider associations conventionally called 'society,' " must become intellectual problems if people are to overcome individual isolation. Thus, the free play of the speculative intellect serves as the organizing principle of social life, that to which all relations between people must answer.

The objectification of social relations into problems to be solved requires of each individual within the social whole a fully developed subjectivity. The premium that Dewey places on perplexities and difficulties requires not only that each individual allow himself to be an object of social inquiry but also that each individual, in whatever he does, participate as an inquiring subject in the process of social inquiry. This subject/object dynamic serves as the basic social relation of Dewey's ideal scientific social order. The subject of this social order relates primarily to an abstract social whole rather than to particular people, yet the "objective direction and outlet" of this individual/social relation has its complement in the intersubjective relations between the various social inquirers: "No scientific inquirer can keep what he finds to himself or turn it to merely private account without losing his scientific standing. Everything discovered belongs to the community of workers. Every new idea and theory has to be submitted to this community for confirmation and test. There is an expanding community of coöperative effort and of truth" (154–55).

Here Dewey presents communication as the essential relation between people in a properly scientific social order. Communication between people presupposes a more basic inquirer-problem relation through which people come to the information they communicate to others: First one investigates a problem, then one submits one's findings to "the community of workers." Dewey sees social life as a process of testing and confirming various accounts of the social whole. The discipline of social life is simply the discipline of the individual-problem relation writ large; in developing one's individuality through encounters with particular problems, one develops society, conceived of as "an expanding community of coöperative effort and truth." Community is communication, and social life is the exchange of information.

The only problem that Dewey sees with this model of social life is that it is "now limited to small groups having a somewhat technical activity": "Suppose that what happens in limited circles were extended and generalized. Would the outcome be oppression or emancipation? Inquiry is a challenge, not a passive conformity; application is a means of growth, not of repression. The general adoption of the scientific attitude in human affairs would mean nothing less than a revolutionary change in morals, religion, politics and industry" (155). Oppression/emancipation, challenge/conformity, growth/repression: these are the dynamics of social life in Dewey's vision of a new individualism. This vision offers "revolutionary change" as a social norm, and reduces social life to a process of pulling the individual out of social life as represented by existing traditions:

> The scientific attitude is experimental as well as intrinsically communicative. If it were generally applied, it would liberate us from the heavy burden imposed by dogmas and external standards. Experimental method is something other than the use of blow-pipes, retorts and reagents. It is the foe of every belief that permits habit and wont to dominate invention and discovery, and ready-made system to override verifiable fact. Constant revision is the work of experimental inquiry. By revision of knowledge and ideas, power to effect transformation is given us. This attitude, once incarnated in the individual mind, would find an operative outlet. (156)

As an organizing principle of social life, science embodies an "attitude" that must be "incarnated in the individual mind," an attitude of "constant revision" that always seems to pit the individual mind against dogmas, external standards, habits, and ready-made systems. Science places the individual mind at odds with everything prior to it and external to it—in effect, everything social, if the "social" is to be something more than the sum of communicated information. Ironically, the "social" nature of the individual thus lies in the ability of the individual to uproot himself from his "conditions" and communicate this process of uprooting to other individuals who are likewise uprooting themselves from their conditions.

The conception of the social whole that Dewey invokes as an antidote to the old individualism is ultimately as fragmenting as that individualism. The new, scientific, communicative individualism replaces the variety of individual desires with the variety of individual problems, and in the face of this variety it, too, establishes a neutral mechanism of arbitration, with communication replacing contract as the nexus of scientific rather than economic exchange. The "more humane age" of science, like its economic predecessor, also "looks forward to a time when all individuals may share in the discoveries and thoughts of others, to the liberation and enrichment of their own experience" (154). Both economics and science depict social life as relations between people's goods rather than relations between people. In the case of science, these goods are "discoveries and thoughts," the products of intellectual labor that undergo the fluctuation of constant revaluation through the constant revision that drives scientific communication. Goods/thoughts and their revaluation/revision stand as a protective buffer between individuals, one that prevents the encroachment of personal domination through an impersonal mechanism geared toward the liberation of all individuals. Science, like economics before it, promises an egalitarian order based on the assertion of individual effort free from the arbitrary, restrictive personal relations of the past.

Scientific rationality may seem to offer a rather cold vision of how people should live together, yet it comes with the appropriate warming antidote. Even as Dewey calls for a rational social order, he also calls for a move from impersonal to personal relations, from atomism to solidarity, from quantity to quality, from the head to the heart—a call that has characterized most critiques of individualism since its inception as an "-ism" in the nineteenth century. Unlike his sentimental predecessors, however, Dewey refuses to relegate this antidote to a realm outside the rational relations of society at large; moreover, he also refuses to imagine a society based on completely personal, emotional relations. Dewey offers his new individualism as a synthesis of the quantitative and the qualitative, one in which the universalization of the impersonal, communicative ethic of science provides the basis for the universalization of personal, emotional relations:

> Society is of course but the relations of individuals to one another in this form and that. And all relations are interactions, not fixed molds. The particular interactions that compose a human society include the give and take of participation, of a sharing that increases, that expands and deepens, the capacity and significance of the interacting factors. Conformity is a name for the absence of vital interplay; the arrest and benumbing of communication. As I have been trying to say, it is the

artificial substitute used to hold men together in lack of associations that are incorporated into inner dispositions of thought and desire. I often wonder what meaning is given to the term "society" by those who oppose it to the intimacies of personal intercourse, such as those of friendship. Presumably they have in their minds a picture of rigid institutions. But an institution that is other than the structure of human contact and intercourse is a fossil of some past society; organization, as in any living organism, is the coöperative consensus of multitudes of cells, each living in exchange with others. (85–86)

Ironically, Dewey defends his new individualism in the very terms that nineteenth-century critics such as Tocqueville attacked the old individualism, that is, he presents an ideal of social life as "but the relations of individuals to one another," or as "the intimacies of personal intercourse, such as those of friendship." There is nothing new, however, about friendship; friendship is the social relation of individualism par excellence, for it is a relation based on choice and consent. For Dewey, relations beyond friendship, such as those of family, locality, and religion are "fixed molds," or "set and external organizations" that threaten the "arrest and benumbing of communication." As a social relation, the personal, emotional relations of friendship thus mirror the impersonal, rational relations of scientific communication.

The egalitarian and consensual nature of friendship drives social life toward an ethic of depth and quality. With no external social context to give meaning to a friendship, meaning must be constructed at the level of "inner dispositions of thought and desire." For the choice of a friend to be something more than arbitrary and trivial requires "the give and take of participation . . . a sharing that increases, that expands and deepens the capacity and significance of" the friends, or in Dewey's terms, "the interacting factors." The emotional exploration of personal friendships thus parallels the intellectual exploration of impersonal scientific inquiry: Both share a model of the individual penetrating depths free from those substantive social relations deemed extraneous to this more basic task. True modern that he is, Dewey reconstructs the vertical social distinctions banished by egalitarianism at the individual level of consensual relations. The limitless emotional depths of friendship provide Dewey's egalitarian society with a substitute for the social hierarchies of old, and depth's defiance of context ensures that no particular depth will ever be established as a fixed or stable limit to individual growth.

As social ethics, both friendship and technical expertise assume that social order can only be sustained by the constant exertion of individual wills. Dewey ultimately rehabilitates the contractarianism of the old individualism through the principle of revision. The dynamism of science and friendship offer an antidote to the "conformity" and "complacency" that result once any particular social contract establishes social relations that escape the direct consent of individuals. Like Jefferson's call for perpetual revolution, Dewey's scientific society of friends implies a kind of routinization of the founding moment of the social contract. Dewey rejects the old individualism for being, in effect, not individualistic enough, for having itself become an established form that limits individual control and growth. True individualism requires the direct reproduction of society by individuals.

The contradictions of Dewey's "new" individualism reveal themselves most clearly in the conflation of organic and contractual metaphors in his description of a properly scientific social order. Dewey's organicism somehow takes the epochal developments of evolutionary biology as a model for immediate, constant, revolutionary social change, and then figures this hyper-evolution as a conscious, directed process. At the end of the passage cited above, Dewey equates social "organization" with the structure of "any living organism" in that both depend on "the coöperative consensus of multitudes of cells, each living in exchange with others." Given all that has come before this formulation, the use of cooperation, consensus, and exchange as metaphors has to be seen as more than merely an awkward choice of words with which to convey a sense of organic relations; rather, it is a perfectly appropriate choice of words to describe a society that depends on communication and conscious interaction for its existence. Unfortunately for Dewey's organicism, living organisms and "organic" societies do not depend on such interaction, are not geared toward constant revision, and do not have as their goal the expansive development of the "cells" that constitute them. Viewed in anything less than an epochal time frame, natural and social organisms work to maintain a certain structure, not transform it. Dewey's metaphor of cellular growth suggests not evolution so much as cancer. With its hostility to fixed structure, Dewey's organicism ultimately owes more to a "mechanical" conception of history rooted in economics than an "organic" conception of evolution rooted in biology.

Individualism Old and New sets the terms for the contradictory condition of much of American social thought during the 1930s. Dewey's closing remarks suggest the shape of things to come:

To gain an integrated individuality, each of us needs to cultivate his own garden. But there is no fence about this garden; it is no sharply marked-off enclosure. Our garden is the world, in the angle at which it touches our own manner of being. By accepting the corporate and industrial world in which we live and by thus fulfilling the preconditions for interaction with it, we, who are also parts of the moving present, create ourselves as we create an unknown future. (171)

Like the old possessive individualism, Dewey's new expressive individualism demands only that individuals accept the necessity of their own liberation. Turning Voltaire's metaphor of cultivation on its head, Dewey figures individual liberation not as a retreat from the world, but as an ever-more strenuous engagement with the world; however, in linking the cultivation of self with the cultivation of the world, Dewey simply reproduces the old economic conception of self and world as resources to be developed.

These continuities have been obscured by Dewey's shift of the locus of creativity from the market to culture. Dewey defines culture as "the type of emotion and thought that is characteristic of a people and an epoch as a whole" (122). He sees his new individualism as a realization of "the distinctive moral element in the American version of individualism: Equality and freedom expressed not merely externally and politically but through personal participation in the development of a shared culture" (33–34). By linking the individual to the idea of culture as an "organic intellectual and moral quality," Dewey hoped to overcome the antinomy of individual and society that characterized the old individualism; however, by linking this synthesis to the principle of development, Dewey paved the way for emotion and thought to be subject to the same exploitation inherent in the "development" of natural resources.

Chapter 4

■

Patterns of Control

A Short History of Culture

JOHN DEWEY hardly needed to rouse his fellow Americans to see the world as their garden. During the nineteenth century, the United States and western Europe had more than made the world their garden through westward expansion and global imperialism. Dewey's vision shifts the focus of this expansionism from economic development to personal cultivation, but in doing so, it draws on an anthropological language of culture that is deeply implicated in the imperial conquests of the nineteenth century. In *Individualism Old and New,* Dewey never addresses the role of the culture concept in the ideological justification of imperialism; instead, he focuses his polemic on the shift from an old, elitist notion of culture as high art to a new, democratic notion of culture as a whole way of life. Historians of American social thought have tended to follow Dewey's account rather uncritically.[1] The meaning of culture in the 1930s, however, lies not in any simple change in meaning but in the particular relation between meanings at a particular time set up by a general structure of transition. Ruth Benedict's *Patterns of Culture* has been taken as a "symbolic landmark" in the history of the culture concept for its popularization of the idea of culture as a pattern of values that organizes the whole way of life of a people.[2] A close examination of this work reveals the persistence of the older, aesthetic notion of culture within the newer, anthropological notion and helps place the culture concept firmly within the tradition of American individualism.

Benedict's book represents a particular moment in the modern writing of culture, a literary tradition with roots in nineteenth-century English and German Romanticism. As Raymond Williams has observed, prior to the nineteenth century, the word "culture" referred to a process of human training, as in the "cultivation" of the mind; however, during the nineteenth century, culture came to stand for a thing in itself, be that thing a body of artistic and intellectual achievement or a whole way of life.[3] By the twentieth century, these two nineteenth-century notions could be seen as opposed to each other, but it is important to realize that they were originally seen as one. According to Williams, for the Romantic artist, "a conclusion about personal feeling became a conclusion about society, and an observation of natural beauty carried a necessary moral reference to the whole and unified life of man."[4] Central to Romantic aesthetics was the notion that the art of a historical period was related to the whole "way of life" of that period.[5] The sense that this natural unity between art and life had been shattered by industrial capitalism led to the notion of art and intellect "as a court of human appeal, to be set over the processes of practical social judgment" precisely because art seemed to offer the wholeness and values lacking in a society operating by the rules of the individualistic, amoral marketplace. This aesthetic ideology saw art not as an escape from social life but as "a militant and rallying alternative" to a particular kind of society, that of industrial capitalism.[6]

The modern conception of culture arose as an idea of wholeness in opposition to the perceived fragmentation of modern social life. By the late nineteenth century, however, the idea of culture itself had undergone a kind of fragmentation, so that art and social life were seen as distinct spheres between which one must choose. In this formulation, art became the province of the poet, and the whole way of life of a people became the province of the sociologist.[7] The critic Matthew Arnold and the anthropologist E. B. Tylor have come to stand as the representative figures of these two poles of the meaning of culture, yet ironically it is the aesthete Arnold whose idea of culture carries the stronger sense of holism.[8] For Arnold, culture was the study and pursuit not just of literary culture but of all aspects of human life.[9] Coming out of the traditions of English Romanticism and German Transcendental philosophy, Arnold saw culture as "both for the individual and for society an organic, integrative, holistic phenomenon."[10] Tylor, in contrast, came out of the traditions of the French Enlightenment and British empiricism; he saw culture in terms of analytic and scientific study, and tended to focus on particular artifacts and manifestations of material culture.[11] Tylor's "comparative method" broke up the whole way of life of a people into its constituent parts so as to place those parts in a hierarchical, evolutionary scheme of cultural stages ranging from the savage to the civilized.[12]

Arnold and Tylor differed in their understanding of the relation of culture to an ideal of wholeness, but they shared a common understanding of culture's relation to freedom and necessity. As George Stocking observes on the nineteenth-century idea of culture,

> Whether in the humanist or the evolutionist sense, it was associated with the progressive accumulation of the characteristic manifestations of human creativity: art, science, knowledge, refinement—those things that freed man from control by nature, by environment, by reflex, by instinct, by habit, or by custom. "Culture" was not associated with tradition—as weighted, as limiting, as homeostatic, as a determinant of behavior. In general, these connotations were given to the ideas of custom, instinct, or temperament, and they were often associated with a lower evolutionary status, frequently argued in racial terms.[13]

This consensus on culture as a realm of freedom began to break down in the early twentieth century with the work of the anthropologist Franz Boas. Early in his career, Boas, following Tylor, tended to equate culture with folklore, or to associate it with formal behavior and discrete, conscious acts of creation; gradually, however, he came to see culture as "the science of all the manifestations of popular life," manifestations that were "unconscious in origin, but central to the maintenance of society."[14] As a result, Boas abandoned the evolutionists' notion that culture consisted of acts of independent invention and creativity that were to be compared to similar acts in other societies. Boas replaced the notion of cultural stages with that of multiple cultures, each of which had to be seen in their own terms as an interrelated, integrated set of activities.

This new conception of culture carried with it a new conception of man. Boas came to see man not in terms of the inventive ways in which he broke from tradition but in the basically uninventive ways in which he reinterpreted the particular tradition in which he found himself.[15] Stocking argues, "It was in this context that the idea of culture, which once connoted all that freed man from the blind weight of tradition, was now identified with that very burden, and that burden was seen as functional to the continuing daily existence of individuals in any culture and at every level of civilization."[16] Boas was the dominant anthropologist of the first third of the twentieth century, and his work shifted the terms of the debate over the meaning of the idea of culture.[17] In the nineteenth century, the notion of freedom united the various conceptions of culture; the question was whether this freedom manifested itself in an organic social whole or in discrete acts of independent creativity. In the twentieth century, integration and synthesis became the unifying assumptions of the various conceptions of culture; the question then became whether this integration would be the basis for a new freedom or a new necessity.

The anxiety surrounding the relation between culture and freedom in the twentieth century has been so great as to structure the very history of the culture concept in twentieth-century America. Thus Warren Susman, who has provided what is still the dominant account of the rise of the culture concept in the 1930s, states the conflict over the meaning of culture in the following terms:

> First, there was in the discovery of the idea of culture and its wide-scale application a critical tool that could shape a critical ideal, especially as it was directed repeatedly against the failures and meaninglessness of an urban-industrial civilization. Yet often it was developed in such ways as to provide significant devices for conserving much of the existing structure. A search for the "real" America could become a new kind of nationalism: the idea of an American Way could reinforce conformity.[18]

Culture as a "critical ideal" or culture as "conformity," culture as freedom or culture as necessity: These are the alternatives of the historical account of culture in the 1930s. These alternatives do not misrepresent the stakes of the culture concept for intellectuals during the 1930s, but simply identifying them as alternatives does not go very far in explaining the meaning of an idea that can be divided into these two alternatives. Every "critical ideal" implies a certain kind of conformity, as every freedom implies a certain kind of necessity. The historical question is thus what kind of freedom and what kind of necessity did "the discovery of the idea of culture" imply for American intellectuals during the 1930s. The answer to this question lies in a close reexamination of one of the key sources for our understanding of the meaning of culture during the 1930s, Ruth Benedict's *Patterns of Culture*.

The Science of Custom

Benedict's book operates on two levels. On one level, it clearly is a "symbolic landmark" in the history of the culture concept. Benedict was a student of Boas, and *Patterns of Culture* presents all of Boas's anthropological theories in a clear and popularizing form. Benedict attacks the old evolutionary anthropologists for the way in which their mere "analysis of culture traits" led to the construction of "a kind of mechanical Frankenstein's monster" of culture-in-general, composed of decontextualized fragments from various cultures.[19] For Benedict, cultures must be seen as "articulated wholes," and her case studies of three "primitive" cultures—the Zuni Indians of New Mexico, the Dobu of New Guinea, and the Kwakiutl of the Northwest coast of America—argue not only for the existence of integration within each culture but also for diversity between cultures (48). These Boasian assumptions, if not shared by all anthropologists, were certainly commonplace enough and legitimate enough by the time of Benedict's writing not to need any rigorous defense against the evolutionists, and *Patterns of Culture* provides no such defense. Benedict dismisses evolutionists more than she argues against them, and she presents the existence of patterning and integration as simply the common sense of the broader scientific community: "The whole, as modern science is insisting in many fields, is not merely the sum of all its parts, but the result of a unique arrangement and interrelation of the parts that has brought about a new entity" (47). Patterning and integration are not the conclusions *for* which Benedict argues, they are the assumptions *from* which she argues. The tension and conflict in Benedict's book lies not in the existence or nonexistence of cultural integration but in the consequences of integration for human freedom.

This tension manifests itself right from the start in Benedict's opening rumination on the role of custom in human activity:

> The inner workings of our own brain we feel to be uniquely worthy of investigation, but custom, we have a way of thinking, is behaviour at its most commonplace. As a matter of fact, it is the other way around . . .
>   . . . John Dewey has said in all seriousness that the part played by custom in shaping the behaviour of the individual as over against any way in which he can affect traditional custom, is as the proportion of the total vocabulary of his mother tongue over against those words of

his own baby talk that are taken up into the vernacular of his family.
(2)

In this initial opposition of thought and the unthought, custom would seem to efface consciousness: The "inner workings of our own brain" are insignificant compared to "the part played by custom in shaping the behaviour of the individual." Indeed, Benedict, and the culture-and-personality school of anthropology to which she belonged, have often been accused of being "conformist," of emphasizing the ways in which individuals are constituted by and harmonized with their culture.[20] Yet the dominance of culture as custom presents itself to Benedict as a problem, not a solution. The significance of the notion of culture as "personality writ large" lies not in the dominance of custom and tradition over individuality but in the parallel structure of culture and the individual (vii). In a sense, Benedict begins her book by moving from mind (personality) to the commonplace (culture), only to reconstruct the commonplace as mind.

Benedict argues for cultural integration as part of a larger scientific consensus on integration as a principle of the natural world. For support, she turns most often to psychology, in particular the *Gestalt* school and its emphasis on the idea of the "whole configuration." For Benedict, a "culture, like an individual, is a more or less consistent pattern of thought and action" (46). Thus, one approaches cultural behavior much like one approaches individual behavior:

> If we are interested in mental processes, we can satisfy ourselves only by relating the particular symbol to the total configuration of the individual . . .
> . . . If we are interested in cultural processes, the only way in which we can know the significance of the selected detail of behaviour is against the background of the motives and emotions and values that are institutionalized in that culture. (49)

Whatever the relation of a particular culture to the individuals within that culture, it would seem that, at the formal level, to talk about "cultural processes" is to talk about "mental processes." Any statement about culture is thus a statement about the individual, and vice versa.

This parallel structure allows Benedict simultaneously to assert and deny the value of the individual and the value of culture. On the one hand, culture is greater than the sum of its parts. Individuals do not create a culture; culture is not the product of the consent or agreement of the individuals within it. On the other hand, Benedict describes culture in terms of a kind of consciousness usually associated with the individual. Culture makes choices and strives to achieve wholeness. Benedict proposes the image of "a great arc on which are ranged the possible interests provided either by the human age-cycle or by the environment or by man's various activities" (24). Cultures select features from this arc and assemble them into the integrated whole that gives a culture its identity. Of course, no culture has access to all human possibilities at any one time; rather, a particular culture "selects from among the possible traits in the surrounding regions those which it can use, and discards those which it cannot. Other traits it recasts into conformity with its demands" (47). As if wary of the anthropomorphic tendencies of her subjectification of culture, Benedict qualifies her equation of culture and consciousness by insisting that the process of selection that goes into creating a culture "need never be conscious during its whole course"; as if wary of the vagaries of the unconscious, she insists that nonetheless the "integration of cultures is not in the least mystical" (47). In search of a metaphor that will reconcile the contradictory aspects of the cultural process, Benedict likens the integration of cultures to the "process by which a style in art comes into being and persists" (47). In this way, culture is both artist and work of art (viii).

The turn to an older, artistic conception of culture, with its connotations of human freedom and self-expression, suggests a certain anxiety on Benedict's part as to the relation between human freedom and the process of cultural integration. The image of a culture forcing traits "into conformity with its demands" links culture to a certain kind of coercion, and this association threatens to undermine her argument for culture as a benign alternative to that more invidious principle of integration, race. For Benedict, what "really binds men together is their culture,—the ideas and the standards they have in common," rather than race, or "common blood heredity" (16). Culture operates in more complex ways than race, for culture "is not a biologically transmitted complex"; moreover, what "is lost in Nature's guaranty of safety is made up in the advantage of greater plasticity" (14). Race represents stasis and conformity, a dull security to which culture offers the liberating alternative of a "greater plasticity." The choice of the word plasticity, and its suggestion of the plastic arts, reinforces Benedict's association of cultural integration with artistic expression. Culture may bind men together, yet it somehow binds them together in freedom.

This freedom manifests itself in the uniqueness, one could say the individuality, of each culture: "Nor are these configurations we have discussed 'types' in the sense that they represent a fixed constellation of traits. Each one is an empirical characterization, and probably is not duplicated in its entirety anywhere else in the world. Nothing could be more unfortunate than an effort to characterize all cultures as exponents of a limited number of fixed and selected types" (238). Benedict expands the notion of integration to include a potentially infinite variety of particular integrations, so that every culture embodies the principles of plasticity and freedom by virtue of the unique integration that it has achieved. No culture is subject to the pattern of another culture, and no culture may be dismissed as unpatterned or unintegrated, for all are by definition integrated: There are no unintegrated cultures, only cultures whose integration has not been sufficiently studied (228). The world is thus a democracy of cultures—each unique, autonomous, and integrated in its own terms.

Such a generous conception of diversity threatens to sap integration of any meaning; by itself, it merely replaces the old evolutionist encyclopedia of cultural traits with a new encyclopedia of cultural patterns. By Benedict's own admission, awareness of the relativity of cultures often elicits only a complacent "shrug of the shoulders," an uncritical acceptance of "the framework . . . that our own culture institutionalizes" (10).

Cultural relativism is, however, the premise, not the conclusion, of Benedict's argument. It is a starting point with a particular direction, a direction that begins to take shape as Benedict moves from the spatial diversity of culture to the temporal diversity of history:

> The fact that the varieties of culture can best be discussed as they exist in space gives colour to our nonchalance. But it is only limitation of historical material that prevents examples from being drawn rather from the succession of cultures in time. That succession we cannot escape if we would, and when we look back even a generation we realize the extent to which revision has taken place, sometimes in our most intimate behaviour. So far these revisions have been blind, the result of circumstances we can chart only in retrospect. Except for our unwillingness to face cultural change in intimate matters until it is forced upon us, it could not be impossible to take a more intelligent and directive attitude. The resistance is in large measure a result of our misunderstanding of cultural conventions, and especially an exaltation of

those that happen to belong to our nation and decade. A very little acquaintance with other conventions, and a knowledge of how various these may be, would do much to promote a rational social order. (10)

This move from space to time, from culture to history, is another step in the larger movement from necessity to freedom that structures the narrative of *Patterns of Culture*. The book begins with the weight of custom and culture as determinative, yet then allows for such a variety of cultures as to turn that determinism itself into a kind of freedom, at least at the level of intercultural comparison. Apart from this comparative framework, however, culture threatens once again to become a principle of determinism. The diversity of cultures granted, people within a particular culture may simply take cultural relativism as an excuse for blindly accepting the particular pattern of culture in which they find themselves. Taken by itself, the integrated wholeness of a particular culture appears limited, almost static. The principle of intracultural historicity rescues particular cultures from this stasis and grants to each culture the dynamism and diversity so apparent between cultures.

As the first law of cultural integration is diversity, so the second law is "the succession of cultures in time." Since each culture is an integrated whole, this process of "revision" extends even to "our most intimate behaviour." Benedict insists on change as inevitable, as a principle of objective reality, yet it is a necessity that makes possible the free exercise of human agency. If cultural integration were static, people would have no choice but to remain mired in the "nonchalance" of an uncritical acceptance of their own culture. The necessity of change, however, forces people to choose between "blind" revision and "a more intelligent and directive attitude," alternatives so loaded as to suggest only one proper "choice," that of the intelligent direction of cultural change. Thus Benedict's cultural relativism, like the evolutionist conception of culture it rejects, has a developmental scheme, a narrative of history. The end point for relativism is not so much "civilization," with its connotation of a certain body of artistic and material achievements, as "a rational social order," which suggests more a process of apprehending culture rather than an ideal of any particular cultural values. For Benedict, a rational social order is one in which the subjective control over cultural change matches the intensity of the objective process of change itself. This subject-object fit in turn demands a particular approach to culture that is anything but relativistic as a process of cognition.

The absolutism of relativism, the necessity that underlies the freedom of cultural diversity, lies in the critical stance that one must take toward one's own culture as a consequence of relativism. For Benedict, the point of becoming culture-conscious is to "accustom ourselves . . . to pass judgment upon the dominant traits of our own civilization" (249). This critical orientation requires a suspension of all loyalties to particular values, however important those values or practices may be, for the "importance of an institution in a culture gives no direct indication of its usefulness or its inevitability." Indeed, "the dominant traits of our civilization need special scrutiny," as if the strong attachment people have to these traits makes them all the more suspect (250). Passion threatens the clear judgment needed to construct a rational social order, and "any cultural control which we may be able to exercise will depend upon the degree to which we can evaluate objectively the favored and passionately fostered traits of our Western civilization" (250). Thus, though the idea of culture as a pattern of values places values at the center of social life, it does so only to decenter them in relation to the process of objectively evaluating the particular values at the center of a particular society.

Cultural consciousness finds its fulfillment in the "self-conscious direction of the process by which . . . new normalities are created in the next generation." Still, it is not yet clear how one could direct the process of change once one has cast suspicion on all the values that might provide change with some direction. Benedict's distinctions between the "culturally conditioned" and the "organically determined," between unessential and essential relations among various fields of experience within a culture, suggest the possibility of some notion of human nature guiding the critical investigation of culture; however, taken in the context of *Patterns of Culture* as a whole, these distinctions amount to little more than a nod to the liberal-humanist piety of the brotherhood of man (16–17, 43). Benedict never follows up on these distinctions with anything like an account of human nature or what kind of relations are essential to all cultures, and the force of these distinctions is to highlight the conditioned, relative nature of all cultural patterns and to debunk any notion of cultural essentialism. In Benedict's account, "the tiny core that is generic in any situation," the essence of man apart from culture, recedes before "the vast accretions that are local and cultural and man-made" (245). The "culturally conditioned," moreover, is ultimately the *merely* culturally conditioned, interesting in its variety and diversity, but commanding no moral or intellectual hold over the allegiance of the cultural investigator.

In this wasteland of cultural diversity, full of values yet lacking value, there is one secure point on which to stand, the point that unites all of these disparate values: the process of cultural conditioning itself. With cultural change the one fact above any particular cultural conditioning, it becomes the value that directs the process of cultural change:

> It is only the inevitable cultural lag that makes us insist that the old must be discovered again in the new, that there is no solution but to find the old certainty and stability in the new plasticity. The recognition of cultural relativity carries with it its own values, which need not be those of the absolutist philosophies. It challenges customary opinions and causes those who have been bred to them acute discomfort. It rouses pessimism because it throws old formulas into confusion, not because it contains anything intrinsically difficult. (278)

The value of cultural relativity thus lies in the way it "challenges customary opinions" and "throws old formulas into confusion." Relativism does not simply reject the old and the customary, for such a simple rejection of the past merely leads to another kind of absolutism, that present-minded hubris by which "we . . . ridicule our Don Quixotes, the ludicrous embodiments of an outmoded tradition, and continue to regard our own as final and prescribed in the nature of things" (272). The present is itself always in the process of becoming the past, and every particular new normality will soon become an old formula. Benedict does not champion any new set of values so much as she champions the move from "the old certainty" to "the new plasticity." The culturally conscious critic seeks not to reject traditional arrangements so much as "to adapt them by whatever means to rationally selected goals" (272). Plasticity allows for a certain continuity amid the constant change that drives the process of cultural integration.

The Political Economy of Culture

Tempered by this sense of continuity, the value of plasticity does not consign the culturally conscious to a meaningless flux of cultural patterns. Benedict realizes that change, while constant and inescapable, is always a threat to social order; while she rejects any notion of a static social order, she also rejects the "wanton waste of revolution and economic and emotional disaster" that comes with the complete rejection of

the existing social order (248). Tradition and revolution are twin abso-
lutisms that must give way to a more balanced notion of "orderly progress" (249). For Benedict, "Real improvements in the social order depend
upon more modest and more difficult discriminations. It is possible to
scrutinize different institutions and cast up their cost in terms of social
capital, in terms of the less desireable behaviour traits they stimulate, and
in terms of human suffering and frustration" (248).

This is one of the few passages in which Benedict suggests a value
to cultural relativism beyond the mere process of cultural change itself.
Cultural change receives its direction from the standard of the alleviation
of "human suffering and frustration"; progress is "orderly" and goals
are "rationally selected" in the degree to which they promote human
happiness. Human suffering and happiness are the only standards that
remain after all others have been relegated to the sphere of the culturally
conditioned. Happiness and suffering are the bottom line of cultural consciousness, the measure of the "social capital" of a culture, the scrutiny
of which proceeds "in terms of profit and loss" (249). Like financial capital, social capital always fluctuates: "No social order can separate its
virtues from the defects of its virtues," and if "any society wishes to pay
that cost for its chosen and congenial traits, certain values will develop
within this pattern, however 'bad' it may be" (248). Thus, orderly progress requires the constant valuing and revaluing of social capital,
weighing the benefits of human happiness against the costs of human
suffering at particular moments in a culture's chosen patterning and re-
patterning of itself.

Benedict presents a profoundly anticultural vision of what should bind
people together. It is precisely what she presents as independent of culture—that is, suffering and happiness—that emerge as the standards by
which to judge cultures. Sympathetic as her accounts of non-Western
cultures may be, Benedict does not suggest that any of these cultures are
patterned to ensure the maximum amount of human happiness. Benedict's cultural relativism may be a safeguard against the condescension
that plagued previous generations of anthropologists, yet it reinforces a
much more insidious Western assumption than the Victorian construction of the primitive, that is, the assumption that human happiness
should be the organizing principle of social life. First fully articulated in
the eighteenth-century social science of political economy, this assumption continued to shape the social vision of the modern West through its
Victorian and anti-Victorian, modernist periods.

Benedict's conception of culture must be seen as a particular moment in this tradition of social thought, a tradition that sees social life in terms of the liberation of individual desires from the arbitrary social restrictions on those desires. Like feudalism and the mercantilist state before it, culture appears as an arbitrary structure of power geared toward repressing individual desire. Benedict's engagement with what she has identified as the source of repression sets her apart from her classical and Victorian predecessors, but the terms of her engagement place her firmly within their concerns for freedom from social restrictions. Benedict embraces culture only to transform it from a principle of necessity to a principle of freedom; to become culture-conscious is to learn how to control culture, and this control justifies itself by its service to human freedom. Benedict not only resolves the conflict between individual and culture but she practically erases the distinction between the two. Culture becomes simply the process of ensuring human freedom and happiness, "by whatever means" (272). This process is never complete, so culture needs constant attention, yet it receives attention only as a means to human happiness, never as an end in itself.

Benedict's simultaneous embrace of and rejection of culture stems in part from her attitude toward that older champion of human freedom, economics. Indeed, *Patterns of Culture* is in many ways an argument for the passing of the torch of human freedom from economics to anthropology. Still, she speaks of culture in terms of "social capital" and of cultural criticism as a kind of cost-benefit analysis (248). These metaphors need not suggest an equation of culture and economics, but neither can they be dismissed as completely fortuitous. Certainly for Benedict economics is an important part of all cultures, and, on one level, economics simply provides another illustration of the variety of cultures. Thus, an economic motive like rivalry has different consequences for different cultures:

> In Kwakiutl life the rivalry is carried out in such a way that all success must be built upon the ruin of rivals; in *Middletown* in such a way that individual choices and direct satisfactions are reduced to a minimum and conformity is sought beyond all other human gratifications. In both cases it is clear that wealth is not sought and valued for its direct satisfaction of human needs but as a series of counters in the game of rivalry. (247–48)

This surface diversity cannot hide a common consequence of rivalry, the distortion of the essential purpose of wealth, which is the "direct satisfaction of human needs." As in *Middletown,* which Benedict takes as an authoritative account of modern American life, culture appears as pathology, as that which represses an authentic core of human needs. Just what those needs are becomes clearer in Benedict's very Lynd-like distinction between rivalry and competition:

> Rivalry is a struggle that is not centered upon the real objects of the activity but upon out-doing a competitor. The attention is no longer directed toward providing adequately for a family or toward owning goods that can be utilized or enjoyed, but toward out distancing one's neighbours and owning more than anyone else. Everything else is lost sight of in the one great aim of victory. Rivalry does not, like competition, keep its eyes upon the original activity; whether making a basket or selling shoes, it creates an artificial situation: the game of showing that one can win out over others. (247)

This is the kind of critical distinction between use value and exchange value that we have seen in a variety of forms throughout the work of Veblen, the Lynds, and Dewey. Relations between people should be a function of a more basic relation between men and things: thus, "providing adequately for a family" should be the social equivalent of an individual's "owning goods that can be utilized or enjoyed." When relations between people take priority over relations to things or operate according to principles other than use, they take on an extraneous exchange value. Benedict attacks rivalry for focusing "upon outdoing a competitor," another person, rather than concentrating on "the original activity," or more precisely, "the real objects of the activity." People are at best secondary to the essential relation between man and object. As a distraction from this essential relation, people take on a kind of exchange value in that awareness of people transforms the ownership of goods, which should merely be a means to using and enjoying goods, into an end in itself. As an end, ownership places value on the mere quantitative accumulation of goods rather than the productive use of them. Thus, as a critical tool, Benedict's cultural relativism merely reinforces an older economic essentialism.

Ultimately, Benedict judges cultures by the very economic standard of their service to "human gratifications." Still, her cultural rewriting of political economy transforms the narrow, utilitarian parameters of pleasure and pain into the broader cultural parameters of "individual choices and direct satisfactions" and "conformity" (247–48). Benedict's defense of competition, as against its neurotic distortion in rivalry, must be seen as part of her broader individualistic attack on conformity: "Middletown is a typical example of our usual urban fear of seeming in however slight an act different from our neighbours. Eccentricity is more feared than parasitism . . . The fear of being different is the dominating motivation recorded in Middletown" (273). Middletown as a symptom shows the cut-throat individualism of rivalry and the retreat from individualism into conformity to be, in effect, brothers under the skin—a brotherhood united against a true individualism that manifests itself in healthy competition.

Benedict's anxiety about conformity in relation to culture parallels Herbert Hoover's anxieties over planning, and the comparison is instructive. Hoover rejected the free market as wasteful and inefficient because of the ruinous competition that it fostered; he also rejected centralized planning as wasteful and inefficient because it threatened to sap individual initiative. His associative idea of cooperative competition was to synthesize the individual initiative of free markets with the rational control of planning. Benedict seeks a similar synthesis in her cultural individualism, and its economic manifestation, competition. Cultural consciousness navigates between the twin evils of "eccentricity" and "parasitism" to unite people in the conscious shaping of culture to serve the needs of individuals. Her idea of culture provides a language for a broader ideal of cooperative competition in which the synthesis of initiative and rationality Hoover advocated becomes the ideal for all aspects of life.

Culture and Creativity

Benedict's fascination with the figure of the shaman throughout *Patterns of Culture* gives some clue as to what kind of person her culture-conscious individual must become. Margaret Mead once commented that Benedict took up the study of culture in part because she was "concerned with the extent to which one culture could find a place for extremes of behavior—in the mystic, the seer, the artist—which another culture branded as abnormal or worthless" (ix). Indeed, by the end of *Patterns of Culture*, the hobo and the artist who reject the value of "the accumulation of property" emerge as representative victims of American culture (260). These marginal men "are unsupported by the forms of their society" and are often frustrated in their attempts "to express themselves satisfactorily"; often the "dilemma of such an individual is . . . most successfully solved by doing violence to his strongest natural impulses and accepting the role the culture honours" (260). Victims of American culture, artists and hobos are martyrs for cultural consciousness. The example of their alienation provides not an ideal to live up to but a cautionary tale to direct the control of culture. A properly controlled culture must foster forms that support people in their efforts to express themselves and liberate natural impulses from the constraints of honored cultural roles that may conflict with those impulses.

Ultimately, cultural consciousness offers a synthesis of parasitism and eccentricity, of conformity and alienation, best expressed by the ideal of tolerance: "At all events, there can be no reasonable doubt that one of the most effective ways in which to deal with the staggering burden of psychopathic tragedies in America at the present time is by means of an educational program which fosters tolerance in society and a kind of self-respect and independence that is foreign to Middletown and our urban traditions" (273–74). The ideal pattern of American culture is that of "self-respect and independence." If people really were independent, if they really did not have to depend on others, then they would not have any reason to conform to other people or make others conform to them. With the passing of conformity comes the passing of its counterpart, alienation. These alternatives are transcended by a creative marginality based on the independence of all individuals. Independence itself seems to imply marginality, for in breaking the power of one person over another it also shatters those constitutive ties that would seem to make cultural integration possible. Yet Benedict places her hope for integration not in culture but in cultural consciousness, which entails first and foremost the consciousness of and acceptance of differences. The rejection of dominant values and the attempt to create one's own values become the integrating pattern of culture; ultimately, the tolerant society is a society of artists whose work of art is their own individuality. Marginality never slips into alienation because in exercising independent self-creation one is embracing the organizing pattern of one's culture.

Benedict's conception of culture overcomes the nineteenth-century opposition of society and the individual by refiguring both in the language of shaping, molding, creating:

> The large corporate behaviour we have discussed is nevertheless the behaviour of individuals. It is the world with which each person is

severally presented, the world from which he must make his individual life. (251)

Most people are shaped to the form of their culture because of the enormous malleability of their original endowment. They are plastic to the moulding force of the society into which they are born. (254)

In making one's individual life, one simply acts out the principle of culture. Much like Veblen's machine process, culture does not control or determine an individual's behavior so much as it sets the terms of that behavior; that is, it establishes a standard of creativity and control which the individual must live up to. In setting this standard, culture reduces itself to the conditions which an individual must work on in the act of self-creation: "Culture provides the raw material of which the individual makes his life. If it is meagre, the individual suffers; if it is rich, the individual has the chance to rise to his opportunity" (251–52).

Thus, though the principle of creativity unites culture and the individual, this union has a particular direction that favors the individual over culture. True, culture shapes individuals, yet this very formulation makes the individual the end or purpose of culture, the standard by which to judge a culture. Thus, a "meagre" culture is one in which "the individual suffers," and a "rich" culture is one in which "the individual has the chance to rise to his opportunity." Like Hoover's associationism, culture is not so much a cure as a challenge; it promises not human happiness but rather the conditions for the equal pursuit of happiness for all individuals who have the drive and determination for such a pursuit. Culture is, in effect, opportunity.

Patterns of Culture is not a book about the idea of culture but a book about the ideal of cultural consciousness. Initially, it presents culture as a process that is both objective and unconscious: Culture shapes individuals and individuals shape culture regardless of conscious intervention on the part of the individual or culture. On one level, culture simply *is*, and the reader must accept this to follow Benedict in her argument. This initial positing of the primal, almost narcissistic union of individual and culture as an objective process is, however, simply the first step in the construction of the union of individual and culture as a subjective process. Awareness of this process leads to a recognition of the diversity of cultural integrations, and a rather anal predilection for analyzing cultures into their constituent parts to expose the arbitrary and unnecessary nature of various integrations. Such a level of culture-consciousness by itself

leads only to a rather immature, unproductive cultural relativism. Culture-consciousness becomes a mature, productive subjectivity when it is
able to direct this knowledge of diversity, to create something from it
that did not exist before.

With all particular cultures deprived of any authority by virtue of their
relativity, the only authority that remains to direct this creative process is
that consciousness which stands outside of all cultures so as to apprehend
them; and the one value that this consciousness may rely on as it wades
through the endlessly documentable diversity of cultures is the seemingly
transcultural value of human happiness. With this figure of the individual
contemplating the various patterns of culture in search of happiness, Benedict completes her journey from "The Science of Custom" to "The Individual and the Pattern of Culture," from necessity to freedom.

To link culture to freedom, as Benedict and many other intellectuals
did in the 1930s, is to link freedom to a particular notion of selfhood.[21]
In arguing for cultural consciousness, *Patterns of Culture* argues for a
particular kind of creativity, that of the intellectual. The subjectivity of
cultural consciousness is the subjectivity of the intellectual as either an
artist or a social scientist. As a model of selfhood, the intellectual corresponds neither to the solid "character" of the producer society of the nineteenth century nor to the fluid "personality" of the consumer society of
the twentieth, at least as these terms have been understood by historians.[22] *Patterns of Culture* suggests an ideal of selfhood that combines all
the control of "character" with all the dynamism of "personality." As
Middletown had its absent center of selfhood articulated by *Individualism Old and New*, so *Patterns of Culture* found its appropriate exegesis
in Robert Lynd's *Knowledge for What?*

Chapter 5

■

Culture for What?

Culture and Commitment

LIKE THEIR LITERARY counterparts, many nonliterary intellectuals underwent an "exile's return" during the 1930s. The revival of social activism inspired by the Great Depression brought social scientists like Robert Lynd back from the epistemological expatriation of detached objectivity. As literary intellectuals forsook alienation and went on the road in search of America, so Lynd returned to Muncie to study the effects of the depression on the people of Middletown. Written within the conventions of professional social science, *Middletown in Transition* nonetheless directly engages the people of Middletown and explicitly offers itself as a guide for progressive social change in a way that contrasts sharply with the detached tone of the original study. Lynd's career during the 1930s suggests a larger intellectual shift from understanding culture as a tool for objective analysis to seeing the idea of culture as itself a normative ordering principle for social life. This shift reached its culmination in Lynd's 1939 work, *Knowledge for What?*

On the most obvious level, *Knowledge for What?* is a polemical call for the unification of the social sciences through the idea of culture and the application of such a unified social science to the task of social reconstruction. The book is a plea for reason in the wake of fascist irrationality, for the value of privacy and individual liberty in the wake of totalizing schemes for a rationally planned society. Yet to sum up the book as, in the words of one historian, a more or less successful attempt "to combine liberal values with the task of socialist reconstruction" leaves unexamined just what such a combination implies as a social vision; such an assessment of the book comes across more as a vindication of Lynd from any charge of extremism than as an actual interpretation of the book in question.[1] Yet *Knowledge for What?* is an extreme book, for it suggests nothing less than the equation of social life with the personal ethic of the social scientist.

The book begins with "Social Science in Crisis," yet immediately figures this crisis in terms of two conflicting personal orientations, two distinct personality types each defined by a particular style of work. Social science is divided "into two blocs of workers: the scholars and the technicians."[2] This division has been growing as these two types of social scientists have moved in opposite directions; "the scholar becoming remote from and even disregarding immediate relevancies, and the technician too often accepting the definition of his problems too narrowly in terms of the emphasis of the institutional environment of the moment" (*KW*, 1). Social science, like Dewey's America, is a house divided against itself; and for Lynd, as for Dewey, the cure for this division lies in the establishment of a proper conception of "the institutional environment of the moment." The irrelevant detachment of the scholar and the uncritical engagement of the technician present false alternatives, for "important problems tend to fall into oblivion between the two groups of workers" (*KW*, 1). The truth, once again, lies in the middle, and that middle, more explicitly than ever before, is culture.

For Lynd, culture serves as the master discipline, the "inclusive frame of reference for all the social sciences" (*KW*, 19). With its roots in aesthetics and the study of "primitive" societies, the word culture carried with it connotations of wholeness no longer available to the word "society," which people like Lynd associated with the anarchy of the capitalist marketplace. Ironically, Lynd's own rendering of the culture concept reproduces the very anarchy he seeks to subdue through the invocation of culture. Lynd decries not only social chaos but also social-scientific order; he attacks the neat formulations provided by sociological rules and exceptions, and he praises the culture concept's ability to render a vision of social life as "a subtly graded, unevenly distributed and continually changing array of behavior" (*KW*, 29). To see culture as a whole way of life is to see it in terms of "all the jumbled details of living" that make up a whole way of life (*KW*, 50). Lynd rejects the notion of culture as having any "inner, ordained teleology" and demands that it be regarded as a "fumbling mass of lags, inconsistencies, right and wrong inferences, and clear and confused motivations" (*KW*, 120). Lynd quotes approvingly Edward Sapir's dismissal of "the tidy tables of contents attached to this

or that group which we have been in the habit of calling 'cultures' "
(*KW*, 30). Freed from its moorings in Victorian anthropology, the concept of culture takes on a certain "fragmentary and confused" quality,
yet it is this very irreducibility that gives the concept of culture its tough-
ness and vitality (*KW*, 30).

In light of this ideal of a fumbling mass of inconsistencies, all other
social visions appear static and reductive. The social sciences, which on
one level appear confused, divided, in need of order, actually suffer from
too much order: "The social sciences have tended to emphasize data
gathered rather than data needing to be gathered, normative theory
rather than the full range of refractory phenomena, and to stress Knowledge and Order rather than the vast areas of the Unknown and Chaotic"
(*KW*, 118). By this formulation, the social sciences seem plagued by the
very qualities often associated with the culture concept in the 1930s; that
is, the stress on integration and order, and the move from a value-free to
a "normative" social science. For Lynd, every integration threatens to
suppress "the full range of refractory phenomena," every order threatens
to gloss over the chaos of reality. Academic social science favors the
"manageably known," and suffers from "the centripetal tendency to
shrink away from the marginal area where insistent reality grinds against
the central body of theory" (*KW*, 118). For Lynd, culture serves not so
much as a principle of order as a reality principle that smashes accepted
theory. Culture carries the social scientist to the margins of inquiry,
where chaos rules; as today's margin and chaos become incorporated
into a new central body of theory, culture pushes inquiry to the new
margins established by the new ordering principle. This is Veblen's savage workman in social-scientific drag. Culture offers not so much the
ideal of an integrated whole as an ideal of integrating a whole that is
always in flux through the process of social-scientific inquiry.

Knowledge for What? does not offer order as an antidote to chaos;
rather, it calls for the constant ordering of a reality perceived as constant
chaos. The fluidity of culture as an object of inquiry demands a compara-
ble fluidity on the part of the social-scientific subject inquiring into culture. This fluidity is transgressive, for it demands that the culture-conscious social scientist "cut cross-lots (as science always must) regardless
of the 'Posted: No Trespassing' signs" (*KW*, 206). The totality of culture
demands the unrestricted access of the social scientist to every aspect of
culture: "If, then, we social scientists set ourselves the common task of
understanding our American culture, nothing in American life escapes

us" (KW, 20). Lynd lauds the physicist P. W. Bridgeman's model for the relation between science and society: "The *utmost* exercise of intelligence means the *free* use of intelligence; [the scientist] must be willing to follow *any* lead that he can see, undeterred by any inhibition, whether it arises from laziness or other unfortunate personal characteristics, or intellectual tradition or the social conventions of his epoch" (KW, 8). The culture concept requires the extension of the autonomy of the natural sciences to the social sciences precisely because the transgressive nature of cultural inquiry so often meets with the resistance of "inhibition," "personal characteristics," "tradition," "social conventions," and perhaps worst of all, "laziness." Indeed, as taboos, these very restrictions constitute the main object of social-scientific inquiry. Social science requires not only complete freedom from them but complete access to them.

Far from a cynical will-to-power on the part of the social scientist against the common citizen, this demand for free and open access must be seen in terms of a persistent democratic concern with openness as a guarantor of freedom and equality. Historians of the United States have observed that secrecy of any kind has often been taken as a cloak for conspiracy or subversion.[3] In this context, sex, the family, and child development, the "problems" which Lynd seems to see as most in need of transgressive, social-scientific investigation, serve the same role for the twentieth century that the Catholic Church, the Masons, and secret societies served for the nineteenth century. Lynd's obsession with these issues should not be taken as prurience, nor should they be traced to any belief in the centrality of sex to social life; rather, the anxiety that these issues arouse stems from a common characteristic of being "areas of study heretofore largely overlooked" (KW, 117). In Lynd's social-scientific rendering, secrecy represents subversion not by conscious conspiracy but by drift. The need to study early childhood development stems not so much from the centrality of childhood development to culture—culture is too complex to be reduced to any one factor—but from the fact that in "our culture the years before starting to school have been largely an institutional vacuum, with which only the individual home has been concerned" (KW, 51). Social science abhors a vacuum, and the greatest fear of Lynd's vision of culture as an inclusive framework lies in the possibility of an "institutional vacuum" for some cultural practice. Of course, the home is an institution in an objective, unconscious sense, as Lynd's study of Middletown makes clear; the institution in relation to which the "individual home" exists in an "institutional vacuum" is social science itself, which transforms the objective and the unconscious into the subjective and the conscious. As in *Middletown*, the "individual home" is, in effect, the isolated home, with all of the connotations of drift, waste, and stagnation that accompany the lack of integration with the larger, social-scientifically organized culture.

If exemption from social-scientific scrutiny smacks of subversion or even conspiracy, the question remains, against what is it a conspiracy? If *Knowledge for What?* is something more than a manifesto for technocracy, on what basis does Lynd justify the complete autonomy of the social scientist in scrutinizing every aspect of human life? Lynd's suspicion of anyone who would object to his social-scientific project and his commitment to a strenuous ethic of inquiry stem from his belief that "social scientists have lost 'the person' below their horizon" (*KW*, 22). Lynd stakes his iconoclastic stance toward orthodox social science on his belief in the centrality of the person to social-scientific inquiry. For Lynd, the withering particularity of culture, its irreducibility to abstract models or general explanations of behavior, demands an "emphasis upon persons as the active carriers, perpetuators, and movers of culture" as opposed to persons as mere objects of larger social forces (*KW*, 25).

Lynd refuses to let the concept of culture become yet another abstract device for explaining social behavior, and he insists that people are not "motivated by a non-personalized 'cultural standard' " but by their own thoughts, feelings, and relations with other people (*KW*, 39). It is just this emphasis on the human person as an active agent, as a subject rather than an object, that demands a greater intrusion into the life of the person by the social scientist. For example, in suggesting the implications of a cultural approach to the human person, Lynd contrasts two ways of studying labor: the old way, with its emphasis on legislation, wages, and unemployment rates, and a new way, an "analysis of labor actually on the job and at home, of labor's motivations and frustrations, and of the kinds of fresh operational theory that will include this living stuff of labor" (*KW*, 35–36). This "living stuff" includes not just the institutions that people live and work in but "what these institutions and problems mean to specific, differently situated people, how they look and feel to these different people, and how they are used" (*KW*, 25).

The general move from surface to depth implied by the move from behavior to experience requires "careful interviewing" and "involves enormous expenditures of time"; Lynd somewhat ironically concedes that "subjects have an annoying habit of proving intractable as one seeks patiently to delve into their personal behavior" (*KW*, 25). This resistance may be unavoidable, but in a world in which social phenomena (including individual persons) increasingly come to be judged in terms of social-scientific accounts of them, this dissection of the person works to uncover the human agency that would remain hidden beneath more general, impersonal studies of institutions. The depth interview, precisely because of its invasion of personal thoughts and feelings, provides the key to understanding how individuals make meaning; this process of inquiry constructs agency and grants it to the individual, rescuing the individual from being constructed as an object, a nonagent, by some less-in-depth social-scientific account.

The issue here is not whether Lynd's approach to the person respects the subjectivity of the person or merely treats the person as an object but what conception of the person is assumed by his social-scientific approach. Certainly no one needs social science to tell them how they act, feel, think, and respond to relations with other people; these perceptions have always existed on a certain commonsense level, and if anything it is a certain kind of social science that has been responsible for downplaying the validity of these experiences. In recovering the importance of the thoughts and feelings of individuals against an older, more objective social science, Lynd does not reassert folk wisdom against scientific orthodoxy. By insisting on the necessity of a social-scientific account of human action, Lynd shifts the standard of human agency from motivated action within a culture to consciousness of oneself as engaging in motivated action within a culture. That is, the stakes of agency shift from having motivations—or perhaps it is safer to say having reasons for one's actions—to explaining reasons and motivations. If people make culture, so, too, culture makes people; to be a conscious person one must be able to see oneself in a causal chain in which one is both cause and effect. To be a person, one must become a social scientist, on the boundaries of one's own culture, transgressing cultural norms.

The social-scientific, culturally conscious character of this self is nowhere clearer than in Lynd's discussion of the place of values in social-scientific inquiry: "Since it is human beings that build culture and make it go, the social scientist's criteria of the significant cannot stop short of those human beings' criteria of the significant. The values of human beings living together in the pursuit of their deeper and more persistent purposes constitute the frame of reference that identifies significance for social science" (*KW*, 189). In his turn to values, Lynd presents himself as boldly willing to go where no social scientist has gone before. Still, Lynd retains a social-scientific suspicion of the "old, aloof ethics," and he insists on approaching ethics as "but a component of the cravings of persons going about the daily round of living with each other" (*KW*, 191). With values brought down to earth and reduced to cravings, they serve as a reality principle capable of guiding cultural inquiry:

> Cravings are not only inescapably parts of the datum with which social science works, but . . . they dictate the direction of emphasis of social science as man's working tool for continually rebuilding his culture. So viewed, "institutions," "social change," "trends," "lags," "disequilibria," and all the other conceptualizations of social science become relevant primarily to the wants and purposes of human personalities seeking to live. The central assumption becomes that men want to do, to be, to feel certain identifiable things . . . and the derivative assumption regarding the rôle of social science is that its task is to find out even more clearly what these things are that human beings persist in wanting and how these things can be built into culture. If man's cravings are ambivalent, if he is but sporadically rational and intelligent, the task of social science becomes the discovery of what forms of culturally-structured learned behavior can maximize opportunities for rational behavior where it appears to be essential for human well-being, and at the same time provide opportunity for expression of his deep emotional spontaneities where those, too, are important. (*KW*, 200)

As critical tools, all the supraindividual "conceptualizations of social science," such as institutions, social change, and social trends, clarify larger social processes only to judge them against the standard of "the wants and purposes of human personalities seeking to live." Classical liberal thinkers separated ethics from social life in hopes of ensuring social order through the liberation of individual self-interest and desire; Lynd's social-scientific reconstruction of this worldview overcomes the split between ethics and social life by reducing ethics to a principle of desire made once again the organizing principle of social life. Classical liberals at least recognized a distinction between ethics and desire; Lynd collapses this distinction. Economics promised a rational social order as the by-product of the release of individual desire; social science, as "man's working tool for continually rebuilding his culture," sets as its task "the discovery of what forms of culturally-structured learned behavior can maximize opportunities for rational behavior." In one sense, social science transforms the person from an assumed means to an achievable end. Precisely because the existence of the rational (and emotionally spontaneous) person cannot be taken for granted, such a person becomes the goal to which all the energies of society—conceived in terms of social science—must be directed.

In the end, however, is the beginning. The person that is the goal of social-scientific inquiry emerges as a reconstruction of the person who is the starting point of that inquiry, the social scientist. Social-scientific inquiry begins with the separation of the social scientist from his object of study and ends with the person distinguished from and set above all the social forces that impinge on him. The social scientist as a studying subject and the person as a studied object are never quite equal, but their interaction provides the essential social relation of a society conceived in terms of the liberation of human cravings. The dynamics of this interaction suggest themselves in Lynd's meditation on the problem of bedwetting:

> Science has brought many new securities to those able to pay for expensive specialized services, and some to those who cannot pay. But it is also creating vast popular awarenesses of new problems as it seeks to discover how to make the hitherto unpreventable preventable. To cite but two commonplace examples, a generation ago thumb-sucking by infants was something they "just got over," and enuresis was handled by telling the child he was naughty and shaming him out of it; but today the whole intricate world of childhood tensions in relation to parental tensions, as antecedents to subsequent adult maladjustment, has opened up before parents. At point after point in daily living the demand for the application of specialized knowledge increases. One cannot know everything, and "everything costs so much money" in a world in which most people have too little money. Almost the entire burden of adaptation is left to the individual by the culture, since the latter recognizes so little responsibility to structure new knowledge into the institutional forms that will encourage and render easy the use in daily living of the best we know. Hence the sinister partial impotence into which progress has led us, despite the fact that ours is physically the most superbly endowed culture on earth. (*KW*, 113)

Lynd's social-scientific vision of social life posits a society based on dialogue in which the relation between the expert and the untutored citizen acts merely as a sociological embodiment of a more basic dialogue between unfulfilled desire and the various means of fulfilling that desire. In this scenario, the freedom of the social scientist guarantees the freedom of the individual citizen.

The social scientist's complete access to every aspect of daily life certainly expands the power of the social scientist, yet it also aids in expanding the consciousness of the average citizen, "creating vast popular awarenesses of new problems." This new awareness demands that people see themselves as existing within a complex chain of causality, so that even childhood problems like bed-wetting and thumb-sucking can be seen "as antecedents to subsequent adult maladjustment." Causality, of course, threatens a determinism that would reduce the individual to a mere "effect," yet consciousness of causality offers the possibility of control, the chance "to discover how to make the hitherto unpreventable preventable." As a response to the popular "demand for the application of specialized knowledge" to "point after point in daily living," this control would be, furthermore, a particularly democratic kind of control. A society truly organized according to social-scientific principles would "structure new knowledge into the institutional forms that will encourage and render easy the use in daily living of the best we know." No mere passive beneficiary of expertise, the citizen of Lynd's social-scientific order must be an active participant in the social scientific project of rational control. Availing oneself of the fruits of social science is itself a process of education, for it demands that, to a greater or lesser degree, one question the previously unquestioned, prevent the previously unprevented, or control the previously uncontrolled. As one makes use of the fruits of social science, one then takes on the values, the model of selfhood, of the social scientist. (Witness in our own time, how the most successful products of drug rehabilitation programs tend to become counselors themselves). Thus, the gap between expert and citizen, while perhaps never completely overcome, tends to decrease with the spread of social science. Ultimately, the distinction between social scientist and citizen becomes a distinction of degree rather than of kind: A good citizen is a good social scientist, and a good social scientist is a good citizen.

At present, Lynd sees an insidious exchange value of "expensive specialized services" restricting the universalization of a liberated use value of social-scientific inquiry. Having equated social science with social life, Lynd divides the contemporary social scene into two groups, "those able to pay" and "those who cannot pay" for social scientific services. Lynd does not ignore issues of power, justice, and equality, yet by addressing

these issues in terms of the relative distribution of social-scientific expertise, his political project becomes one of making "the partial and imperfect application of progress to the whole round of daily living" in effect
total and perfect (KW, 109). Far from offering a conflict-free, totally
administered society, Lynd's utopian vision, if it may be called that, suggests rather an ideal of struggle finally placed on the right footing, conducted in the right terms. With the demise of restrictive pecuniary interests and the universalization of social science, people will be able to
engage freely in the rational dialogue of desire between their cravings/
values and the social-scientific means to realize those those cravings/
values.

Knowledge for What? has been interpreted by some historians as a
fall from the more tempered criticisms of Middletown, a lapse into vulgar
technocracy.[4] Such a reading, however, fails to account for the persistent
coupling of social-scientific expertise and individual agency in Lynd's
book, as well as in the writings of Veblen, Dewey, and Benedict. These
writings make their arguments not by setting off expertise against agency
and then siding with one or the other but by setting "a large and pervasive extension of planning and control" against "casual individual initiative," or, more generally, by opposing matter of fact to rule of thumb
(KW, 209). The opening up of all aspects of life to social-scientific inquiry signals not a surrender to technocratic domination but a surrender
of one's previously casual attitude toward one's own life. It is, ultimately,
a call to heroic agency on the part of all citizens of a democratic society.

There is certainly a paradox in the idea that one can plan freedom,
that "deep emotional spontaneities" can somehow "be built into culture" (KW, 200). Lynd addresses this paradox directly:

> Our task here as social scientists is to try to discover what sort of
> culture that sort of culture would be which utilized its best intelligence
> systematically at point after point to plan and to coordinate the institu-
> tionalized ways of doing things which are important to us as persons.
> Nobody wants to be planned into the routine status of a robot. But
> here the problem for social science is to determine which is baby and
> which is bath, and not to allow both to be thrown away in the frothy
> suds of indiscriminate "freedom." (KW, 209)

Lynd wants to engineer the conditions that foster individual agency. Of
course, Lynd's own work insists on the interconnectedness of the individ-

ual and his conditions: Too much planning of conditions reduces the individual to "the routine status of a robot" while too little abandons the individual to the "frothy suds of indiscriminate 'freedom.' " Lynd's ideal seems to be one of spontaneity as a kind of planned casualness, and the paradoxical nature of this ideal only leads to a redoubling of the social-scientific project: Not only must we use "intelligence systematically at point after point to plan and to coordinate the institutionalized ways of doing things which are important to us as persons" but we must apply intelligence to the process of applying intelligence to society. The solution to the potential problem of social science is more and better social science. Thus, the social-scientific critique of economic anarchy results in the rejection of one self-regulating mechanism, the market, for another, social science.

We distort the character of this shift from the market to social science to speak of it, as Lynd and the writers of his time did, as a shift from laissez-faire to planning. Social science itself embodies a kind of laissez-faire spirit, particularly in its call to tear down traditional restrictions and taboos so as to allow for the free flow of inquiry. If anything, social science offers an even more rigorous assault on traditional restrictions than does laissez-faire economic ideology. As free-market ideologues ceased to be outsider-adversaries to an entrenched feudal order and became the status quo, they made certain compromises with their initial assault on tradition. In particular, the nineteenth-century ideology of "separate spheres" seemed to exempt the domestic realm of family life from the market's assault on traditional social relations.[5] It is just this Victorian sentimentalization of the family and private life that elicits so much of Lynd's social-scientific indignation. However much the invasion of the home by mass-produced commodities had long since undermined the validity of any notion of separate spheres, in Lynd's time, this doctrine still had a certain power at an ideological level. It is as if the market had experienced a failure of nerve in its assault on tradition, with only social science left to take up the fight.

In taking up this fight, Lynd takes up the all-or-nothing rhetoric of his laissez-faire predecessors: that is, man will never be free until all traditional restrictions to action are eliminated. The more ominous passages in *Knowledge for What?* should be read with this rhetorical frame in mind. Thus, Lynd's concluding passage on the fate of a public hostile to change: "Social science cannot perform its function if the culture constrains it at certain points in ways foreign to the spirit of science; and at all points where such constraints limit the free use of intelligence to pose problems, to analyze all relevant aspects of them, or to draw conclusions, it is necessary for social science to work directly to remove the causes of these obstacles" (*KW*, 249).

Lynd's book suggests two publics. The passage above refers not to the public in general but to a particular kind of public, one trapped "within the grooves of traditional folk assumptions" and aligned with "the rigidities of institutionalized habit or human inertia"; such a public threatens "to block the march toward desirable cultural change," and indeed has much to fear from social science (*KW*, 145, 206). This public will suffer the same fate at the hands of social science that priests and kings suffered at the hands of the free market. Indeed, crucial to the establishment of a reign of social-scientific freedom is the elimination—or at least neutralization—of all who might perceive "the free use of intelligence" as itself an act of coercion or domination. This public must go the way of the Indian. *Knowledge for What?* suggests another public as well, one committed to the values of critical intellect and cultural change. This public assumes "that wherever our current culture is found to cramp or to distort the quest of considerable numbers of persons for satisfaction of basic cravings of human personality, there lies a responsibility for social science" (*KW*, 205). This public experiences the bracketing of all assumptions, the detachment from all loyalties not voluntarily entered into, and the relentless examination of every aspect of one's life as liberation. This public has everything to gain from the ascendency of the social-scientific worldview of *Knowledge for What?*, a worldview that demands only that everyone submit to the discipline of becoming self-creating individuals.

Citizenship as Transition

Before Lynd offered a theoretical formulation of the proper relation between social scientist and citizen, he offered a practical example of his own relation to his citizen/objects in his 1935 work *Middletown in Transition: A Study in Cultural Conflicts*. The subtitle of this book suggests a contrast with the original *Middletown*, whose subtitle was *A Study in American Culture*. Of course, conflicts abound in *Middletown*, which is certainly no less a study of cultural conflicts than its sequel. Even the highly touted addition of the X-family and their "pattern of business-class control," Lynd's supposedly Marxist turn, offers no serious revision of the original study; business-class control is all over *Middletown* in the form of the dominance of the money medium of exchange. The importance of *Middletown in Transition* lies not in its lengthy "reinterpretation" of Middletown life but in its nine-page defense of the process and perspective of interpreting and reinterpreting all of American life.

The most obvious problem with the social-scientific perspective is the gap between the social scientist as a studying subject and ordinary people as objects of study. In what may be the only meaningful acknowledgment that anyone can make when writing a work of social science, Lynd addresses this problem from the very start of *Middletown in Transition:*

> Most of all, this report is indebted to the people of Middletown. Not only did they cooperate generously during the period of adding to and checking the data, many individuals have been endlessly helpful in assembling material, making special studies at certain points, and in reading and criticizing sections of the report. It is the hope of the writers that Middletown will not regard this study as an attempt to single out Middletown, or groups or individuals in the city, for praise or blame. The reason for undertaking such a study as this lies in the assumption that there is so much that is common to tendencies in the broader culture of the nation in a Middletown that a detailed interwoven analysis of the single community will throw light on the situation we all face at this stage of our American civilization.[6]

Having properly humbled himself before the people of Middletown, Lynd proceeds with yet another social-scientific dissection of Middletown life.

Between this acknowledgment and this dissection, however, there lies a defense, a preface to dissection. Lynd must answer the charge of dissection leveled at him by the people of Middletown. Lynd cites a review of *Middletown* by a local editor: "Of course, Lynd has the provincial view of the highly trained specialist in humanology, if there is such a word which I doubt greatly. He likes to take a mind apart, especially a rather inferior mind, to see what makes it tick, if it does" (*MT,* xi). It is clear from Lynd's account of the response of the people of Middletown to *Middletown* that many were upset by the book's account of their lives; however, even the editorial cited above ultimately concedes the legitimate authority that such a social-scientific study of Middletown has over Middletown itself. The editor goes on to state: "I was startled to discover that in a rather large way his conclusions . . . were the things that had occurred to me time after time" (*MT*, xi). For all of its unpleasantness, the Lynds' account "rings true" (*MT*, xi). Ultimately, the editor concludes that if "you have not read *Middletown*, you have not taken proper stock of yourself" (*MT*, xi). Thus, *Middletown* succeeds in establishing itself as a necessity, as constitutive of Middletown life itself, and as a legitimate formalization of the common sense of Middletown.

At this point, Lynd has rhetorically neutralized the question of why this common sense needs to be formalized through social science. One would think that a study of people that simply tells them things that had already occurred to them "time after time" would be of little consequence, but the importance of *Middletown* lies not in what it says but in the way that it says it. According to Lynd's account of Middletown's initial response to *Middletown*, many people were "proud of the fact that the city 'had been written up in a book' " (*MT*, xii). Aestheticized and formalized by *Middletown*, Middletown life has taken on the character of a book, or more precisely a novel; and in the modern world, one cannot ask for more than the opportunity to lead a novelistic life. (Lynd explicitly compares his dilemma to that of the midwestern novelist [*MT*, xiv]). The people of Middletown proudly accept the new status conferred on them by *Middletown*. The question now becomes, Is *Middletown* a good novel or a bad novel?

What makes a novel good or bad? According to Lynd, the "central criticism of *Middletown* by the Middletown people is . . . that, while true, it tends to be cold, an aggregation of facts lacking some of the vital tissue that makes the city live" (*MT*, xii). This is the cruelest criticism one can level at Lynd, for it is precisely the warmth of the "vital tissue that makes the city live" that he sought to capture by his "new" method of social anthropology. Lynd defends *Middletown* as a social-scientific attempt "to make larger gains by digging vertically rather than by raking together the top-soil horizontally," and he attacks what he sees as the "disproportionate amount of energy in current social research [that] appears . . . to be going into the latter sort of work" (*MT*, xi). In this sense, Lynd and the people of Middletown are in perfect agreement. Lynd wanted to give a "deep" account of Middletown life, and the only objection by the people of Middletown is that he did not go deep enough into their lives. Lynd reports that on his return to Middletown in 1935, "there were bantering reproachful remarks that 'you sorta made us out as a town of hicks,' but everywhere the cooperation was marked and spontaneous" (*MT*, xiii). Middletown may think that *Middletown* got it wrong, but Middletowners are more than willing to help Lynd get it right this time. The task now is to write a better novel, a task which Lynd sees as a collaborative venture between the social scientist and the people he studies. The only thing greater than living a novelistic life is actually writing a novel oneself, and here, as in his acknowledgments, Lynd raises the people of Middletown to the status of coauthors of the novel that is their life.

Still, the collaborative nature of the social-scientific endeavor cannot completely efface the gap between the perspective of the social scientist and that of his objects of study. According to Lynd:

> An inescapable gulf separates the points of view of Middletown and of an investigator who comes in from outside to study it, for the latter is under no emotional compulsions to defend Middletown. He is not a permanent part of its life, his future is not its future, his hopes need not be its hopes. In this difference in emotional need to emphasize local integrity lies the genesis of many of the criticisms of "superficiality" and "unfairness" that are leveled by the people against the outside observer. (*MT*, xiv)

The difference in emotional investment leads to "a rather fundamental difference in the way investigator and community view cultural processes" (*MT*, xiv). The "professional equipment" of the social scientist provides him with "unfamiliar ways of looking at familiar things" (*MT*, xiv). Thus, while a community may be aware of its symbols and rationalizations, the social scientist is aware of "its symbols . . . *as symbols*, its rationalizations *as rationalizations*"; the people of a community are concerned with "manipulating the going system" of symbols and rationalizations, while the social scientist is concerned with "appraising" that system (*MT*, xiv). This difference in perspective manifests itself in different assumptions about how the world works. The people of Middletown see human nature as free and rational, while Lynd, versed in modern psychology, tends to see it as emotional and irrational. Middletowners think of their institutions in moral terms as being good, while Lynd thinks in functional terms of how they operate. Most important, the people of Middletown are hostile to change, while Lynd is sensitive to the fact of change and the issue of cultural lag (*MT*, xv–xvi).

Having set up this rather stark opposition, Lynd proceeds to break it down. For Lynd, both perspectives are flawed as ideal types. The insider perspective of the people of Middletown is always in danger of sliding into mere boosterism, while the outsider perspective of the social scientist verges on a smug, cynical superiority (*MT*, xiv). The answer to this problem of perspective, like all answers in the *Middletown* universe, lies in the middle, between two worlds, between two perspectives: "The object of a penetrating study is to combine both procedures; to understand through intimate participation how the persons who carry the culture within their skins feel toward it, and yet to avoid the contagion of local enthusiasm enough to be able to analyze the how's and why's of the local scene against the generalized knowledge of comparative cultures" (*MT*, xiv). Thus, Lynd will be a better novelist by being both an insider and an outsider.

As part of his rejection of a purely objective or "outsider" social science, Lynd rejects the fact/value dichotomy of that social-scientific tradition. The social scientist, too, is a creature of values, a person with a particular point of view. Lynd argues that precisely because he has values and a point of view, he is able to give a deep, warm, human account of other people who have values and points of view. Still, it would be too simplistic to reduce social science to a mere question of values:

> No social scientist works without "values" in the *selection* of his problems—though the "good" scientist seeks to test his hypotheses rather than to prove his values. What he tries to do is to make his values with which he approaches and selects problems internally coherent and as close as possible to reality as he sees it, to curb those values that are in his judgment inappropriate to a given research situation, and, when his values diverge from those commonly held, to make his point of view explicit. (*MT*, xv)

Values are clearly a danger, yet they are a danger that must be confronted, not avoided. The admission of the role of values in social research is an occasion for greater self-control, for a more rigorous, exacting discipline than a naively "value-free" social scientist could ever imagine. The admission of a particular point of view calls for a similar effort of self-control:

> The recognition by the investigator of these differences in point of view means that he has tried constantly to correct for any bias they might introduce. On the other hand, research without a point of view is impossible. If research were mere photography science would stand still,

swamped in the mass of undifferentiated and unoriented detail. Science depends upon sensitized, coherent points of view oriented around reality. (*MT,* xvii)

The self-disciplined social scientist is thus the key to intellectual progress. This social scientist "is honest and self-critical, he does not seek to bolster his own intellectual position but rather to marshall all relevant data" (*MT,* xvii). This self-discipline allows him to overcome the threat of the stagnation, the standing still, the "mere photography" of a supposedly objective social science. By confronting and controlling his own subjectivity, the social scientist is able to differentiate and orient the mass of detail that swamps and extinguishes the consciousness of objective social science.

The discipline required of the social scientist by virtue of his insider/outsider status demands that he constantly move back and forth between fact and value, between his perspective and the perspective of those he studies, between what Lynd calls "data" and "insight":

The attempt to apply such labels as "superior" and "inferior" to insight *as over against* the careful marshalling of data seems to the investigator irrelevant and misleading; for knowledge cannot advance without both insight and data, and the need is obviously for the maximum admixture of both, the one constantly checking the other in the endless game of leapfrog between hypothesis and evidence as understanding grows. (*MT,* x)

This "endless game of leapfrog" is nothing other than Veblenian boundary crossing, the borderland existence of the savage, the handicraftsman, the modern interchangeable worker, the Jewish intellectual. For all of Lynd's criticism of the cynicism and pretention of objective social science, his defense of his modified, subjective objectivism leaves him in an even more pretentious position than the objectivists who came before him. He claims not only a mastery of the techniques of objective social-scientific understanding (data) but also a certain kind of mastery over the subjective feelings of ordinary people (insight). Lynd offers a vertical, surface/depth study that seeks to understand people's deepest feelings in terms of a larger social context, but he never seems to recognize the heightened arrogance of his modified objectivism.

Still, Lynd's perspective must be understood as not simply arrogance but a social relation. To understand it on this level, we must consider

Middletown and *Middletown in Transition* as particular works of social science that embody a more general social-scientific structure of thought. In these books, Lynd locates the privileged point of understanding on the border between two worlds—between, if you will, the social and the scientific. Lynd approaches this border from the scientific world through the act of writing *Middletown*. Once at this border, he observes the social world of the people of Middletown and is transformed by this experience. Theoretically, Lynd can never look at the world in the same way again after writing *Middletown;* conceivably, he could even permanently cross the border into that social world, "go native," and never write *Middletown*. The people of Middletown also have access to this boundary-crossing experience. They approach this border from the social world through the act of reading *Middletown*. Once at this border, they observe the scientific world of Lynd's writing and are transformed by this experience. Theoretically, they can never look at the world in the same way again after reading *Middletown;* conceivably, they could even permanently cross this border into the scientific world, assimilate, and then write their own account of Middletown (or of some other town, for that matter).

Middletown and *Middletown in Transition* propose a democratic utopia of reading and writing, of intellectual labor, where all people read and write about their lives and the lives of others, where the fundamental relation between people is that of "the one constantly checking the other" (*MT*, x). The observed self is also the observing self, and even though each person exists as potential "data," they also exist as potential "insight." *Middletown* and *Middletown in Transition* establish an ideal of surveillance as the desired relation between men in a society conceived of as an aggregate of individuals who are always both observing and being observed. If surveillance is the ideal social relation, then the essential tension—the tension which keeps this social relation vital, disciplined, dynamic, and progressive—is the tension between a surveillance that represses, restricts, isolates, objectifies, and one that liberates, expands, integrates, subjectifies. This essential tension is itself maintained by the constant leapfrogging between the objective/repressive and the subjective/liberating modes of surveillance.

Eternal surveillance is the price of liberty, a certain cost with certain benefits. If one is willing to pay the price of social-scientific self-discipline, then one gets the opportunity to achieve the keen intellectual sense and sophisticated emotional sensibility of a mature mind that can see the world for what it is and face the flux of experience without surrendering to it completely. Although one can never completely control change, one can understand it, and this understanding is itself a kind of control for, and of, the individual. Lynd's closing reflections on his relationship to the people of Middletown give the best sense of the sensibility of this individual:

> If he has missed the "great warm heart" of Middletown, he is nevertheless not unaware of a deep emotional kinship with these open-hearted folk so many of whom he thinks of as his friends. On more than one late evening in June, 1935, he refused his hospitable host's offer to drive him back to his hotel, in order to walk back alone the quiet, shaded streets pondering the birthright that he, along with other midland boys migrated to large cities, has relinquished for the debatable advantages of the metropolis. (*MT*, xvii)

A society organized according to the principles of humanistic social science allows everybody to be caught between two worlds, be it country and city, past and future, ethnic and W.A.S.P., black and white, working class and middle class, male and female.[7] At this border region all have the opportunity to ponder their maturity and to assess their allegiances to the two worlds they are caught between, whatever those two worlds may be. In this sense, social-scientific works like *Middletown* and *Middletown in Transition* enact a kind of democratization of a classic American literary narrative of self. The people of Middletown now have a chance to be marginal men, like the outsider/artist heroes and "knockers" who appear on the margins of the story in the Middletown books.

The last chapter of *Middletown in Transition* is titled "Middletown Faces Both Ways." Although the title refers to the plight of Middletown in the wake of the Great Depression, Middletown has been facing both ways all along, even in the prosperous 1920s. Constantly facing both ways, Middletown—and by implication, modern American life in general—*is* transition. The purpose of Lynd's books is to lay out this situation to the people of Middletown so that they may transform their objective, "in-itself" transition to a subjective, "for-itself" transition. This subjectivity is nothing other than the mature modern consciousness—a consciousness that is always developing, always transforming itself, always overcoming itself.

Culture and Carnival

The meaning of the idea of culture in the 1930s cannot be reduced simply to a "drive for unity and conformity" that often "threaten[ed] the survival of individualism." Nor can we characterize the cultural approach to the individual as one which "nowhere suggests a rebuilding of the ego so it can stand alone."[8] Benedict and Lynd argue for nothing if not the setting apart of the ego, not in isolation from but in control of culture. In Lynd's words, the point of cultural understanding is "to rebuild the culture so as to adjust the situation to the individual" (*KW*, 231). The relation of the individual to culture is neither that of sentimental conformity nor of existential struggle but one of strenuous creativity, with culture as a resource for the development of a distinct individuality through a process of relentless self-examination through the examination of others.

Perhaps the significance of Benedict's *Patterns of Culture* as a "symbolic landmark" in the rise of the culture concept in the 1930s stems not from its satisfaction of some popular need for belonging to a group but from the way that it draws upon and reformulates the classic American ideal of the self-reliant individual. There is more than a little irony in an ideal of self-reliance that seems to require such an apparatus of expertise, but this is an irony rooted in the very idea of self-reliance: Nineteenth-century Emersonians, after all, had to read "Self-Reliance" before they could be self-reliant. By the twentieth century, however, the stakes of self-reliance had changed. One could no longer rest content at being above the narrow prejudices and social norms of the mass of men, for in the new social-scientific world view, self-reliance was also threatened by innumerable unseen "social forces." In such a world, one needs not only an Emerson to tell one to be self-reliant but an endless array of experts to assess the quality of that self-reliance in relation to hidden determinative forces unknown to the untutored individual.

This said, we cannot recast Benedict as cultural critic. Clearly Benedict was a critic, and clearly she favored, in the terms of one historian, a "beneficent" rather than a "manipulative" social science.[9] Taken as terms of opposition, these adjectives tell us more about the character and motives of particular social scientists than they do about the character and motives of a society that has a place for any kind of "cultural critic," be she beneficent or manipulative, of a literary or a social-scientific bent.

At this point, it is instructive to consider one of the most significant contributions to the rise of the idea of culture in the 1930s, the social documentary. William Stott's classic study of 1930s documentary argues that the documentaries often lapsed into nostalgia or sentimentality despite the critical impulses that initially inspired many of them. [10] The sentimental/critical distinction is to documentary, however, what the manipulative/beneficent distinction is to social science. In relation to the idea of culture, the significance of documentary does not lie in the way it presented nostalgic images of America that played on the emotions of those who viewed them. Instead, documentary contributed to the idea that it was somehow necessary to produce an image of America, for people to see themselves objectively as a culture in all their diversity and particularity, even for people to argue about the validity of the images presented to them, and that such a process of self-reflection was an essential response to an economic crisis such as the Great Depression.

The significance of the rise of the serious study of popular and folk culture during this period lies not in the particular representations that were produced but in the general phenomenon of this process of representation itself, which brought about a formalization of the folk, the popular—those aspects of life previously characterized by their informality. The notion of culture as a whole way of life, combined with the representational means of rendering this whole way of life through a variety of media, ultimately led to an aestheticization of the everyday whereby people learned to approach the everyday in a way once reserved for objects of high culture. Aestheticization need not imply trivialization; if anything, it demands a much more serious attitude toward the everyday. Consciousness of the everyday implies a certain objective distance from it, a distance induced by the process of presenting a culture to itself. Not only does the everyday come to be something which can be debated (How do people live? What is their life really like?), but this debate takes place on a certain level, so that, for example, debate over the plight of Southern tenant farmers is, in effect, a debate over the relative merits of *You Have Seen Their Faces* and *Let Us Now Praise Famous Men*. Participation in this debate requires a certain education to taste and discrimination, suspension of the sentimental, and a premium on critical distance. In short, it requires something like what the Lynds called "literacy" in *Middletown*.

The rise of the idea of culture carries with it the rise of the figure of the cultural critic. Herein lies what can be called the social relations of the culture concept. The development of the idea of culture in the work of Benedict and Lynd establishes the cultural critic as the ideal citizen of a democratic society. The ethic of cultural criticism, that detached-yet-engaged stance toward one's social world, has its origins in the rather narrow world of the middle-class intellectual, but the point of *Patterns of Culture* and *Knowledge for What?* is not to assert this ethic over against the untutored masses but to universalize this ethic by incorporating the masses into it. As much as any Marxist, Benedict and Lynd have a profoundly classless vision of the utopian society, one in which all traditional hierarchies have been abolished, leaving only the hierarchy of reason to order social life.

Short of the achievement of this "utopia," the social relations of the culture concept can be seen as the end point in the change in the relation between elite and popular culture since the dawn of the modern era. Peter Burke argues that in early modern Europe, nobles and peasants to a large degree shared a common culture that allowed for a kind of promiscuous intermingling foreign to the cross-class relations of developed bourgeois societies. With the rise of the middle class, this promiscuity gave way to a period of withdrawal, which in turn gave way to the "discovery" of the people whereby the educated classes recovered the everyday as something strange and exotic. The culture concept, as developed by Benedict and Lynd, represents a kind of rationalized promiscuity where educated elites neither share a common culture with the "people" nor withdraw from or exoticize the "people." In one sense, the culture concept embodies the kind of elite/popular intermingling that Burke, following Mikhail Bahktin, calls the carnivalesque.[11] The study of culture is one grand ritual of reversal, in which the uneducated instruct the educated, the illiterate guide the literate, the unconscious uplift the conscious. The study of culture requires the suspension of the rules of culture; the cultural critic brackets all presuppositions, as "ought" surrenders to "is" and the ideal surrenders to the real.[12] The human cravings that Lynd sees as the object of cultural inquiry must be allowed to act themselves out free from the judgments of the social scientist.[13]

Still, the social scientist never simply records the polymorphous perversity of culture, and the engagement with culture "as it is" never loses the taint of the objective detachment that serves as the starting point for cultural inquiry. This dialectic of detachment and engagement itself gives the study of culture its direction, as cultures—in particular American culture—come to be judged by the degree to which they allow for a detachment that preserves autonomy and an engagement that provides the support of human fellowship so essential to a "healthy" sense of self. As the basis for a new kind of class mixing, the culture concept offers the possibility of the spread of this dialectical self from those who study culture to those who are studied as culture. Thirties documentaries were, after all, supposed to transform the consciousness of those who viewed them. That they did so in varying degrees and in different ways does not change the general meaning of documentary as a form of expression, a meaning best expressed by the masterpiece of the genre, Evans and Agee's *Let Us Now Praise Famous Men,* a book as much about its authors' detached/ engaged consciousness as it is about dust-bowl tenant farmers.

Of course, Evans and Agee's book is far from the last word on the problem of middle-class intellectuals studying the "people." If anything, the status of *Let Us Now Praise Famous Men* represents not the canonization of its particular vision, but the canonization of a certain intellectual problematic as necessary to the kind of society that America wants to be. As a model of class mixing, the culture concept represents a kind of routinization of the carnivalesque. Rather than temporarily suspending norms and inverting hierarchies only to reassert the dominant order, it renders all norms in a constant state of suspension. The study of culture replaces all traditional hierarchies with a hierarchy of consciousness that is static in its standard of detached engagement, yet fluid and dynamic in what it is able to incorporate into this standard. The success or failure of *Let Us Now Praise Famous Men* may always be open to question, but the necessity of the documentary undertaking (and the documentary undertaker) remains above question.

In *Knowledge for What?* Robert Lynd observes that "no informed person questions nowadays the indispensability of objective data-gathering and of the exhaustive statistical analysis of those data for all they are worth. The only question that is being raised here concerns the need to ask, '*What* are they worth for *what?*' " (*KW,* 128). The truth of this statement lies in its tautology. By 1939, "objective data-gathering" and "the exhaustive statistical analysis of those data" had come to define the terms of being an "informed person." The culture concept, as developed by Benedict and Lynd, provided a language that promised to be as much at home with objective data as with the values that might direct "man in continually understanding and rebuilding his culture" (*KW,* ix). It is misleading, however, to see this fusion of fact and value simply as a turn to the anthropological notion of culture as a whole way of life. The culture concept developed by Benedict and Lynd owes as much to an older Romantic notion of man as the creator of value and meaning as it does to anthropology; if anything, it combines art and science to return the idea of culture to its original sense of cultivation, of human training. This new cultivation, however, is process without telos. Culture as a whole way of life exists merely as a resource for the cultivation of one's inner depth, a depth limited only by one's commitment to scrutinize it. No nostalgic nod to premodern wholeness, the culture concept of Benedict and Lynd transcends the dichotomy of *Gemeinschaft* and *Gessellschaft*: by reaffirming personal relations so long as they open themselves to social-scientific scrutiny, it reestablishes values as central to social life so long as those values are freely chosen, and it reasserts the organic unity of social life so long as that unity is constructed by conscious, mechanical means.

Toward Consensus

The outbreak of World War II brought about a subtle change in the political meaning of the idea of culture as developed in the work of Dewey, Benedict, and Lynd. From an argument for social engineering which explicitly recognized serious problems with American society, the idea of culture came to be used primarily as a defense of a particular culture, the "American way of life," against its perceived antithesis, the fascism of Nazi Germany. Far from abandoning the values of social engineering, this move from critique to celebration tended to equate those values with the values of the American way of life itself. American culture was democratic, which meant that it was tolerant, pluralistic, and respectful of individual differences; fascism, by contrast, was authoritarian, which meant that it was intolerant, monistic, and disrespectful of individual differences.[14]

The relation between this ideal of tolerance and the values of social engineering becomes clearer when we look at the consequences of this conception of American culture as a normative guide to action. Here the work of Margaret Mead, a leading ideologue of the American way of life and, like Ruth Benedict, a student of the anthropologist Franz Boas, becomes particularly important. No vulgar cheerleader for American culture, Mead felt that the prized freedoms of the American way of life brought with them certain problems. The fluidity and mobility that characterized the American social structure induced a certain anxiety about order, a reform impulse that often expressed itself in a moralistic sense of mission to remake not only American society but the world.[15] For Mead, this sense of mission could slide into fascist intolerance unless Americans could be made to realize the values that defined them as Americans, namely, tolerance and respect for individual liberties. Only then could America lead the fight to rid the world of "every social limitation of human beings in terms of heredity, whether it be of race, or sex, or class."[16] Thus, even in its nationalist mode, the culture concept effectively effaced all distinctions between culture and cultural consciousness. After one has proscribed "every social limitation," be it of race, sex, or class, it is not clear what kind of culture one has left, apart from a residue of quality-less individuals free from all social restrictions, that is, a residue of culturally conscious individuals.

The irony of this simultaneous celebration of American culture and the devaluation of all that could be deemed cultural only deepened after the war, as the reflection on American culture took a historical turn. Initiated by a critical dissatisfaction with the banalities of the American way of life, which now seemed to represent the last best hope for mankind, Richard Hofstadter's *American Political Tradition* (1948) nonetheless found many of these banalities borne out by the historical record. Surveying American political statesmen from Jefferson to F.D.R., Hofstadter found "a kind of mute organic consistency"—language that suggests the influence of the culture concept on the historical thinking of this period—in American political life.[17] This "consistency" consisted of a belief in economic individualism, competitive capitalism, and the moral value of owning property, all of which Daniel Boorstin and Louis Hartz would later enshrine under the rubric of "Lockean liberalism."[18] With varying degrees of approval, Hofstadter, Boorstin, and Hartz called this consistency a "consensus." It was the political equivalent of culture in that it declared the values of Lockean liberalism to be the enduring pattern of American political life.

That these historians should have arrived at something like Lockean liberalism as the unifying pattern of American political culture suggests a certain symbiotic relation between the idea of a liberal culture and culture as a liberal idea. As developed during the 1930s and 1940s, the culture concept inherited from Enlightenment liberalism a general suspicion of all circumstances of race, sex, family, and received social position as somehow external to a more basic individuality of persons. For Enlightenment thinkers such as Locke, this individuality found its fullest expression in the exercise of economic rationality, the calculation and pursuit of self-interest. Those who developed the culture concept tried to rescue self-interest from the taint of filthy lucre, but in doing so they only reaffirmed ever more stridently the Enlightenment liberal ideal of the individual as the bearer of certain (arbitrary) desires that have priority over all would-be social restrictions on them. To speak of any culture, even a specifically "political" culture, as expressing a "consensus" itself suggests a certain contractual model for cultural life, as if at some point individual Americans got together, expressed their desires, and agreed to create a Lockean-liberal culture.

The culture concept's reaffirmation of the primacy of economic relations is no where clearer than in the place of political "conflict" within "consensus" thought. Borrowing concepts from Max Weber's historical sociology, consensus thinkers such as Hofstadter distinguished between two kinds of political conflicts, those based on "status" and those based on "interest." Status politics refers to conflicts over noneconomic, that is, cultural, issues; it finds its expression in "symbolic tensions and cultural antinomies" which, for consensus thinkers, were less real and more "subjective" than hard economic issues.[19] (Perhaps the most famous example of historical interpretation that uses the concept of "status" politics is Richard Hofstadter's dismissal of Populism as an irrational revolt driven by nostalgia for the "agrarian myth" of the yeoman farmer in the face of the "reality" of economic "improvement" brought on by the changes—that is, the rise of agribusiness—that the Populists protested).[20] "Interest" politics, by contrast, refers to conflicts over the distribution of material resources, conflicts that are real in that they reflect certain "objective," economic conditions. As good Weberians, consensus thinkers saw interest politics as a politics of "fact," of quantitatively measurable, thus partible, thus negotiable, material resources; in turn, they dismissed status politics as a politics of "value" that involved totalizing moral commitments that could not be compromised or negotiated.

Consensus thought did not deny the presence of conflict in American history, yet it tended to dismiss the most volatile of those conflicts as somehow epiphenomenal, as neurotic distortions of properly economic conflicts. Similarly, while it acknowledged real conflicts of economic interest, even "class" conflict of a sort, it tended to devalue such conflict for being contained within the framework of a Lockean-liberal respect for private property. Many consensus thinkers were ex-socialists of one sort or another, and most concluded that American history lacked "real" conflict because they saw "real" conflict as ideological in nature. The tremendous religious, ethnic, racial, and regional conflicts, as well as the bloody class warfare that accompanied the industrial revolution in America, all failed to meet the stringent criterion of real ideological conflict because they failed to offer the possibility of a socialist alternative to the liberal value of private property. The reservations about, and often dark musings on, American culture by consensus thinkers attest to their sense of there being a real difference between liberalism and the socialist ideal, and their sense of the seeming impossibility of a viable socialism in America. Liberalism seemed to be all that America had—indeed all the world had outside of totalitarian communism—and one could do no more than make the best of life after utopia.

Liberalism and socialism may have substantive differences, but both are clearly economic ideologies that see economic issues as the reference point for reality. Thus, within the dynamics of consensus thought, American culture was being judged as at once too economic—too mired in the bland calculations of liberal economic man—and not economic enough—too lacking in the radical, transformative vision of a socialism that took the democratic promise of capitalist productivity even more seriously than did liberalism. This obsession with economics worked to devalue the particulars of American culture, yet it also served to perpetuate a dynamic central to the general idea of culture as developed during the 1930s. In the dynamic of consensus thought, socialism as a critical principle stands in relation to liberalism as the culture-conscious individual stands in relation to culture in Benedict's work: Socialism is that which could have, or should have, broken out of the deterministic framework of Lockean liberalism. Apart from any explicit concerns of consensus thinkers, we can see that socialism and cultural consciousness share a common enemy, Lockean "possessive" individualism. Apart from the protests of advocates of socialism and/or cultural consciousness, we can see that the social ideal of a critical liberation from all potentially coercive or determinative frameworks has its roots in an ideology of economic individualism.

For economic individualism, revolutionary socialism, and cultural consciousness, all that is solid melts into air. The promise of nineteenth-century socialism had been that this constant flux and fluidity could be channeled into something substantively more progressive and liberating than mere flux and fluidity. A commitment to true socialist fluidity as opposed to mere capitalist fluidity ostensibly distinguished the radical from the liberal, but this distinction was never made very clear; attempts to define it had led to factionalism and splintering within socialist ranks. For consensus thinkers, this distinction had lost its meaning as a language with which to conduct practical politics, even though socialism survived as a critical ideal by which to judge the failures of American political culture. Those who did not despair completely of meaningful political action were left with making the best of capitalist fluidity, and this entailed augmenting classic liberalism with a welfare state that would provide at least the minimum of material security needed by individuals to pursue their happiness as they saw fit. Hope for anything more was pure chiliasm, with definite totalitarian tendencies.

This rejection of political utopianism carried with it disturbing doubts as to the possibility of any kind of transcendence. The "sense of the whole" promised by the idea of culture seemed to manifest itself less in solidarity than in bureaucracy, and many intellectuals came to judge bureaucracy to be even more "conformist" than the market it was intended to replace. As dissent became orthodoxy, new conditions seemed to reproduce old problems. Ambivalence toward economic values grew to a larger ambivalence toward modernity in general and the social-scientific values that underlay it. The postwar world would see a "consensus" not on the values of liberal culture but on an ambivalence toward the values of liberal culture.

Chapter 6

■

The Sociological Imagination

The Fourth Epoch

THAT LYND COULD argue so passionately for a certain kind of social science is a measure of how, by 1940, social science of some kind or another had come to be incorporated into the institutional structure of American life. The expansion of governmental activities under the New Deal offered unprecedented employment opportunities for social scientists in the public sphere. Even with this expansion, most social science during the Depression years was financed by private funds. With the outbreak of World War II, however, social science became an integral part of the daily functioning of the federal government.[1] *Knowledge for What?* marks a turning point in the history of social science as a social institution; moreover, it appeared at an equally momentous turning point in the history of social science as a structure of thought. Ironically, social science was gaining institutional acceptance at the very moment when its intellectual foundations were coming under fierce attack in what Richard Gillam calls the "general 'reorientation' of American social thought after 1940."[2] Unlike previous attacks on social science, the criticisms that led to this reorientation did not come from the defenders of religion and tradition but from secular thinkers who had once placed so much faith in the Progressive belief in human perfectability and the rational control of society. The rise of totalitarianism and the outbreak of World War II destroyed this Progressive belief. Faith in progress gave way to a heightened awareness of complexity, paradox, limitation, and, above all, irony as the defining characteristics of human history.[3]

The master trope of irony both threatened to undermine and functioned to sustain the social-scientific project of rational control. If social science seemed morally and intellectually questionable, it also seemed technically and practically workable. If anything, this seeming contradiction between theory and practice provided yet another paradox that confirmed the ironic worldview of which social science was to be a central component. Still, after 1940 even the most strenuous advocate of social science had to offer some kind of defense of social science as a form of knowledge, a way of seeing the world. Most historians, themselves deeply indebted to this social-scientific worldview, have tended to treat this fundamental attack on and defense of science as an interesting digression from the main story of social science during the 1940s and 1950s: its rise to institutional prominence, its corruption by those institutions, and the transformation of its liberating theory into repressive practice.[4] This narrative of declension-via-institutionalization is, however, central to the self-conception of the very critical, humanistic social science to which many critical, humanistic historians of social science are the intellectual heirs. The more interesting story of social science during this period lies in the fate of this self-conception in light of the growing sense during the 1950s that the "corruption" of social science might have its source within social science as an intellectual worldview.

For this story, the critic C. Wright Mills emerges as a figure crucial to understanding midcentury social science—not a marginal figure at all, but in some sense the paradigmatic midcentury intellectual.[5] Mills's importance does not lie in his criticism of conformity, his analysis of stratification, or even his political radicalism. His major studies—the trilogy of *New Men of Power, White Collar,* and *The Power Elite*—represent not simply a more-or-less accurate, more-or-less dated account of American society at midcentury but a specific moment in the tradition of social-science writing. Whatever the "scientific" value of their particular findings, these studies are bound together by a commitment to exposing the divorce of knowledge from power in modern America. Wherever Mills looks—in labor unions, office buildings, or the Pentagon—he finds at best the absence of reason, at worst the corruption of reason by the vested interests. To understand this overarching narrative, some attention should be given to the conception of reason embodied in Mills's opposition of knowledge to power. Such an examination requires a move from Mills's particular studies to his own extended reflection on social science in general, *The Sociological Imagination.* A book with many parallels to Lynd's *Knowledge for What?, The Sociological Imagination* argues not simply for the necessity of social science but for the very possibility of social science.

Mills's last major work, *The Sociological Imagination* (1959) offers a personal and methodological reflection on the preceding two decades of sociology, asking both whence and whither the discipline as a whole. The book begins, appropriately enough, with "The Promise" of sociology, the possibility of understanding and controlling social life for the betterment of man. Next, it assesses the methodological abdications of this promise by the dominant schools of sociology during this period—grand theory and abstracted empiricism—showing how these methodologies reflect and in part shape "The Bureaucratic Ethos" of the institutions within which they operate. Finally, taking the social and intellectual contingency of these methodologies as a sign of hope, Mills sketches an outline of a possible nonbureaucratic sociology that could "make reason democratically relevant to human affairs in a free society, and so realize the classic values that underlie the promise of our studies."[6]

The sociological imagination represents the possibility of sociology triumphant over its conditions. Mills's polemic aside, in this respect it differs little from its methodological adversaries. Grand theory and abstracted empiricism assume nothing if not a transcendent perspective set over against objectified social "conditions"; the sociology-of-knowledge component of Mills's sociological imagination simply turns this perspective on knowledge itself, so that even sociological methodologies can be seen as objects of study. The sociology of knowledge affirms a basic perspective that can accommodate a variety of conflicting methodologies, yet as the logical end point of the self-reflexive project of modernity, it also represents a crisis in that perspective, a crisis which makes it impossible to talk about that perspective with the same confidence that one could have before it was turned on knowledge itself.

The Sociological Imagination cannot simply offer an alternative to the reigning social-scientific orthodoxy. It must somehow offer a defense of the social-scientific project as a whole, a project so much a part of a "modern" world that Mills sees as passing away. Mills situates his book in a "postmodern period" which, following the previous periods of Antiquity, the Dark Ages, and Modernity, he calls The Fourth Epoch: "The ideological mark of The Fourth Epoch—that which sets it off from the Modern Age—is that the ideas of freedom and reason have become moot; that increased rationality may not be assumed to make for increased freedom" (166–67). This abandonment of the ideas of freedom and reason marks "a giving up of the central goal of the secular impulse in the West: the control through reason of man's fate. It is this goal that has lent continuity to the humanist tradition, re-discovered in the

Renaissance, and so strong in the nineteenth century American experience."[7] The crisis in Western humanism has led to a revival of conservatism, "the search for tradition rather than reason as guide; the search for some natural aristocracy as an anchor point of tradition and a model of character."[8] Liberalism has done little to remedy this crisis, for "the current doubts are secular, humanistic—and often quite confused" (15–16). In the wake of total war, death camps, and the possibility of nuclear annihilation, liberals themselves have come to fear science and technology and to doubt the possibility of progress.

Ultimately, Mills does not take the revival of conservatism too seriously.[9] In classic "consensus" fashion, the problem of The Fourth Epoch becomes the problem of liberalism, of the legacy of an ideal of reason, free from tradition, directed toward the control of man's fate. Mills takes some comfort in the persistent appeal of this ideal at some level, but he concedes that "if the moral force of liberalism is still stimulating, its sociological content is weak; it has no theory of society adequate to its moral aims."[10] The Sociological Imagination is, in effect, Mills's attempt to give classic liberal moral aims an adequate theory of society.

Mills figures this disjunction of morality and theory as a contrast between eighteenth-century ideals and twentieth-century reality.[11] Classical liberals saw freedom and security thriving in a world of small, property-owning entrepreneurs, yet modern liberals experience anxiety over the lack of widespread ownership of property. Classical liberals assumed a world of small communities capable of generating public opinion to which individuals could be held accountable, but such communities no longer exist. Classical liberals sought the autonomy of different institutional spheres such as religion, politics, and the economy, yet modern America has seen a fusion of these spheres with the rise of vast economic, political, and military bureaucracies. Classic liberals saw rationality residing in the individual, whereas the modern world locates rationality in large institutions. Finally, classic liberals assumed a certain explicitness of authority, an ability to know who exercises power and then to debate it, obey it, or reject it, whereas in the modern world the problem has become one of locating who actually has power.[12]

These contradictions made obsolete the alternatives of "drift" and "mastery" that had shaped liberal views of the social order from the eighteenth to the twentieth centuries. On the one hand, this obsolescence seemed to mark a positive intellectual advance, for neither the idea of the pure drift of aimless pluralism or the mastery of simple domination offered much potential as a guide for sophisticated sociological inquiry; however, the obsolescence of these terms also threatened certain values dear to Mills's sociological imagination itself, namely "drift" as a kind of libertarian *freedom* from coercion and "mastery" as the control and direction of social life by *reason*. Nineteenth-century free-market liberalism tended to pit the positive notion of drift as freedom versus the negative notion of mastery as domination, while twentieth-century corporate liberalism, perhaps best represented by Walter Lippmann's *Drift and Mastery,* tended to pit the rational directedness of mastery versus the anarchy of pure drift.[13] Postwar America seemed to offer both the best and the worst of both worlds of drift and mastery. For mainstream liberal thinkers, the American welfare state approximated an ideal of rational control as distinct from domination and allowed for civil liberties short of anarchic drift; for a critic like Mills, postwar America seemed to embody domination without control and atomistic anarchy without freedom. For mainstream liberals, the obsolescence of drift and mastery ensured the preservation of freedom and reason; for Mills, it signaled the obsolescence of freedom and reason.

Of course, this states the case too starkly. *The Sociological Imagination* is nothing if not a statement of faith in the continuing power of freedom and reason in human affairs. Any meaningful solution must, however, begin with an honest statement of the problem:

> The underlying trends are well known. Great and rational organizations—in brief, bureaucracies—have indeed increased, but the substantive reason of the individual at large has not. Caught in the limited milieux of their everyday lives, ordinary men often cannot reason about the great structures—rational and irrational—of which their *milieux* are subordinate parts. Accordingly, they often carry out series of apparently rational actions without any ideas of the ends they serve, and there is the increasing suspicion that those at the top as well—like Tolstoy's generals—only pretend they know. That the techniques and the rationality of science are given a central place in a society does not mean that men live reasonably and without myth, fraud, and superstition. Science, it turns out, is not a technological Second Coming. Universal education may lead to technological idiocy and nationalist provinciality, rather than to the informed and independent intelligence. Rationally organized social arrangements are not necessarily a means of increased freedoms—for the individual or for the society. In fact, often they are a means of tyranny and manipulation, a means of expro-

priating the very chance to reason, the very capacity to act as a free man.[14]

In The Fourth Epoch, one can no longer simply bring reason to bear against unreason, knowledge against power, for "it seems that knowledge leads to powerlessness"; intellectuals "continue to know more and more about modern society, but . . . find the centers of political initiative less and less accessible." [15] These developments have reached their "*postmodern* climax" in the cold war conflict between the United States and the Soviet Union, for these two superpowers best embody the ironic conjuncture of an unprecedented power to shape history and an unprecedented collapse in the ideology of history-making. Ultimately for Mills, that "collapse is also the collapse of the expectations of the Enlightenment." [16]

Mills argues the case for despair a bit too well. With no plausible social agency for freedom and reason, he can only suspend his disbelief and turn to social science as a sphere of activity that is relatively autonomous from the debilitating contradictions so characteristic of The Fourth Epoch. To write a book like The Sociological Imagination, Mills must assume that man is free and can to some extent make history, however slim the "sociological" evidence may be. In The Sociological Imagination, Mills states bluntly that he is "not now concerned to debate the *values* of freedom and reason, but only to discuss under what theory of history they may be realizable" (181). Given the social and historical context that Mills establishes for social science, his book becomes a kind of existential affirmation of the "moral and the intellectual promise of social science . . . that freedom and reason will remain cherished values, that they will be used seriously and consistently and imaginatively in the formulation of problems" (173).

In his essay "The New Left," written a year after The Sociological Imagination, Mills asks not "What is to be done?" (Lenin's classic modernist revolutionary question), but "Where do we stand?" [17] Mills does not elaborate on the significance of this revision, and although he appears to be groping for meaningful continuities with an older revolutionary tradition when he asks his question, it is the differences suggested by these two formulations that illuminate the intellectual context of The Sociological Imagination. Lenin faced one kind of social-scientific failure—the failure of history to bear out Marx's prediction of the revolutionary radicalization of the working class—with the confidence that a more rigorous and exacting scientific inquiry could tease out the true course of revolutionary change; that is, Lenin could supplement Marx's conception of the revolutionary working class with the notion of a vanguard party and still claim to be acting in accordance with the scientific laws of history. Mills, too, wrote in the wake of dashed historical hopes, but at a time when the belief that the meaning of history could be deciphered by ever-more rigorous social-scientific inquiry no longer seemed self-evident. Lenin's crisis issued in practical and tactical reflection, whereas Mills's crisis issued in theoretical and methodological reflection; Marx and Lenin saw reason and freedom *in* history, whereas Mills sought to formulate a "theory of history" that could realize the values of reason and freedom (181). This disjunction accounts for the I'll-take-my-stand character of so much of Mills's defense of the sociological imagination.

The existential tone of Mills's methodological reflection entails no retreat from "real" social life. As with Sartre, Mills's existentialism issues in an ever-more rigorous engagement with history and society as the stage on which man makes his own essence. If anything, *The Sociological Imagination* conflates, even equates, methodology with social life in general: In figuring out where he stands methodologically, Mills figures out where the postmodern everyman stands socially.

The Big Picture

The Sociological Imagination begins with the problem of society as a problem of knowledge. The problem of knowledge, in turn, must be seen as a problem of locating oneself in society:

> Nowadays men often feel that their private lives are a series of traps. They sense that within their everyday worlds, they cannot overcome their troubles, and in this feeling, they are often quite correct: What ordinary men are directly aware of and what they try to do are bounded by the private orbits in which they live; their visions and their powers are limited to the close-up scenes of job, family, neighborhood; in other milieux, they move vicariously and remain spectators. And the more aware they become, however vaguely, of ambitions and of threats which transcend their immediate locales, the more trapped they seem to feel. (3)

This image of the befuddled everyman should be familiar by now; it has provided critical, humanistic social science with its reason for being at least since *Middletown*. The source of this befuddlement again stems from a problem of placement—in particular, the isolation of common people in "their private lives," "their everyday worlds," what they "are directly aware of," "the private orbits in which they live," "the close-up scenes of job, family, neighborhood." These "limited" locations have become "a series of traps," for as soon as people stray from them, they become confused and passive, "they move vicariously and remain spectators." As in *Middletown*, the problem lies not so much in a widespread state of pure isolation, but in the pervasiveness of a confusing midpoint between isolation and integration with a larger world. People are not so isolated as to be blissfully ignorant, nor are they integrated enough to overcome an anxiety about their sense of place. In the modern world, people are "aware . . . however vaguely, of ambitions and of threats which transcend their immediate locales" yet, unable to trace a clear connection between these larger ambitions and threats and their own locales, such awareness only leaves them feeling more trapped than ever.

In Mills's formulation, the postmodern everyman finds himself caught between two worlds, facing both ways. In one direction lies the local, particular, almost material world of the "close-up scenes of job, family, neighborhood"; in the other direction lies the general, almost intellectual world of which people are only vaguely aware, a world that transcends the local yet still somehow acts upon it. People could conceivably resolve their confusion by moving completely in either direction, but clearly for Mills any simple return to the local would constitute a retreat to childlike innocence, and any simple leap into the general would constitute a retreat from the messy particulars that make up "reality." Mills wants to rehabilitate this in-betweenness in a way that resolves itself in favor of both the particular and the general.

This resolution demands that people think about problems in order to solve them and that people adopt a certain mode of consciousness appropriate to a particular historical period, The Fourth Epoch, the "Age of Fact," the age of information:

> What they need and what they feel they need, is a quality of mind that will help them to use information and to develop reason in order to achieve lucid summations of what is going on in the world and of what may be happening within themselves. It is this quality, I am going to contend, that journalists and scholars, artists and publics, scientists and editors are coming to expect of what may be called the sociological imagination. (5)

The way out of confusion thus lies in a certain "quality of mind" that can encompass both the general and the particular, "what is going on in the world" and "what may be happening within themselves." The intellectual character of this resolution demands not an abandonment of the material, the local, but a specific attitude toward it:

> The first fruit of this imagination—and the first lesson of the social science that embodies it—is the idea that the individual can understand his own experience and gauge his own fate only by locating himself within his period, that he can know his own chances in life only by becoming aware of those of all individuals in his circumstances. In many ways it is a terrible lesson; in many ways a magnificent one. (5)

The sociological imagination enables people to locate themselves temporally within a "period" and spatially within "circumstances," yet this placement of self also involves a certain dis-placement of self. In order "to understand his own experience and gauge his own fate," the individual must not only discover his own place in society, but also become aware of the experiences "of all individuals in his circumstances." There would, of course, be no point in comparing these experiences if all of them were the same. For the sociological imagination, every individual's experiences are particular and unique, but never so particular that they cannot benefit from comparison with those of individuals who share their same general circumstances. In understanding others' experiences, individuals also understand others' "chances in life," which would seem to increase an individual's own chances in life. The sociological imagination enables one not only to get out of the "traps" of one's circumstance but also to return to one's own circumstances with an imaginative experience that is capable of transforming those circumstances into chances through the awareness of alternatives.

The sociological imagination thus offers not so much a placement of the self as a process of constant re-placement or dis-placement of the self through comparison with others. This process of imaginative displacement requires more than simply moving from individual to individual within similar circumstances. The exhausting of the "chances" of one's immediate circumstances will lead to the examination of ever-wider contexts—the circumstances of one's circumstances, so to speak. This requires not simply a shuttling between the experiences of individuals within a certain context but the shuttling back and forth between seemingly disparate and unrelated contexts themselves:

Whether the point of interest is a great power state or a minor literary mood, a family, a prison, a creed—these are the kinds of questions the best social analysts have asked. They are the intellectual pivots of classic studies of man in society—and they are the questions inevitably raised by any mind possessing the sociological imagination. For that imagination is the capacity to shift from one perspective to another—from the political to the psychological; from examination of a single family to comparative assessment of the national budgets of the world: from the theological school to the military establishment; from considerations of an oil industry to studies of contemporary poetry. It is the capacity to range from the most impersonal events and remote transformations to the most intimate features of the human self—and to see the relations between the two. Back of its use there is always the urge to know the social and historical meaning of the individual in the society and in the period in which he has his quality and his being. (7)

Once again we see how the sociological imagination embodies a conception of the whole beyond the liberal/modernist alternatives of drift and mastery. American social thought of the first half of the twentieth century offered the figure of the expert as the last stand of mastery in the face of a social complexity that had made the nineteenth-century, frontier jack-of-all-trades obsolete. As a social type, the expert represented the passing of the frontier and the rise of an interdependent, bureaucratically organized society. In part, Mills writes *The Sociological Imagination* as a polemic against the degeneration of expertise into mere technique, yet he offers no simple return to the unreflective wholeness or self-sufficiency of the frontiersman. The sociological imagination claims the whole world as its object of study—"from the most impersonal and remote transformations to the most intimate features of the human self." But the sociological imagination conceives of that whole as a pastiche, or must first conceive of that whole as a pastiche in order to arrive at any mature, meaningful account of society as an ordered whole. Mills's conception of the whole bears the stamp of the bureaucratic fragmentation of the whole into its constituent parts. This analytic fragmentation does not preclude synthesis, but it fosters a particular kind of synthesis: synthesis by juxtaposition. The sociological imagination conceives of the sweep and variety of human life primarily by the coupling of alien, disparate, seemingly unrelated social phenomena, such as politics and psychology, a single family and a national budget, an oil industry and a poem. These couplings establish a potentially unlimited number of relations that need to be discerned, of boundaries or borders that need to be crossed. Juxtaposition as an initial, defamiliarizing move is a prelude to a true sociological insight that can "see the relation between the two" seemingly disparate phenomena. The sociological imagination reconstitutes the frontier experience within society itself, for it sees every aspect of social life as existing on a border with the alien. Social phenomena exist not so much to be contextualized as to be constantly recontextualized to achieve what Mills, after Kenneth Burke, calls the "perspective by incongruity" (215). In this sense, the sociological imagination stands for a primacy of perception over the things perceived, of relation over the things related.

For Mills, the point of this process of inquiry is nothing less than a radical "transvaluation of values" (8). As with most Nietzschean formulations, Mills's conception of the sociological imagination suggests both a heroic affirmation of the human capacity to exert power and control and an underlying anxiety about the meaninglessness of all that strenuous bluster. The sociological imagination renders society infinitely complex, yet this complexity makes accounts of particular social relations obsolete upon formulation. Pastiche offers an excess of meaningful relations, an excess which stands as both its virtue and its vice. Depending on the amount of energy one has, the initial defamiliarization by the pastiche mode may issue in either a bemused, ironic resignation to the arbitrariness of relations between events or a commitment to the strenuous ordering and reordering of relations in defiance of a seeming arbitrariness.

To be fair to Mills, these do seem to be the logical alternatives once one assumes the condition of man to be one of "alienation" in the sociological sense of that word. Given this rather loaded assumption, the sociological imagination would indeed seem to be "the most fruitful form of this self-consciousness" (7). Mills concedes, however, that this man-as-outsider feeling reflects not only certain objective social conditions but also the rise of historical and cultural relativity as the dominant modes of human consciousness (7). The significance of *The Sociological Imagination*, in turn, lies in its inability to question seriously these modes of consciousness as the lenses through which one understands social life. Ultimately, Mills's book represents the triumph of historical and cultural consciousness as the organizing principles of American culture.

Mills argues for the sociological imagination as a "style of reflection" (13). The sociological imagination is becoming "the major common denominator of serious reflection and popular metaphysics in Western societies" (14). As such, "men ... state their strongest convictions in its terms; other terms and other styles of reflection seem mere vehicles of escape and obscurity" (14). The sociological imagination has not yet fully arrived, but all other orientations have lost their credibility. The physical and biological sciences were the common denominator of the modern era during which the "technique of the laboratory" provided "the accepted mode of procedure and the source of intellectual security" (14). Total war and the threat of nuclear annihilation have undermined the faith in science to the extent that, for most people in the present postmodern period, "the technological ethos and the kind of engineering imagination associated with science are more likely to be frightening and ambiguous than hopeful and progressive." Moreover, the traditional secular alternative to science—humanism—does not seem capable of filling the void left by the decline of scientific authority (16). Literature, "the essence of the humanistic culture," simply cannot compete with "the historical reality and political facts of our time" (16, 17). People "want 'a big picture' in which they can believe and within which they can come to understand themselves"; they want "orienting values," "suitable ways of feeling and styles of emotions," and proper "vocabularies of motive," yet they can find none of these in contemporary literature (17).

With the waning of the modern era and the seeming obsolescence of science and literature, the sociological imagination stands in as the style of reflection appropriate to The Fourth Epoch:

> In factual and moral concerns, in literary work and in political analysis, the qualities of this imagination are regularly demanded. In a great variety of expressions, they have become central features of intellectual endeavor and cultural sensibility. Leading critics exemplify these qualities as do serious journalists—in fact the work of both is often judged in these terms. Popular categories of criticism—high, middle, and low brow, for example—are now at least as much sociological as aesthetic. Novelists—whose serious work embodies the most widespread definitions of human reality—frequently possess this imagination, and do much to meet the demand for it. By means of it, orientation to the present as history is sought. As images of "human nature" become more problematic, an increasing need is felt to pay closer yet more imaginative attention to the social routines and catastrophes which reveal (and which shape) man's nature in this time of civil unrest and ideological conflict. Although fashion is often revealed by attempts to use it, the sociological imagination is not merely a fashion. It is a qual-

ity of mind that seems most dramatically to promise an understanding of the intimate realities of ourselves in connection with larger social realities. It is not merely one quality of mind among the contemporary range of cultural sensibilities—it is *the* quality whose wider and more adroit use offers the promise that all such sensibilities—and in fact, human reason itself—will come to play a greater role in human affairs. (14–15)

Mills clearly conceives of the sociological imagination not as an alternative to science or literature but as a higher synthesis of the two. In the preceding passage, art seems to overshadow science, but elsewhere Mills insists that the sociological imagination "requires orderliness and system" (127). There may be no single way to exercise this faculty, but it "does always require a developed carefulness and attention to detail, a habit of being clear, a skeptical perusal of alleged facts, and a tireless curiosity about their possible meanings, their bearings on other facts and notions" (126–27).

This concern with synthesizing science and art through some sociological account of the whole is central to the rise of the culture concept in writers like Dewey, Benedict, and Lynd. Mills describes the "sociological" as an attempt to gain "a conception of the whole" somewhat after the manner of cultural anthropology, and *The Sociological Imagination* is in many ways a rewriting of Lynd's *Knowledge for What?* (137).[18] Mills's choice of "the sociological imagination" as opposed to "culture," however, suggests that Lynd's book, and his larger intellectual project, needed revision. By 1959, the word "culture" lacked the critical-yet-synthetic edge that it had in 1939. Mills's methodological writings reveal his critique of American society to extend beyond the mere unmasking of the banalities of "consensus" politics to a deep engagement with the intellectual foundations of the idea of "consensus" itself—in particular, the culture concept.

In his essay "The Professional Ideology of Social Pathologists," Mills attacks the use of "liberal totalities" such as society, the social order, the social organization, the mores and institutions, and perhaps most of all, American culture on intellectual as well as purely political grounds. For Mills, these totalities represent "undifferentiated entities" and assume "a homogeneous and harmonious whole"; as such, they offer only a "formal emptiness" and a "low level of abstraction."[19] These empty abstractions are the legacy of the "processual" or "organic" view of society, one in which "nothing is fixed or independent, everything [is] plastic and takes influence as well as gives it." According to Mills, this view has plagued liberal social thought at least since the work of Charles Horton Cooley during the Progressive Era.[20] This intellectual fuzziness has often served a particular political program. The "social" took on a normative as well as a descriptive meaning during the late eighteenth century as the rising bourgeoisie invoked "society" against "the state" as a principle of order. In these ideological wars, the bourgeoisie presented society as a naturally democratic order that made unnecessary any interference by the state.[21] The twentieth-century descendants of the eighteenth-century bourgeoisie may have overcome their ancestors' hostility to all state interference, but they are still able to invoke totalities such as "society" when any "outside" interference threatens to place restrictions on their freedom.

The culture concept provides the language for one of the most egregious of these liberal totalities: "American culture." Mills objects to the tendency of the cultural approach of Benedict and Mead to ignore the political context of the "whole way of life" that it may be studying at a particular time, yet this objection should not be taken to be as crucial to Mills's critique of "culture" as some historians have made it out to be.[22] Given Benedict's argument for cultural consciousness in *Patterns of Culture,* the more interesting objection of Mills is that in the concept of culture "there can be no bases or points of entry for larger social action in a structureless flux" because "no set of underlying structural shifts is given which might be open to manipulation, at key points."[23] With the rise of the ideology of consensus, "organicism" had emerged as a two-edged sword: It provided the longed-for "sense of the whole," but, as a liberal totality, it lacked the critical edge that could direct that "whole" toward novel ends. Sensitive to both the possibilities and the limitations of "culture," Mills cannot simply dismiss the term. In *The Sociological Imagination,* Mills states that "the concept 'culture' is one of the spongiest words in social science, although, perhaps for that reason, in the hands of an expert enormously useful" (160). Mills's alternative to culture—"social structure"—can be seen as the culture concept in the hands of an expert, for ideally it offers all of the fluid interrelatedness of a liberal totality, but it provides an explanatory account of causality that would allow for activist intervention into social life.

Given the interventionist argument of a work like *Patterns of Culture,* this attack on the culture concept should not be taken at face value. Instead, the move from culture to social structure should be seen as a particular instance of a more general structure of transition that is central to the tradition of critical, humanistic social science that binds Mills to Benedict: the move from mere "understanding" to causal "explanation." Mills does not make the culture concept the whipping boy of *The Sociological Imagination*, but his attack on the reigning schools of social science of his day—grand theory and abstracted empiricism—is of a piece with the polemics that gave shape to the culture concept in the 1930s. The anxious tone of crisis that pervades *The Sociological Imagination*, along with the promise of undreamed of power and control should the crisis be overcome, echoes the narrative pattern of Lynd's *Knowledge for What?* Mills's grand theory plays the role of Lynd's armchair scholarship in that both are too removed from real problems to affect any change; abstracted empiricism shares the weaknesses of Lynd's practical technician in that, for all of its immersion in the real world of fact, it lacks any theory that could order these facts in an explanatory context (33, 67–68).

Mills's writing appears even more anxious than Lynd's. This is due in part to the ironic failure-in-success of postwar social science, that is, its social acceptance as a servant rather than critic of power, and in part to a certain narrative necessity of a work like *The Sociological Imagination* to place itself in a unique historical position, a moment of crisis unlike all that have come before it. In his very construction of this uniqueness, however, Mills locates the sociological imagination in the far-from-unique position of the privileged middle. The sociological imagination locates sociological truth "between abstracted empriricism and grand theory" and thus carries on the task of the "classic" or "macroscopic" work of the European sociological tradition (124). According to Mills, "classic social science, in brief, neither 'builds up' from microscopic study nor 'deduces down' from conceptual elaboration. Its practitioners try to build and to deduce at the same time, in the same process of study" (128). The reigning social-scientific orthodoxy has oscillated between deductive detachment and blind inductive engagement, yet the critical sociological imagination moves social science toward the privileged position of criticism—the middle that somehow embodies both extremes that situate it. Subjectively, this means that the sociological imagination claims as its proper object of study not so much man and society, biography and history, self and world, as the interaction between the poles of these and other such antinomies (4). A critical social science concentrates on the *intersection of* and the *relation between* the polar terms of such oppositions (4, 6).

This boundary region, this point of intersection, need not be limited to conventional oppositions such as self and world. As we have seen, the sociological imagination freely constructs boundaries between aspects of social life with seemingly no relation to one another. Boundaries, relations in need of description and explanation, exist everywhere, between a single family and the national budgets of the world, between poetry and the oil industry, and so forth; moreover, the sociological imagination demands that the social scientist be able not only to shuttle back and forth on either side of ever-new and exotic boundaries but also "be able to shuttle between levels of abstraction *inside each phase* of our simplified two-step act of research."[24] The sociological imagination offers the ideal of an infinite number of boundaries, as well as an infinite number of boundaries within boundaries, a seemingly infinite regress.

This vision of an infinitely complex methodology appropriate to an infinitely complex object of study would seem to lead Mills into the relational flux of the liberal totalities for which the sociological imagination was to be an antidote. Mills's analytic precision threatens to fall into the trap of abstracted empiricism, with relations, interactions, and boundaries replacing the contextless facts of that methodology; his insistence that all of these boundaries are somehow interrelated threatens to fall into the wishful generalizing of grand theory. My point, of course, is not simply to expose the contradictions of Mills's argument but to explore the meaning of those contradictions. We have seen such aporias recur too often in the work of Veblen, Lynd, Dewey, and Benedict simply to dismiss them as failures of intellectual rigor. Failures they may be, but they are failures that require more rigor than many intellectual successes. Indeed, *The Sociological Imagination* seems to offer the tension inherent in the constant shuttling back and forth between all levels of experience as the best argument against any less anxiety-producing methodologies whose easy formulas might require something less than the constant intellectual motion of the sociological imagination.

Still, mere free-floating intellectual anxiety would offer no meaningful alternative to the assurances of liberal totalities. Mills seems to conceive of the sociological imagination as a kind of directed, constructive anxiety attack, and he gives this anxiety direction in two ways. First, for all the constant shifting of perspective required by the sociological imagination, Mills subsumes the infinite number of boundaries within the social whole under one master boundary, one master relation: that between "the personal troubles of milieux" and "the public issues of social structure" (8). Sociological investigation seeks primarily "to understand the larger historical scene in terms of its meaning for the inner life and the external career of a variety of individuals" (5). This understanding demands both an account of relations by analogy or homology and a formulation of "the causal connection between milieux and social structure" (130). This need to establish causal relations brings us to the second ordering principle of the constructive anxiety of the sociological imagination, empirical inquiry. Mills's apostrophes to complexity may suggest a rather mushy notion of the sociological whole, but *The Sociological Imagination* is in the end a call to action, a call to a certain kind of practice that could relieve social science of the vagaries of "the sense of the whole." Operating within the basic framework of connecting personal troubles and public issues, the sociological imagination issues in a practical engagement with the inner lives of individuals in society. To understand the meaning of the sociological imagination, we must understand the meaning of this engagement.

The Human Variety

For all of his criticisms of social-scientific orthodoxy, Mills could hardly contain his enthusiasm or the ascendancy of social science as a social/intellectual practice. Misanthrope that he was, Mills nonetheless expressed the hope that in a time "when few aspects of American reality are not being studied by U.S. social scientists, their work is slowly resulting in a wider awareness of how American society actually works."[25] Indeed, for all of Mills's criticism of liberal totalities, the pluralism embedded in those concepts suggested, as Edward Purcell observes, "a fascinating range of problems and hypotheses that seemed to be empirically testable," and therefore had much to offer a thinker like Mills.[26] For the satisfaction of these empirical desires, the sociological imagination offers not "society," but "the human variety" (132).

Genial and tolerant though the phrase may sound, "the human variety" stands as a tough, empirical alternative to the easy formulas of drift and mastery that plague sociological orthodoxy. For Mills, cold-war political dualisms led consensus thinkers into the intellectual error of reducing social life to the alternatives of freedom or domination. The reality of social life lies instead in the "numerous forms of 'social integration' " that exist between the freedom of a "common value system" and the necessity of a "superimposed discipline" (40). The human variety is that which cannot be reduced to pure consent or pure coercion but must be studied in its particularity, a particularity that is, however, a unique and individualized amalgam of consent and coercion.

Mills's article "Mass Media and Public Opinion" provides a telling example of the consequences of the sociological imagination's recovery of the human variety. This article addresses one of the recurring themes of Mills's work, the fate of the democratic public in modern mass society. Mills traces the modern notion of the public back to the eighteenth-century ideal that rooted authority in face-to-face communication, in discussion circles that held speakers accountable for their words.[27] Mills charts changes in the public by analogy to changes in the commodity market: In the eighteenth century, both functioned as "widely scattered little powers"; by the end of the nineteenth century, they developed into centralized, powerful monopolies; and by the middle of the twentieth century, these private communication and economic monopolies were incorporated into the state, resulting in totalitarianism.[28] In keeping with his general Fourth Epoch scenario, however, Mills figures postwar America as beyond the historical shift from the free market to totalitarianism. The United States has entered a new phase of history, beyond democracy and totalitarianism: "Today in the United States a synthesis of these two stages of thought is coming about: both mass media and person-to-person discussion are important in changing public opinion. It is a question of which is the more important in different areas of opinion, at different times, and of just how the two, as forces causing opinion change, sometimes work together, and sometimes clash."[29]

This passage certainly belies the common characterization of Mills as a critic driven by nostalgia to bemoan the decline of "publics" into "masses."[30] Mills retains these terms for their heuristic value, but he clearly sees them to be inadequate to the task of describing postmodern realities. Faced with the obsolescence of the modernist alternatives of public and mass, Mills does not call for a "third way" beyond those alternatives; he calls on people to realize that the third way is here, whether or not they like it. Given the "fact" of this third way, the task becomes one of turning this objective third way into a more constructive, subjective third way. People must be made aware of the various integrations of mass media and person-to-person discussion through the social scientific study of these integrations.

Mills establishes the objective goal of his study as the rendering of the fusion point, the boundary that unites face-to-face communication and the mass media. So, too, he frames the subjective process of grasping this relation as a kind of boundary situation. Mills introduces his empirical investigation of public opinion as a "study of Decatur, Illinois, recently completed by Columbia University's social science laboratory in New York City." [31] There is more than a trace of irony in the disjunction between the small town and the big city, the Midwest and the East Coast, the social-scientific specimen and the laboratory of a major university. The choice of Decatur must be seen in the tradition of the search for the "typical" or "average" that goes back at least as far as *Middletown;* for Mills, as for the Lynds, the typical becomes the alien in relation to the subjective center of the study, New York City. In Mills, however, this foreignness suggests that which is *human* in the human variety. Decatur as the "average" is more complex, more unpredictable, more human precisely because it lies between the very predictable extremes of "public" and "mass." This complexity offers the ultimate challenge to the principle of the "social science laboratory," for it resists all easy formulations and fixed conclusions.

The complexity of public opinion in Decatur does not stem from the quality or sophistication of that opinion but from the way that opinion takes shape. Mills describes his research project as designed not only to find out what opinions people hold but also *to find out how opinions change, how these people, as members of the public, actually made up their minds.* [32] To this end, the research plan included a return research trip a few months after the initial trip; any observable changes in opinion were to be followed up with questions as to what people had seen, read, or experienced in the intervening period, all with an eye toward explaining the change, if any, in opinion. Such a research plan suggests that any rigorous study of public opinion must also be a study of the causes of public opinion, a relating of the actual thoughts of people to the environment that shapes those thoughts. This environment may include conscious experiences, such as a conversation with a friend, the reading of a magazine article, the death of a loved one; however, in Mills's explanatory scheme they become in a sense unconscious, or that which shapes consciousness. In many ways, the study of the formation of public opinion is an attempt to explain people's explanations; such a project renders people's opinions inherently suspect, a mere surface hiding an explanatory depth unknown to the citizen and in need of penetration by the social scientist.

This suspicion serves as the first step in the proper valuing of those opinions. The next step, the social-scientific technique that complements this suspicion, is the depth interview. Richard Gillam posits that this technique was central to Mills's major work, *White Collar* and that he tried to incorporate this technique into all of his projects. Mills defined his social-scientific task as follows: "I am trying to be absolutely definitive in so far as factual materials existent are concerned, to exploit fully (given my small amt [*sic*] of money to spend) the new techniques, especially the intensive interview and to write it in such a way as [to] be 'literature.' " [33] Like the proponents of the culture concept he so sharply criticized, Mills saw his work as a synthesis of science and art. His heroes were Weber *and* Balzac, which should come as no surprise given the strong affinities between the social-scientific and the novelistic attempt to grasp "the whole." (Perhaps one of the enduring legacies of the culture concept is the way in which the expression of literary aspirations by a social scientist has served to exempt him from the status of a mere technician.)

The literary aspirations that led Mills to adopt the technique of the depth interview must be seen in terms of a larger novelistic/social-scientific anxiety concerning "reality." In *The Sociological Imagination* Mills criticizes social-scientific "technicians" for having "forgotten that social observation requires high skill and acute sensibility." He suggests "that discovery often occurs precisely when an imaginative mind sets itself down in the middle of social realities" (70). Much like Lynd's comparison of the old and the new sociology of labor in *Knowledge for What?*, Mills states that "Alfred Vagts' one volume *History of Militarism* and the wonderful reportorial techniques for getting up close to men in battle, used by S. L. A. Marshall, in his *Men under Fire,* are of greater substantive worth" than Samuel Stouffer's more prestigious, four-volume study *The American Soldier* (53–54). The depth interview is the key to Mills's version of the move from a merely quantitative to a truly qualitative social science; it is the immersion into the flux of direct, immediate experience that enables the truly human encounter with reality that is necessary for an accurate rendering of the human variety.

In the interviews Mills did for the "Everyday Life in America" project, he made it a point to document every aspect of his interviewees' lives, especially their dreams.[34] According to Gillam, "Mills also scoured novels bearing on his subject, drew upon the reminiscences of a Macy's floorwalker for 'intimate' material, and eventually went so far (or so he later claimed) as to post stenographers in women's rest rooms to catch the offguard chat of salesgirls."[35] Whether Mills actually posted the stenographers is debatable, but the ideal expressed by such a maneuver is central to any social-scientific project that sets as its task the investigation of the most intimate details of people's lives.

A women's room presents an obvious barrier to the male social scientist. Mills's conception of empirical research seems to require some kind of native informant, someone who could move freely in a forbidden area and capture experience relatively undistorted by native suspicion of social-scientific outsiders. As we return to the empirical investigation of "Mass Media and Public Opinion," we find another troublesome boundary, the enormous social, intellectual, and regional gulf between Decatur and New York City. Significantly, Mills makes a point of stating that his research staff trained housewives and young unmarried women to go out and interview people for the study. Thus, a truly human account of human variety would seem to require that the objects of inquiry become, at least in part, inquiring subjects.

Still, the depth interview and the recruitment of natives into the process of inquiry do not provide immediate access to experience. Mills insists on the interview as superior to more distanced techniques, yet he concedes that "if you have ever seriously studied, for a year or two, some thousand hour-long interviews, carefully coded and punched, you will have begun to see how very malleable the realm of 'fact' may really be" (72). This malleability, however, does not preclude the grasping of reality, instead, it holds out hope for the possibility of grasping many realities by shuttling between the many perspectives offered by the many interviews. The qualitative assessment of each particular perspective thus takes on greater significance by association with the seemingly more quantitative process of relating a large number of perspectives to each other and to other variables.

"Mass Media and Public Opinion" offers a perfect illustration of this dialectic of quantity and quality. After describing in great detail the variety of questions involved in the personal interviews conducted for the study, Mills describes, without a hint of irony, the process by which he and his staff processed the personal experiences they recorded: "This information gave us a list of all the possible influences at work in this sample of opinion changes. So we began to analyze the figures, running six or seven thousand tables over a period of months, some of them with as many as 10 variables in them which enabled us to answer rather complicated questions on a statistical basis."[36] This passage would seem to suggest the kind of scientistic, overly technical sociology so often attacked by Mills, yet Mills sees his own quantitative research as rising above mere technique by being directed toward the truly human in the human variety. Figures, statistics, and tables—"some of them with as many as 10 variables"—are necessary, but not sufficient, to any meaningful sociological account of human life. The quantitative complexity of this passage has its complement in the qualitative complexity of Mills's conclusions:

> The American public is neither a sandheap of individuals each making up his own mind, nor a regimented mass manipulated by monopolized media of communication. The American public is a complex, informal network of persons and small groups interchanging, on all occupational and class levels, opinions and information, and variously exposed to the different types of mass media and their varying contents. There are many influences at work upon those publics and masses and within them, and there are many resistances and counter-forces to these various influences. But today it is still the case that the most effective and immediate context of changing opinion is people talking informally with people. "All conversion," Ralph Waldo Emerson once wrote, "is a magnetic experiment."[37]

The dialectic of quantity and quality reaffirms the irreducibility of human experience, experience which is ultimately personal (that is, "people talking informally with people") and, in its own way, given the nod to Emerson, creative and artistic.

By giving priority to the influence of interpersonal communication over that of the mass media, Mills's study offers a kind of social-scientific recovery of the everyday. As an act of recovery, this study embodies one of the chief narratives of critical, humanistic social science in twentieth-century America: the pastoral of autonomy. This narrative may be called a pastoral not because it always tells a story of loss but because it can at best only tell a story of recovery. In the case of Mills's study, even the refutation of the idea that the mass media dominates all personal communication carries with it the threat of impending loss: "The network of discussion and the flow of influence which move through the streets and over fences of the city are not formally organized by any centralized power. . . . The informal flow of opinion is still autonomous and cannot be said to be weak."[38] A conclusion about the present, this passage nonetheless sounds like a nostalgic ode to the past. The mere presence of the possibility of discussion being "formally organized" by a "centralized power" suggests that even though it is not so organized at present, it soon may be. The very terms of present hope suggest the threat of future despair.

Mills's study does more than assert a tension between personal communication and the mass media. As the bearer of its own cultural logic, the article links the objective autonomy and informality of everyday life with the subjective process of social-scientific inquiry into the everyday. By formalizing previously informal relations through a process of social-scientific textualization, "Mass Media and Public Opinion" concludes that people still communicate on a person-to-person level but also, and more importantly, that "you can only know for sure if you get your own facts together and study them carefully."[39] To this end, Mills's article refuses to present itself as the last word on public opinion; indeed, as a study in the causes of the *change* in public opinion, it has the need for further research built into its very subject matter. Ultimately, Mills's third way between naively democratic and dismissively totalitarian views of public opinion establishes a floating, nodal point of synthesis between face-to-face communication and the mass media—a point of tension that does not need to be relieved but articulated by the constant social-scientific scrutiny of public opinion.[40]

In keeping with this tension, the relative strength of personal relations at a particular place and time does not change the fact that, as Mills states in "The Cultural Apparatus," "men live in second-hand worlds."[41] The mere presence of mass media, whatever its power to indoctrinate the masses, makes people "aware of much more than they have personally experienced."[42] A later essay, "The Cultural Apparatus" is much less sanguine than "Mass Media and Public Opinion" on the persistence of personal relations as a point of resistence to the mass media: "For most of what he calls solid fact, sound interpretation, suitable presentation, every man is increasingly dependent upon the observation posts, the interpretation centers, the presentation depots, which in contemporary society are established by means of what I am going to call the cultural apparatus."[43] The point here is not to try to figure out which assessment represents the "real" Mills. Clearly both do by virtue of their shared conception of the problem of communication as a problem of mediation apart from the substance of what is actually being mediated. In this respect, Mills reads a postmodern problematic into the entire history of the modern public. For eighteenth-century democratic theorists, the problem of the public was not one of immediate versus mediated discussion but was that of "free" discussion versus the repression of that discussion by the arbitrary authority of church and state. To be sure, the waning legitimacy of arbitrary power relations and the spread of the "free" exchange of ideas led to a gradual reconception of power as somehow internal to the communicative process itself, rooted in the distorting effects of the various degrees of mediation. Although it was a "public" issue as early as the Dewey-Lippmann debate of the 1920s, the problem of mediation as the defining problem of public life should be seen as intellectually specific to Mills's own time, The Fourth Epoch.

Far from excluding each other, the ideas of "personal" relations and a cultural apparatus presuppose each other. In a kind of pastoral dialectic, face-to-face relations can be dismissed as nostalgia and yet be recovered as resistance. For Mills, there is no turning back from the secondhand world of modern mass communications; still, relatively immediate, personal communication remains possible, and a critical social science can investigate the conditions that foster this communication and the possible ways in which mediation can actually purify otherwise distorted communication. Clearly Mills's critical social science is as much an "interpretation center" as the evening news, yet it conceives of itself as a counter to popular media myths—in the case of the study of Decatur, the myth of people's freedom from or domination by the mass media itself. The sociological imagination stands as that true, deep mediation that seeks to recover the immediacy of the human variety: Witness "Mass Media and Public Opinion," which provides people with a secondhand account of the persistence of firsthand experience in a town that most people will only know through the mediation of a sociological report. The logic of the sociological imagination demands both sweeping statements about the cultural apparatus and case studies of particular interactions between people and the media. Mills's attempt to synthesize the particular and the general does, however, tend to resolve itself in favor of the particular, that is, particular syntheses of the general and the particular, of which "Mass Media and Public Opinion" is but one example.

In this way, the sociological imagination threatens to turn into its nemesis, the ideology of "liberal practicality" and "pluralistic causation," the belief that "the causes of social events are necessarily numerous, scattered and minute" (85). In The Sociological Imagination, Mills criticizes this ideology on the kind of political practice that issues from it. At its worst, liberal practicality suggests political paralysis, for it implies the suspension of action until all the facts are in, which they really never can be in the terms set by liberal practicality's notion of pluralistic causation. For Mills, this "principled pluralism" is as dogmatic as a "principled monism": All facts are not equally important and there must be a level of verification that will allow social scientists "to study causes without becoming overwhelmed" (71, 86). At its best, when not completely overwhelmed by causes, liberal practicality issues in "a liberal politics of 'piecemeal' reform" (88). In true sociological fashion, Mills explains this political position in terms of the social position of those who hold it:

> Liberal practicality is congenial to people who by virtue of their social positions handle, usually with a degree of authority, a series of individual cases. Judges, social workers, mental hygenists, teachers, and local reformers tend to think in terms of "situations." Their outlook tends to be limited to existing standards, and their professional work tends to train them for an occupational incapacity to rise above a series of "cases." Their experience and the points of view from which each of them views society are too similar, too homogeneous, to permit the competition of ideas and the controversy of opinions which might lead to an attempt to construct the whole. Liberal practicality is a moralizing sociology of milieux. (88)

Ironically, this indictment suggests deep affinities between liberal practicality and the sociological imagination. With its insistence on the particularity of experience, the sociological imagination, too, thinks in terms of "cases" and "situations." [44]

Mills's attack on liberal reform as stemming from an artificial homogeneity that stifles "the competition of ideas and the controversy of opinion" is of a piece with the liberal attack on Mills's "radical" idea of a monolithic "power elite" as too dismissive of the pluralistic distribution of power in America. The liberal attack certainly overemphasizes the "monolithic" nature of the power elite in Mills's account, yet to be fair, one could say that Mills overemphasizes the homogeneity of liberal social workers. His indictment implies that the battles fought within social-service bureaucracies over the theory and practice of casework are somehow not "real," a charge that at best merely echoes the consensus historians' dismissal of class conflict in America for not being "real," that is, radical, socialist, European, class conflict.

In Mills's work, as well as in that of other consensus figures, the distinction between liberal and radical would seem to lie in the "attempt to construct the whole" (88). Mills codes this positively, whereas more conventional consensus figures tend to code it negatively, but it is this construction of the whole that seems to separate the casework of the sociological imagination from that of mere liberal practicality. Consensus figures like Daniel Bell and Richard Hofstadter would approve of this distinction, for, viewing the intellectual attempt to grasp the whole as of a piece with totalitarianism, they prided themselves in possessing a liberal-pluralistic aloofness to questions of "the whole." Still, conventional consensus figures were never very convincing at fitting enormous military, political, and economic bureaucracies into a liberal-pluralist disregard for totality. The amount of control that these bureaucracies were able to exercise may be debatable, but that the intention of these bureaucracies was the rational management of the "whole" is undeniable.

Mills recognizes the liberal welfare-warfare state as some kind of integration of the whole. At times, he can hardly contain his admiration for the enormous potential for technical control that exists in the bureaucratic structures presided over by the power elite (182). Still, Mills most often invokes integrating "the whole" as a possibility, as something that does not yet exist but which can serve as a utopian guide to thought and action. Just how this whole differs from the liberal whole is difficult to say, for at every point of comparison the two have parallel terms (pluralism/the human variety, casework/case study), the distinction between which seems to depend on the by-no-means self-evident distinction between a deep and a superficial "social whole." This parallel structure exemplifies how Mills operates in the same intellectual continuum with "establishment" consensus figures.

The differences between Mills and establishment consensus figures stem not from a misleading distinction between liberalism and radicalism but from the varying degrees to which Mills and his liberal adversaries take seriously the Enlightenment values that seemed so suspect in the postwar intellectual world. Consensus figures still believed in freedom and reason, but they tended to feel that those values were best served by not being taken too seriously. The domestic welfare state and the regulated (as opposed to "planned") economy best represent this ideal of a rationally managed, but not too rationally managed, society that would balance order with freedom. Halfway covenants are always a sign of an explanation system in trouble, and for Mills such compromises signaled nothing less than an abdication of the promise of the Enlightenment. The rehabilitation of freedom and reason required a redoubling of efforts on the part of intellectuals to realize these values in everyday practice. Mills realized that, given the conditions of his time, such practice would have to begin on the "as if" level, but he believed that in acting "as if" freedom and reason were adequate guides to conduct, they would in fact become adequate guides to conduct (189).

The centrality of intellectuals to Mills's social vision, and the often blatant vanguardism of his recipes for radical change, have been a point of confusion in the interpretation of Mills and much of the rest of twentieth-century American social thought. Even his most sympathetic interpreters seem willing to concede his "elitism," and it is this "elitism" that irredeemably links him to his consensus adversaries.[45] It is precisely on this issue of elitism, however, that Mills differs from consensus figures. Nowhere was the consensus school's chastened affirmation of freedom and reason more egregiously a sign of bad faith than in its reformulation of democratic theory. Not all consensus intellectuals were vulgar celebrators of American society, but they did all tend to agree that the United States, for all its faults, represented the best of all possible worlds. America was still a democracy of and for the people, but it could no longer be a democracy by the people in the nineteenth-century understanding of political participation.

The problems facing any modern society had become too complex and too technical to be subject to mass democratic consideration; moreover, the experience of totalitarianism seemed to show mass political participation to be irrational and ultimately detrimental to the true goals of democracy. The imperfections of American society needed to be addressed, but they were to be addressed as technical problems by trained experts with no direct accountability to the public at large. The goals of democracy—which by the 1950s had been reduced for all practical purposes to economic prosperity and national security—were best served through the rational management of society by experts. Popular participation in the political process had a place in this vision of democracy only as a check on the possible abuse of power by politicians and their administrative/technical support staffs. Participation was best kept to a minimum so as not to interfere with the technical problem solving that was the essence of this new vision of democracy.[46]

Mills's indictment of the social-scientific "technician" is part of his larger indictment of this consensus vision of politics. As a merely technical conception of social science prevents the social scientist from ever properly questioning the framework in which he works, so an overly technical vision of politics prevents politicians from ever questioning the consensus within which they work, that is, the bureaucratic welfare/warfare state. More important, both technocratic social science and consensus democracy have no real place for the ordinary person: Social science either loses the ordinary person through the vagaries of grand theory or reduces him to a mere statistical fact through the quantifications of abstracted empiricism, while consensus political theory reduces the ordinary person to a passive consumer of technically administered services. For Mills, the promise of the sociological imagination is not merely a radical change in social science; it is a radical change in social life. Mills shares with his consensus adversaries the belief in the centrality of social science to political life, yet he extends to all citizens the ideal of political man as social scientist—not as technocrat, however, but as intellectual, as the critical, framework-questioning practitioner of the sociological imagination. For Mills, a social-scientifically alert citizenry is both the means and the end of any meaningful public life in the postmodern era of The Fourth Epoch.

Building the Postmodern Public

The problem of the relation between the intellectual and the public brings Mills to contemplate once again the disjunction in democratic theory between eighteenth-century ideals and twentieth-century realities: "The root problem of any 'democratic' or 'liberal'—or even humanist—ideals is that they are in fact statements of hope or demands or preferences of an intellectual elite psychologically capable of individually fulfilling them, but they are projected for a population which in the twentieth century is not at present capable of fulfilling them."[47] Mills is not the first intellectual to doubt the ability of the common man to live up to the standards of democratic citizenship. The anxious tone and sense of crisis that pervade his writing could be matched by any nineteenth-century reformer. The sense of crisis persists, yet the terms of that crisis change. Nineteenth-century reformers sought to solve the problem of the democratic public by instituting a system of public education, but for Mills education has been problematized by elaborate bureaucracies and a mass media network that undermine rational communication. Thus, the task for a twentieth-century democrat like Mills is not simply the education of the public but the investigation of the conditions under which the public is educated.

This sensitivity to "conditions" should not be seen as a reconciliation of the "demands or preferences" of an eighteenth-century "intellectual elite" and the means of modern mass communications. As the context for communication shifted from the small group to the mass media, so the intellectual ideal that was to be communicated underwent a transformation. The intellectual twin brother of the mass media, social science, as it developed in the late nineteenth and early twentieth centuries, greatly expanded the field of study deemed proper to intellectual life. Politically, this new intellectual ideal meant a new ideal of the requirements for active citizenship: One no longer had to be educated to a moral ideal of public virtue but to a social-scientific sensitivity to the complex web of interdependence that structures society.

Mills's defense of the "classic" values of freedom and reason bears the stamp of the social-scientific revision of those Enlightenment ideals:

> But the values threatened in the era after World War Two are often neither widely acknowledged as values nor widely felt to be threatened. Much private uneasiness goes unformulated; much public malaise and many decisions of enormous structural relevance never become public issues. For those who accept such inherited values as reason and freedom, it is the uneasiness itself that is the trouble; it is the indifference itself that is the issue. And it is this condition, of uneasiness and indifference, that is the signal feature of our period (12).

As with everything in The Fourth Epoch, discussion of knowledge and politics has shifted to the "meta" level. Postmodern politics is not defined in terms of any set of political issues but by a condition of "uneasiness and indifference" on the part of the citizen with respect to all political issues. Classic democratic theory made the citizen the basis for democratic government, but the social-scientific revolution of the late nineteenth century transformed the individual from an assumed means to an achievable end. The fundamental political task becomes that of explaining the citizenry to itself so that it may become aware of the threat to freedom and reason, acknowledge these as values worth preserving, and so work to preserve them.

Politics thus becomes education, but education in the broadest possible terms. For Mills, the main duty of the social scientist as educator is

"to make clear the elements of contemporary uneasiness and indifference," yet he sees this as fundamentally a "political and intellectual
task—for here the two coincide" (13). As an educator, what the social
scientist "ought to do for the individual is to turn personal trouble and
concerns into social issues and problems open to reason" (186). Far from
presenting an alternative to social or political action, Mills's idea of education sets as its task making connections between the intellectual and
the political, between "personal troubles" and "social issues."

The articulation of personal uneasiness contrasts sharply with the administration of therapeutic services. For Mills, "the end product of any
liberating education is simply the self-educating, self-cultivating man and
woman; in short, the free and rational individual" (187). The sociological imagination does not address particular problems so much as the
character of those who have to deal with these problems. The individual
is the beginning and the end of the political/intellectual energy loop of
the sociological imagination. Inquiry begins by translating personal "indifference into issues," personal "uneasiness into trouble"; it continues
by admitting "both troubles and issues in the statement of our problem";
and it ends by helping "the individual become a self-educating man, who
only then would be reasonable and free" (131, 186). Education is politics
and politics is education, for the "first and continuing task" of a liberating education is "to help produce the disciplined and informed *mind* that
cannot be overwhelmed. . . . to help develop the bold and sensible individual who cannot be overwhelmed by the burdens of modern life." [48]
This conception of politics completes the Deweyan-Progressive project of
breaking down the distinction between school and society, a distinction
that stood for all of the "artificial" barriers that distort or inhibit the
basic social relation of the social-scientific worldview: that of "the free
and rational individual" confronting "modern life."

For Mills, any truly democratic education must occur within a political context broad enough to address questions of power. This distinction
between education (knowledge) and politics (power) once again collapses, however, in Mills's own definition of power:

> Power has to do with whatever decisions men make about the arrange-
> ments under which they live, and about the events which make up the
> history of their times. Events that are beyond human decision do hap-
> pen; social arrangements do change without benefit of explicit deci-
> sion. But in so far as such decisions are made, the problem of who is

involved in making them is the basic problem of power. In so far as they could be made but are not, the problem becomes who fails to make them?[49]

With power defined as the restriction of access to the means of decision making, the democratic political project becomes that of expanding participation in decisions that affect the arrangements under which people live and "the events which make up the history of their times." This expansion would seem to require an initial inquiry into existing restrictions, into the power relations that limit access to the means of decision making. The sociological imagination provides the means of inquiry, yet it also provides the very object of inquiry, for it is hard to imagine what "decision making" could mean for Mills apart from the sociological imagination. To make decisions in the modern world, one needs the sociological imagination; meaningful access to the means of decision-making requires access to the sociological imagination. The problem of power is a problem of knowledge, of the relative distribution of knowledge in society. Politics thus begins and ends with the sociological imagination: It is an investigation into the means of decision making so as to liberate decision making from all that would restrict it.

In equating politics with power and control, Mills's democratic ideal mirrors the technocratic reality against which it is set. The increasingly strident declarations of difference suggest suspicions regarding the distinctions so central to his polemic: "To say that 'the real and final aim of human engineering' or of 'social science' is 'to predict' is to substitute a technocratic slogan for what ought to be a reasoned moral choice" (117). The distinction between the "reasoned moral choice" of radical democracy and the prediction and control imperatives of technocracy would seem to depend on his account of the values that could make a choice "moral" as opposed to merely technical. The guiding values of radical democracy are, of course, freedom and reason, yet these, too, need to be distinguished from the freedom and reason that guide technocracy.

For his exercise in values clarification, Mills once again adopts the rhetorical strategy of the "third way." Decision making may be at the heart of democratic politics and knowledge, but decisions cannot be guided simply by a naively democratic notion of *"what men are interested in"* or a dogmatically technocratic notion of *"what is to men's interests"* (194). Freedom in The Fourth Epoch requires a kind of synthesis of rights and duties, of liberties and obligations:

Freedom is not merely the chance to do as one pleases; neither is it merely the opportunity to choose between set alternatives. Freedom is, first of all, the chance to formulate the available choices, to argue over them—and then, the opportunity to choose. That is why freedom cannot exist without an enlarged role of human reason in human affairs. Within an individual's biography and within a society's history, the social task of reason is to formulate choices, to enlarge the scope of human decisions in the making of history. The future of human affairs is not merely some set of variables to be predicted. The future is what is to be decided—within the limits, to be sure, of historical possibility. But this possibility is not fixed; in our time the limits seem very broad indeed. (174)

In The Fourth Epoch, freedom and reason mean both more and less than they did in the eighteenth century. On the one hand, people in the postmodern world must not only be free to make choices but also to formulate the alternatives from which they choose. In this way, reason works "to enlarge the scope of human decisions in the making of history." On the other hand, the mature, responsible mind must realize that it is not free to do as it pleases, that reason only functions "within the limits . . . of historical possibility."

Despite this somewhat chastened view of human freedom, Mills still sees freedom exclusively in terms of making decisions. He declares that "the social task of reason is to formulate choices," and the "future is what is to be decided"—a declaration as stubbornly silent as to normative context or direction as any technocratic slogan. The only standard that Mills seems to be able to offer as a guide to this freedom is the limits of the possible, which from a moral standpoint is no standard at all. With an almost willful refusal to clarify the meaning of democratic freedom in terms of any specific ends or values, Mills rests the weight of his argument for the meaning of "a reasoned moral choice" on the openness of the decision-making process itself, irrespective of the decisions made.

Democratic freedom requires that all people have access to the decision-making process. It also requires that the decision-making process have access to all people. Mills clearly does not want to reduce people to "some set of variables to be predicted," but to exercise decision-making power in the postmodern world (that is, to exercise the sociological imagination), people clearly have to be willing to treat themselves and others as just such variables. This is nowhere more clear than in Mills's conception of historical inquiry: "We study history to discern the alternatives within which human reason and human freedom can now make history.

We study historical social structures, in brief, in order to find within them the ways in which they are and can be controlled. For only in this way can we come to know the limits and the meaning of human freedom" (174). Controlling social structures inevitably entails controlling the people who live in those social structures, and Mills's vision of history evokes a multitude of technocratic sins: It is a vision in which all social structures may be open to question and revision, a vision in which all that is solid melts into air, its contingency exposed by proper placement within the causal sequence of "the structural mechanics of history" (116). With every normative social arrangement leveled by its contingency, democratic individuals would then be able to exercise "some kind of collective self-control," directing this flux of contingency toward chosen ends, restrained only by the limits of the possible and the preferable (116). Completing the dialectic of democratic control, Mills insists that his vision of control is only possible if "there are dominant within a society the kinds of publics and the kinds of individuals I have described" (188). Such a vision is distinguishable from technocracy only by the number of people it would include in a basically technocratic project; yet, since to be included in the decision-making process one must first internalize the values of technocracy, it is hard to imagine how this inclusiveness could substantially change the technocratic project.

Mills seems to have trouble distinguishing between democracy and technocracy, and more often than not argument gives way to simple assertion: "Is it possible to speak of 'control' in any perspective other than the bureaucratic? Yes, of course it is." (116). There may be a control that is not bureaucratic, but Mills fails to provide a convincing picture of it. He shares too deeply the technocratic worldview of options and decisions that are bounded only by vague, contextless value preferences and the limits of the possible. Ironically, this hostility to any normative, ordering contexts itself initiated Mills's own attack on one of the leading schools of "technocratic" social science, abstracted empiricism. Mills saw the sensitivity to issues of social, cultural, and historical context as one of the distinguishing features of the sociological imagination, yet if one imagines the sociological imagination practiced on a mass scale, one can see the relatively neutral "facts" of abstracted empiricism giving way to the relatively neutral "contexts" of the sociological imagination. Lacking a master context or a metanarrative, history becomes a smorgasbord of contingencies democratic/technocratic citizens/scientists choose from in constructing their preferred society.

Mills cannot give an account of an objective context by which the sociological imagination could adjudicate between the endless variety of particular contexts it is capable of generating. He does, however, provide a subjective context for the reasoned moral choices of the sociological imagination. Never explitly stated as such, the root of Mills's "ethics of inarticulacy" lies not in any particular kind of morality but in a particular kind of self.[50]

The Postmodern Craftsman

The opposition of technocracy and democracy, so central to Mills's writings, collapses in his own terms. Mills's affinity with technocracy does not stem from his elitism or his intellectual vanguardism but from his commitment to the democratic expansion of the social-scientific worldview of technocracy. If he "privileges" intellectuals as a class, he is only rewriting the nineteenth-century democratic "privileging" of the working class: For both, the idea of a "universal" class privileges not a restricted group of people but a restrictive ideal that must be applied to all people. Mills takes up the vanguardism of Lenin, yet this seems inevitable for anyone who despairs of spontaneous revolution and fears a future of bureaucratic muddling-through. Charges of elitism and indictments of vanguardism tend to distract attention from the more substantive issues at stake, that is, To what end are the democratic or undemocratic means of the sociological imagination to be directed?

Irving Louis Horowitz interprets *The Sociological Imagination* as a "throwback to the Saint-Simonian vision of social science as creating possibilities for a world of thirty million Shakespeares and Newtons."[51] This is true in one sense, for clearly Mills models his ideal citizen on some kind of intellectual; however, the proper model is not Shakespeare or Newton but Martin Luther. Somewhat jokingly, Mills declares that "the slogans we ought to raise are surely these: Every man his own methodologist! Methodologists! Get to work!" (123). This almost parodic echo of Luther's "priesthood of all believers" is the culmination of the ideal relation between work and social life developed in the tradition of critical, humanistic social science stretching from Veblen to Mills. Twentieth-century social science, with its relentless examination of everyday life, represents the ironic, but inevitable, negation of Luther's initial rehabilitation of the everyday from medieval otherworldliness.[52] The "this-worldly asceticism" of Calvinism that followed from the simultaneous re-valuing of the everyday and the universalization of the formerly otherworldly office of the priest made the everyday world a stranger and more alien place than it ever could have been for those content to escape it through mystical transcendence. The gap between the human and the divine had to be overcome by an ever-more rigorous ordering of the world through one's work as an outward sign of inward grace.[53]

It is precisely this inward grace that Mills sees lacking in the "cheerful robots" who populate the white-collar world and the "technicians" who serve as their counterparts in the social-science profession. This inner emptiness, this lack of grace does not stem from a distance from God but from a distance from one's own personality. For Mills, these lost souls lack "any passionate curiosity about a great problem, the sort of curiosity that compels the mind to travel anywhere and by any means, to re-make itself if necessary, *to find out.*" Because they lack this passion, their "intelligence itself is often disassociated from personality and is seen by them as a kind of skilled gadget, that they hope to market successfully" (105, 106). In this way, the technician has separated his work from his life, and it is the reunification of work and life that drives critical, humanistic social science: in Veblen's call to free the instinct of workmanship from the fetters of pecuniary interest so that it might truly structure all of social life; in the Lynds's indictment of the meaninglessness of modern work in Middletown as the symptom of all of Middletown's problems; and in Dewey and Benedict's call for a perpetual re-making of self as the unifying pattern of a revitalized American culture. In all of these manifestations, "work" means not so much a making of things as a making of self, a self that could serve as the basis of a social order directed toward . . . well, the production of that kind of self.

The consequences of the proposed unity of work and life are nowhere clearer than in the appendix to *The Sociological Imagination,* Mills's essay "On Intellectual Craftsmanship." Mills's choice of the term "craftsmanship" should not be taken as a nostalgic nod to the preindustrial organization of work. Mills is the most modern (or postmodern) of thinkers, and his opposition of technique to craft is a thoroughly modern way of understanding work. In such an opposition, the problem of work becomes a problem of meaning. Particular tasks are relatively undifferentiated, for the key to work is the way that one engages in whatever one engages in, the degree to which one's work is somehow unified with one's life (195). Thus, "Scholarship is a choice of how to live as well as a choice of career; whether he knows it or not, the intellectual workman forms his own self as he works toward the perfection of his craft" (196). Given the abstract nature of the modern idea of work, its emphasis on a generalized process and method over particular tasks, what Mills says of the scholar stands for a universal ideal open to all workers, to all citizens. Truly, everyman must be a methodologist, for all work approaches method. In this generalized approach, the intellectual craftsman is the ideal type of worker, for his work literally is his "life," and the lives of others; that is, the sociologist's work is the study of everyday life.

Grand theory and abstracted empiricism show that even everyday life can become lifeless, distanced from reality, if approached in the wrong way. Mills would counter the objectifying tendencies of these methodologies by having the intellectual craftsman take his own subjectivity as the starting point for sociological inquiry:

> What this means is that you must learn to use your life experience in your intellectual work: continually to examine and interpret it. In this sense craftsmanship is the center of yourself and you are personally involved in every intellectual product upon which you may work. To say that you can "have experience," means, for one thing, that your past plays into and affects your present, and that it defines your capacity for future experience. As a social scientist, you have to control this rather elaborate interplay, to capture what you experience and sort it out; only in this way can you hope to use it to guide and test your reflection, and in the process shape yourself as an intellectual craftsman. But how can you do this? One answer: you must set up a file, which is, I suppose, a sociologist's way of saying: keep a journal. Many creative writers keep journals; the sociologist's need for systematic reflection demands it. (196)

To be meaningful, the writing of society must also be a writing of self; to be more than merely subjective or arbitrary, this writing of self must be directed by a methodology, the sociological imagination. This methodology has as its key ordering principle the key ordering principle of society in general in The Fourth Epoch: the file.

Mills's invocation of the file is perhaps the clearest instance of the relation between critic and object of criticism in the humanistic social science of twentieth-century America. The file is, in one sense, the epitome of the bureaucratic organization of modern life. With an obvious nod to e. e. cummings's World War I novel *The Enormous Room*, Mills titled chapter 9 of his *White Collar* "The Enormous File." This chapter describes the reality of a world only foreshadowed by cummings's novel, a world organized by total institutions peopled by mindless automatons:

> As skyscrapers replace rows of small shops, so offices replace free markets. Each office within the skyscraper is a segment of the enormous file, a part of the symbol factory that produces the billion slips of paper that gear modern society into its daily shape. From the executive's suite to the factory yard, the paper network is spun; a thousand rules you never made and don't know about are applied to you by a thousand people you have not met and never will. The office is the Unseen Hand become visible as a row of clerks and a set of IBM equipment, a pool of dictaphone transcribers, and sixty receptionists confronting the elevators, one above the other, on each floor.[54]

For Mills, as for other critical humanists, visions of complete domination coexist with utopian visions of complete control. In this coupling, domination reduces people to objects, while control raises people to the level of subjects.

As with Dewey's new individualism and Benedict's conception of culture, this move from object to subject takes on a certain aesthetic quality, with a subjectifying social science approaching the richness and fullness of art. Mills liked to refer to *White Collar* as his "little work of art," and the reviews that hurt him most were those that attacked the book on stylistic grounds.[55] Mills's own comparison of the sociologist's file to the creative writer's journal suggests a certain uneasiness about the file as an organization form, a felt need to somehow remove the bureaucratic taint of the enormous file by associating it with art. The moral authority of art in the modern (and postmodern) world makes this aestheticizing move understandable: What could be more moral or just than to demand that the sociologist, and by implication the citizen, become an artist? This demand for creativity, however, must itself be examined.

Although art has always been about human "experience," the meaning of "experience" changed dramatically with the rise of the modern intellectual traditions of which social science is a part. Dante and Shakespeare wrote about "experience" and sought to render an account of "reality," but it was not until the rise of the novel and the conventions of what Ian Watt calls "formal realism" that experience and reality took on a purely empirical character apart from all normative ordering forms.[56] With this empirical imperative to show life as it "really is" apart from formal idealizations of it, art, and the novel in particular, came to depend more on actual observation of everyday life than on the replication or development of artistic forms.[57] The lack of a normative, formal context in the novel led to many attacks on the novel as a corrupt and corrupting art form; ultimately, it led to the moralization of the content of the novel in the nineteenth century. Mills himself is evidence of the success of this moral rehabilitation of the novel, for he need only identify the social scientist with the novelist, and social science with the novel, to legitimize the whole project of the sociological imagination.

Mills's file shares with the novel and more conventional social science the imperative "to engage in the controlled experience" (197). In the context of Mills's work it is especially important to see the roots of the novel and social science in an older, religious literary form, the Puritan diary. All three forms demand the relentless scrutiny of everyday life, but none with quite the ferocity of the diary. In this tradition, Mills's file is first of all an act of *self*-scrutiny. Mills admonishes the intellectual craftsman: "Whenever you feel strongly about events or ideas you must try not to let them pass from your mind, but instead to formulate them for your files and in so doing draw out their implications, show yourself either how foolish these feelings or ideas are, or how they might be articulated into productive shape" (197). In this way, the file "encourages you to capture 'fringe-thoughts': various ideas which may be by-products of everyday life, snatches of conversation overheard on the street, or, for that matter, dreams. Once noted, these may lead to more systematic thinking, as well as lend intellectual relevance to more directed experience" (196). By keeping a file, one develops strenuously "self-reflective habits" so as "to keep your inner world awake" (197). Mills's file-keeping intellectual craftsman is thus the antithesis of the cheerful robot: Eternally vigilant, the intellectual craftsman makes all his experience the object of conscious scrutiny, thus distinguishing himself from the poor lost souls who merely muddle through their lives of quiet desperation.

If Mills's file is a kind of postmodern Puritan diary, its postmodernity lies in part in its conception of salvation. The file/diary no longer directs itself toward God, but this does not mean that the "controlled experience" lacks direction. Far from representing "work without salvation," the file represents a very particular kind of salvation. The file offers a redemption of everyday life through "more systematic thinking" and "more directed experience," a working of the "by-products of everyday life" into "productive shape." The demands of self-consciousness can be exhausting, and the file "enables you to conserve your energy" by "serving as a check on repititious [sic] work" (196). To ask how the energy conserved by the file is to be used is to miss the point. The file is not a prelude to intellectual production; rather, the "maintenance of such a file *is* intellectual production" (199). In the world of the file, the values of system, productivity, and efficiency are directed toward ever-more strenuous orderings of experience, which in turn create an ever-more systematic, productive, and efficient self. The file eliminates the extremes of both transcendence and solipsism by directing its attention toward the observable (broadly conceived) and the everyday, insisting that one can know oneself only after a strenuous engagement with the world. This process of engagement, of moving back and forth between self and world, becomes an "end" in itself, the salvation offered by the file.

At first glance, and even at second and third glance, no one would seem more deserving of the label "cheerful robot" than this file-keeping intellectual craftsman. He is controlled, systematic, productive, and efficient in everything he does; what is more, he actually likes being that way. He enjoys subjecting every aspect of his life to this discipline because it results in an expansion of his consciousness (even if it is ultimately only consciousness of his own self-control). Indeed, this standard of consciousness, a rather vague quality of intellectual productivity, is all that separates the intellectual craftsman from the cheerful robot. The two types are the qualitative and quantitative alternatives within a shared framework of bureaucracy. The intellectual craftsman is conscious of the bureaucratic structure within which he lives, but he is able to use it in a positive, active, "productive" way; the cheerful robot may at some basic level understand that he works within a giant bureaucracy, but, unable to direct himself toward that structure in a critical manner, he becomes a mere passive object controlled by a system larger than himself.

Apart from any explicit statement by Mills, his work shows that the true cultural meaning of bureaucracy does not lie in its ability to repress more "natural" social relations but in its ability to set the terms for both repression and liberation. On one level, Mills is highly critical of bureaucratic repression. In his article, "Two Styles of Social Science Research," for example, he defends what he calls the "macroscopic" style of research, which is in the grand European tradition of Durkheim and Weber, against the "molecular style" of abstracted empiricism, which he sees as a mere "bureaucratization of reflection . . . quite in line with dominant trends of modern social structure and its characteristic types of thought." This overly statistical approach to reality is tainted not only by its bureaucratic nature but also by its origins in market research, so once again bureaucracy and pecuniary interest appear as partners in repression.[58] In the same article, however, Mills concedes the necessity, even the desirability, of large-scale bureaucracies for achieving the synthetic goals of the macroscopic tradition in a world in which Max Webers are few and far between:

> Perhaps we cannot hope, except in rare instances, to have combined in one man all the skills and capacities required. We must proceed by means of a division of labor that is self-guided, in each of its divisions, by an understanding of and a working agreement upon a grand model. When as individuals we specialize in one or the other phases of this model, we must do so with a clear consciousness of the place of that phase within the model, and thus perform our specialist role in a manner likely to aid another specialist in the architectonic endeavor. The development of such clear consciousness, in fact, is the complete and healthy significance of discussion of the method of the social studies.[59]

As in most humanistic defenses of modern organizational structures since the Progressive Era, a proper sense of the whole transforms a repressive bureaucracy into a liberating one. The modern division of labor, symbolized for Progressives by the factory and for Mills by the office building, may be redeemed by "a working agreement upon a grand model," the division of that model into specialized phases, and "a clear consciousness of the place of that phase within the model" on the part of individual specialists. The redeeming value of an authentic bureaucracy is thus a "clear consciousness." Ultimately, Mills's work does not offer a bureaucratization of consciousness but an ideal of consciousness as a bureaucracy; its account of bureaucracy suggests not an internalization of bureaucracy on the part of individuals but bureaucracy as itself the external manifestation of the consciousness of certain great individuals like Max Weber. Consciousness precedes bureaucracy; bureaucracy is effect, not cause. Bureaucracies are substitutes for a certain kind of self. They must exist because "we cannot hope, except in rare instances, to have combined in one man all the skills and capacities required" to do the macroscopic work of the sociological imagination.

Despite his admiration for Weber (and a certain kind of bureaucracy), Mills refuses to resign himself stoically to the necessity of an "iron cage" of bureaucratic rationality. Weber did not reduce modern life to this iron cage, but in classic modernist fashion he did see the bureaucratic structures of modern society as the basically meaningless setting in which man must make meaning as an existential subject; the difference between Weber and Mills can be seen as the difference between the modern and the postmodern. If modernism looks for meaning in the brief gasp between clichés, then postmodernism gives up on the gasp and looks for meaning in the clichés themselves, or more properly, in the juxtaposition and recontextualization of clichés. The file represents more than simply an increase in the scope and precision of sociological investigation, and Mills's ideal of organizing information "into a master file of 'projects,' with many subdivisions" suggests nothing more than the common sense of the white-collar world Mills himself so vilified (198). In a world oppressed by an excess of "facts" which, taken by themselves, have become clichés incapable of producing meaning, Mills's file distinguishes itself not by the amount of information that it accumulates but in the way that it organizes that information.

Describing one research project, Mills states: "After making my crude outline I examined my entire file, not only those parts of it that obviously bore on my topic, but also those which seemed to have no relevance whatsoever. Imagination is often successfully invited by putting together hitherto isolated items, by finding unsuspected connection. I made new units in the file for this particular range of problems, which of course, led to new arrangements of other parts of the file" (201). Mills's postmodern bureaucratization of reflection leads to a "liberating" fluidity. As in the pastiche passages quoted above, Mills's description of the file shows the essence of the sociological imagination to lie in the juxtaposition of seemingly unrelated parts, the constant arrangement and rearrangement of the decontextualized constitutent parts of the human variety. Indeed, the bureaucratic fragmentation of social life embodied in the endless divisions and subdivisions of the file seem to be a prerequisite for the liberating recombination that is the sociological imagination.

The sociological imagination assumes the essential arbitrariness of all relations to be the starting point of any serious reflection on those relations. This initial assumption is, in effect, a bracketing of all assumptions, all normative ordering frameworks external to the intellectual craftsman. Thus, the initial experience of human life through the lens of the file is that of complete chaos, which exists to be heroically ordered by the sociologist:

You simply dump out heretofore disconnected folders, mixing up their contents, and then re-sort them. You try to do it in a more or less relaxed way. How often and how extensively you re-arrange the files will of course vary with different problems and with how well they are developing. But the mechanics of it are as simple as that. Of course, you will have in mind the several problems on which you are actively working, but you will also try to be passively receptive to unforeseen and unplanned linkages. (212)

The sociological imagination demands an "attitude of playfulness" (212). Its creativity lies not so much in thinking as in re-thinking and in making connections that are the least obvious. It demands that one see the world as a pile of disconnected folders, with no ordering principle other than that imposed on it by the heroic intellectual craftsman—and the true heroism of this craftsman lies in his refusal to accept as permanent any order that he has constructed. The sociological imagination demands not order but constant re-ordering. Pastiche is its privileged trope, for juxtaposition incites the articulation of hitherto unthought connections; these connections, in turn, are never more than stillborn, for the sociological imagination, like Veblen's instinct of workmanship, makes one connection only to move on the next juxtaposition.

Mills advises the would-be intellectual craftsman "to think in terms of a variety of viewpoints and in this way to let your mind become a moving prism catching lights from as many angles as possible" (214). It is this "capacity to shift from one perspective to another, and in the process to build up an adequate view of a total society and of its components," that distinguishes the intellectual craftsman from the mere technician and signals the unity of work and life demanded by the sociological imagination (211). Ironically, with this formulation of intellectual craftsmanship, Mills achieves a greater unity of work and life than he ever could have imagined. His conception of the sociological imagination is, more than grand theory or abstracted empiricism, "in line with dominant trends of modern social structure and its characteristic types of thought" for it represents the best that modern life has to offer. The sociological imagination provides the intellectual style appropriate to a social/intellectual ideal of unfettered, unrestrained mobility: of capital and information, of institutions and ideas.

■

Conclusion

> You may say that all this is an immoderate and biased view of America,
> that America also contains many good features. Indeed that is so. But you
> must not expect me to provide A Balanced View. I am not a sociological
> book-keeper. . . . A balanced view is usually . . . merely a vague point of
> equilibrium between platitudes.
>
> —C. Wright Mills, "Culture and Politics"

MILLS'S FILE STANDS as the culmination of the tradition of conspicuous criticism. It is critical in that it demands that one approach self and
society with no assumptions or preconceptions; that one accept no relation between people, or between people and their physical environment,
as "natural"; and that one engage in a rigorous process of inquiry that
will issue in some "new" perspective on self and society. It is conspicuous, moreover, in that it is capable of producing an infinite number of
conflicting perspectives; that each perspective becomes obsolete upon
formulation, the fodder for some other act of critical inquiry; and that it
offers no way of adjudicating between these perspectives other than engaging in a more rigorous version of the kind of inquiry that produces
the chaos of perspectives it seeks to order. Ultimately, the file is the factory that produces the commodified perspectives which flood the free
marketplace of ideas. This intellectual marketplace is the only social ideal
that the tradition of conspicuous criticism can offer as an alternative to
the capitalist market of goods and services.

The orderly chaos of constant revision, the persistence of a larger critical perspective despite the planned obsolescence of all particular critical
perspectives, remains the dominant ethos of intellectual life in postmodern America. With this fundamental agreement on social and intellectual

values, it is not surprising that "On Intellectual Craftsmanship"—which is, unlike most of Mills's work, primarily a statement of those values rather than an attack on those who fail to live up to them—should have become, as Irving Louis Horowitz puts it, "the most universally praised part of *The Sociological Imagination.*"[1] For all of his disagreements with Mills, Richard Hofstadter, the greatest of the consensus thinkers, praised "On Intellectual Craftsmanship" as a model of intellect in the "right state" and compared it to vocational literature such as Richard Steele's *The Tradesman's Calling* and Cotton Mather's *Essays to Do Good.*[2] Richard Gillam writes suggestively of Hofstadter and Mills being bound together by a "Critical Ideal": the belief that the scholar must be engaged and political, but that critical intelligence must be autonomous, above any party line. For Gillam, this Critical Ideal spared Hofstadter and Mills the "failure of nerve" that afflicted others of their intellectual generation. Although Hofstadter and Mills stressed "the ambiguous interconnections of mind and reality," they also "reserved a belief in the liberating power of ideas used critically to unmask or debunk whatever was outmoded or untrue."[3] Since Mills's time, this Critical Ideal has accommodated both a radical skepticism with regards to the limits of reason and a rigorous testing of those limits in an attempt to order human society in accord with reason.

Alas, the Critical Ideal's vaunted sensitivity to complexity has proven itself to be nothing more than a capitulation to irony. Intellectuals of all political persuasions have by and large given up on the Enlightenment's quest for philosophic certainty, but they have nonetheless committed themselves to the ever-more strenuous construction and administration of some rational, bureaucratic institution rooted in that quest, whether it is the corporation (for conservatives), the federal government (for liberals), or the sociological imagination (for radicals). This ironic disjunction between ideas and institutions has found its most explicit defense in the recent writings of Richard Rorty. Rorty's ideal of "postmodernist bourgeois liberalism" is of a piece with the ironic self-consciousness fostered by intellectual elites of the consensus era; appropriately enough, the leftist political critique of Rorty merely rehashes Mills's attack on orthodox consensus thinkers. Both Rorty and his critics share the same social vision: maximum material prosperity for all combined with an "aestheticized culture" of self-creating individuals. This schizophrenic consensus on social meliorism and philosophic nihilism would have people shuttle back and forth between a practical quest for certainty in their "public," social lives, and an equally practical rejection of all certainty in their "private," individual lives. Acceptance of this schizophrenia then stands as the mark of a mature, responsible, ironic self.[4]

Clearly many people today are comfortable with such ironic disjunctions. Encompassing everything from Rorty to MTV, ironic disjunction stands as the closest thing to a pattern of culture in contemporary America. I am decidedly uncomfortable with this culture of irony, and I have tried to make my objections to it clear by laying out the social and intellectual implications of one significant strand in the genealogy of modern irony, the tradition of critical, humanistic social science stretching from Veblen to Mills. To those committed to irony in its modern or postmodern expressions, I have nothing more to say. For those willing to engage premodern thought in an attempt to live within some kind of nonironic social and intellectual world, I can only suggest the outlines of an ethos that seems to be emerging from the various antimodern critiques of the Enlightenment that have persisted despite the dominant irony of our era. In an attempt to bridge the gap between the modern and the premodern, I begin my account with a consideration of the premodern understanding of the values of complexity and uncertainty so dear to modern ironists; next, I consider the work of Christopher Lasch as the most sympathetic and sophisticated encounter with tradition on the part of a modern American critic; finally, I turn to the philosophy of Hannah Arendt as suggesting the most promising sites for the engagement with premodern thought.

The serious engagement with premodern traditions would be greatly served by a proper understanding of modernity's self-proclaimed monopoly on complexity and uncertainty. By misreading a quest for certainty into the entire history of Western thought, such twentieth-century intellectuals as John Dewey were able to perpetuate a progressive reading of history in which the present stood to the past as adult to child: complex rather than simple, mature rather than immature, tolerant of ambiguity rather than demanding of clarity. Such a reading renders premodern philosophy and theology as imperfect versions of modern science, as if modern and premodern thought were somehow commensurable due to a common concern for controlling nature. Given this assumption, the aspects of premodern thought directed toward this control may be dismissed as primitive or outdated, while the vast areas of premodern thought not directed toward this control may be dismissed as irrelevant web-spinning. The charge of web-spinning often suggests the presence of a complexity one either does not understand or cares not to understand. Giving moderns the benefit of the doubt on their technical abilities, I am willing to concede that most simply do not care to understand premodern complexity; however, I am also willing to charge that this lack of concern stems not simply from the subject matter of premodern inquiry but also from its social relations.

The notion of complexity I have in mind here stems from Roberto Unger's insistence on the acceptance of a certain "ambiguity of meaning" as a central trope of the "ancient humanistic arts" that he calls the "dogmatic disciplines," namely, theology, law, and grammar. This ambiguity suggests a certain quality of mind as well as a certain relation between people within a community of inquiry.[5] Unger illustrates this relation best through the example of theology, the dogmatic discipline which, more than any other, modern science set out to replace. According to Unger, the process of interpreting scripture or theological texts assumes an inevitable disjunction between the meaning intended by the original writer and the "purposes or interests" of the person interpreting the writing. The resolution of this ambiguity "is possible to the extent that interpreter and interpreted participate in the same community or tradition of shared beliefs, beliefs that are both understandings and values." Since "the community of intention is never perfect and . . . is always threatening to fall apart . . . the ambiguity of meaning cannot be resolved completely or with finality." The acceptance of ambiguity ensures not only that no particular interpretation will ever be final but also that no particular interpretation will ever be obsolete, for its meaning "must always be rediscovered by an interpreter, who has his own purposes and his own form of existence." Through this process of rediscovery, theology participates in the development of the religion it studies, "helping define its shape and determine its directions." As an intellectual and a social practice, theology offers "an elaboration of some point of view already present in the community with which [it] is associated." Since the doctrines of theology "are drawn from the very traditions they expound and develop," theology recognizes no clear distinction between "the object accounted for and the account itself," and thus no clear distinction between description and evaluation.[6]

All this contrasts sharply with the modern, scientific heir to theology, the sociology of religion. Unlike theology, a science or sociology of religion attempts to give an account of religion in general. It treats the conception of religion "prevalent in specific societies as part of what has to be explained instead of as part of the explanation." As a science, the sociology of religion distinguishes clearly "the dimension of [its] subject matter from the dimension of the theory" with which it describes a religion. For the sociologist of religion, the "greater the independence a science achieves from the pretheoretical views of any one group, the more universal and objective it supposedly becomes."[7] This self-reflexive, scientific suspicion of the object of study issues in a radically self-reflexive suspicion of the very process of studying the object; science seeks independence from not only the pretheoretical, but also the past theoretical. To claim for his or her work the status of science, a sociologist of religion must "improve" on Weber and Durkheim in a way that a theologian can never really "improve" on Augustine or Aquinas. Against the process of reinterpretation offered by the dogmatic disciplines, modern science offers a process of revision, a refinement of method that incorporates and explains both a greater number of facts and a greater number of relations between facts in such a way as to make previous accounts obsolete. Science may indeed acknowledge its past, but it characteristically does so through a "history of science" or a "history of sociology," which simply treats previous scientific accounts as those accounts treated nature or society, that is, as objects in need of explanation.

Unlike the sociology of religion and science in general, theology assumes that questions of knowledge unavoidably involve relations between people. As Alasdair MacIntyre writes, a tradition like theology assumes "that reason can only move towards being genuinely universal and impersonal insofar as it is neither neutral nor disinterested, that membership in a particular type of moral community, one from which fundamental dissent has to be excluded, is a condition for genuinely rational enquiry and more especially for moral and theological enquiry."[8]

This conception of knowledge as rooted in a moral community assumes a certain kind of tautology as a precondition for rational inquiry. The tautology of tradition operates on the level of being as well as the level of knowing. To think rationally within a tradition, "the enquirer has to learn to make him or herself into a particular kind of person if he or she is to move towards a knowledge of the truth"; paradoxically, "only insofar as [the enquirer has] already arrived at certain conclusions [is he or she] able to become the sort of person able to engage in such inquiry so as to reach sound conclusions." As inescapably a relation between people, this tautological transformation requires not only that the mind conform "itself to the object . . . presented for its attention" but that the enquirer accept the rational teaching authority of a mentor within the moral community of the tradition as necessary for achieving this conformity of mind and object.[9] This submission amounts to an act of faith, which in the Catholic tradition implies faith in the community and faith in the God to whom this community has submitted. In rejecting the priority of the moral community as a guarantor of rationality, the modern turn to epistemology has fostered a social ideal of an isolated individual consciousness as existing somehow prior to or apart from a community of inquiry; however, this break from tradition has not resulted in an escape from circularity but in a shift from the tautology of community to the solipsism of the individual.

Modern social science has dedicated itself to solving a series of problems bequeathed by the initial bracketing of all traditions, beliefs, and "social conditions" that gave birth to the modern subject. At its most humanistic, social science has sought to code the solipsism of the modern subject positively as "autonomy," and then construct a rational social order geared toward maintaining and developing the autonomy of the individuals within it. This rational social order, figured most often as the "social whole," has in many ways been a substitute for the premodern notion of tradition; it has presented itself as a set of enabling, constitutive "pre-conditions" that nonetheless allow for, even demand, an autonomous, transcendental subject. This social synthesis, established as intellectual orthodoxy by the end of the eighteenth century, has never been stable, and autonomy always seems to be in danger of sliding into mere alienation. In nineteenth-century America, the idea of community emerged as a nurturing, supportive alternative to the potentially alienating objective social whole of the market. During the twentieth century, the idea of culture emerged as a nurturing, supportive alternative to the potentially alienating objective social whole of bureaucracy. At its height in the "consensus" era of the 1950s, the idea of culture as a whole way of life promised to synthesize tradition (necessity) and the individual (freedom). Culture has since proven itself to be yet another objective social whole engaged in a ceaseless dialectical struggle with autonomous subjects.

Consensus thinkers accepted culture as a "fact" of social life, yet maintained their critical detachment from, and even hostility to, not only American culture but all particular cultures. The jeremiad of consensus may be seen as expressing a discontent with America in particular and with modernity in general. Reflection on the dialectic of enlightenment—

the ironic juxtaposition of modernity's emancipatory promise and its alienating threat—has served as a characteristic mode of public address for intellectuals across the political spectrum. The particular location of modernity's promise and threat differs with various political positions, but everywhere we are cautioned that too much toothpaste has been squeezed out of the tube, that we must take a balanced view and be careful not to throw the baby out with the bath water.

The career of the late Christopher Lasch suggests the fate of this jeremiad. More than any other intellectual since the 1950s, Lasch carried on the struggle with modernity as it took shape in the tradition of conspicuous criticism. As he makes clear in the personal memoir with which he opens his *True and Only Heaven,* Lasch was raised in the tradition of Midwestern progressivism that we have seen in the works of Veblen, the Lynds, Dewey, Benedict, and Mills. His domestic and foreign-policy sympathies grew out of a Midwestern, secular-Protestant moralism; he believed in the New Deal attempt to improve social life through an activist government, and he supported Henry Wallace in his attempt to come to some peaceful coexistence with the Soviet Union. Much of Lasch's writing from the 1960s through the early 1970s can be seen as of a piece with the critique of American society offered by C. Wright Mills; however, as the political issues of the cold war began to recede with the American withdrawal from Vietnam, the moral concerns that had driven Lasch's political critique began to take center stage. Lasch had tended to side with student radicals against the American war machine, yet he became increasingly suspicious of the way in which the new left "indiscriminately condemned all institutions and equated 'liberation' with anarchic personal freedom." By the mid-1970s, Lasch came "to question the left's program of sexual liberation, careers for women, and professional child care." Lasch arrived at his supposed cultural conservatism through a deep engagement with the writings of the cultural left itself, in particular the work of the Frankfurt School and English Marxists such as Raymond Williams and E. P. Thompson. The latter in particular exposed Lasch to "a sympathetic account, not just of the economic hardships imposed by capitalism, but of the way in which capitalism thwarted the need for joy in work, stable connections, family life, a sense of place, and a sense of historical continuity." Lasch spent the last twenty years of his life trying in incorporate these concerns into some "moral consensus" that could serve as the basis for "legitimate authority." [10]

In his rejection of progress and his refusal to play the benefits of modernity against its costs, Lasch transcended the tradition of conspicuous criticism. Still, Lasch's persistent concern with the fate of America as a moral order ties him to a jeremiad tradition that stretches back at least to the reform movements of the Jacksonian era.[11] The socially secularized Protestantism that inspired so many reformers in the nineteenth century saw in moral conduct a substitute for the spiritual order banished by denominationalism and a secular constitution. Based on the Enlightenment fiction that morality has an objective basis apart from any spiritual or ontological order, the quest for a moral order initially saw its task as getting people to behave properly, but it has subsequently foundered on the problem of what precisely constitutes proper conduct. Slogans such as "safe sex" are no less moralistic than ad campaigns that declare "real men don't do porn." Radicals and conservatives may disagree on particular moral issues, but they agree that the future of America depends primarily on the conduct of each individual American citizen. The attempt to get beyond this individualism by addressing America as a culture has simply conferred upon this individualism the status of a unifying pattern of values. American individualism may deserve this status, but this leaves American moralists in the ironic position of addressing a people bound together only by a belief in their inalienable right not to be bound to anything.

Lasch's moral individualism transcends the sentimentality of the nineteenth-century ideology of "separate spheres" by its insistence on the unity of work and family life. It transcends the sentimentality of contemporary bourgeois conservatism by rejecting the economic libertarianism of free-market capitalism; it transcends the sentimentality of contemporary bourgeois radicalism by rejecting the cultural libertarianism of libidinal anarchy. Unable to transcend the everyday world of work and love, however, Lasch's moralism threatens to naturalize that affirmation of ordinary life which, since the Reformation, has ironically issued in the exploitation of everyday life.

In his later work, Lasch was much more likely to quote Jonathan Edwards than Sigmund Freud, but Edwards's metaphysical and spiritual insights appear in Lasch's work as something like equipment for living rather than as objects for contemplation. The moralism that has dominated American intellectual life since the nineteenth century is quite foreign to even so Protestant a thinker as Edwards, whose early-modern theology looks back to a premodern order of piety more than ahead to a fully modern order of moralism.[12] Lasch does not reclaim Edwards merely for his practical "usefulness," but neither does he submit to the teaching authority of Edwards, much less of the Bible; rather, he incorporates Edwards into his own usable past, a genealogy (in the non-Nietzchean sense) of a populist tradition characterized by a respect for limits and a deep suspicion of progressive improvements. Wrenched from its moorings in a premodern ontology, Edwards's conception of limits appears as a personal ethic that guides and sustains a life whose meaning is exhausted in the joys and sorrows of the bourgeois world of work and love. As admirable a personal ethic as this may be, it cannot serve as any basis for social unity in the face of the bewildering variety of options that the world of work and love now presents to individuals.

Lasch's genealogy of populism takes its place alongside the usable pasts of his socialist and feminist critics in that its very recovery of a tradition as marginal—if not in the past, at least in the present—only reinforces the notion of the centrality of liberal individualism to American culture. Ultimately, these marginal traditions always seem to struggle with, to accommodate and resist, the liberal tradition outlined by consensus thinkers in the 1950s. Indeed, the whole project of constructing a usable past—the promise suggested by C. Wright Mills's phrase "every man his own methodologist" and Carl Becker's "every man his own historian"—speaks to the dominance of individualism in America's approach to the past. These alternative histories are often driven by an intense moral passion, but however much one may share the values of these genealogies—and I share much with Lasch's—no particular genealogy can hope to represent the values of so individualistic a group of people as "we Americans." [13] The religious denominationalism of the nineteenth century has been succeeded by the moral denominationalism of the twentieth, and there seems about as much hope for resolving moral differences as there is for resolving religious differences. One can no longer invoke the "practical" nature of morality as opposed to religion. People once felt that society could not exist apart from religious unity, yet for much of American history some kind of society has existed apart from any officially recognized sacred order. I imagine some kind of society can exist beyond the moral order of right and wrong. Risking melodrama, I would venture to say that such a society already exists in America, and seems to get along okay in its own imperfect way.

For most of the modern era, morality has been invoked as an alternative to nihilism. In our present postmodern moment, morality has revealed itself to be nihilism. Moral jeremiads of the type found in the tradition of conspicuous criticism must fail. Calls for moral responsibility are pointless apart from some context of shared values, and the only values Americans share are the procedural norms of a libertarian social order, the thinness of which incite the anxiety that drives the jeremiad in the first place. In the current intellectual climate, attempts to revive public life or public culture by incorporating moral debate into politics seem misguided, even dangerous; most people, "experts" and intellectuals especially, have no idea what constitutes a moral argument, and any attempt to engage in debate over moral issues will likely only confirm people's commonsense belief that morality is arbitrary, emotive, and irrational. The way out of this nihilism lies in an abandonment of the notion of society as a moral order.

In America, the abandonment of modern moralism entails an abandonment of the language of work. Even so seemingly benign a phrase as "the need for joy in work" carries with it the seeds of an instrumental worldview that figures man as the maker of meaning. As Hannah Arendt argues in *The Human Condition,* the universalization of instrumental rationality brought on by the rise of political economy deprived contemplation of its monopoly on truth. The premodern world insisted that "no work of human hands can equal in beauty and truth the physical *kosmos,* which swings in changeless eternity"; for premoderns, truth rested in the contemplation of this order. Against this, the modern world has insisted "that man can know only what he makes himself"; as a result, thinking has shifted from its premodern role as the handmaid to contemplation to its modern role as the handmaid to doing. The instrumentality of work implies a mastery over the object worked upon, and the linking of work to meaning makes man the master of meaning. To see man as the master of his "ends" is to justify all means in the furtherance of those ends: As Arendt insists, "the definition of an end [is] precisely the justification of the means," and "it is not enough to add some qualifications, such as that not all means are permissible or that under certain circumstances means may be more important than ends." Writing in the wake of the Holocaust, Arendt was well aware of the "murderous consequences" of the instrumentalization of meaning.[14]

The abandonment of the language of "work" makes possible the acceptance of the locus of meaning as lying in an objective world outside of the self. Against the modern objectivity of the social whole, this objective world resembles what Arendt refers to as the "common world" of premodern philosophy, in which "reality is not guaranteed primarily by the 'common nature' of all men who constitute it, but rather by the fact that, differences of position and the resulting variety of perspectives not withstanding, everybody is always concerned with the same object." Recovery of this common world requires acceptance of the premodern insistence that God, not man, is the measure of all things, and that man connects himself to God through ritual, prayer, and contemplation, not work.[15]

The revival of contemplation does not signal a simple retreat into otherworldliness. The contemplative life of the premodern world may have set itself above the vulgar world of the active life, but it never set itself against activity in the way that modern "work" has attacked contemplation. At its high points in ancient Greece and the Catholic Middle Ages, the contemplative life was conceived as part of a larger social/natural order that included the active life. The abandonment of work as the locus of meaning points not only to a revival of the contemplative life but also to a revival of those aspects of the active life marginalized by the modern universalization of instrumental rationality. Drawing on classical Greek conceptions of the *vita activa,* Arendt figures these other aspects in terms of "labor," the realm of necessity, and "action," the realm of freedom.

First, let us consider labor. Arendt defines labor as "the activity which corresponds to the biological process of the human body, whose spontaneous growth, metabolism, and eventual decay are bound to the vital necessities produced and fed into the life process by labor."[16] By presenting the ancient Greek *oikos* (household economy) as the ideal embodiment of the life of labor, Arendt links labor to violence and force, as in the father's power over his wife and children; she even concedes that the understanding of necessity embodied in the life of labor amounts to something like slavery. This strong conception of necessity is about as palatable to the modern world as submission to God. Still, Arendt insists that freedom, even life itself, has no meaning apart from the necessity associated with labor: "Necessity and life are so intimately related and connected that life itself is threatened where necessity is altogether eliminated. For the elimination of necessity, far from resulting in the establishment of freedom, only blurs the distinguishing line between freedom and necessity."[17]

I am not prepared to, and I would be suspicious of any attempt to, construct out of whole cloth a "natural" biological order of necessity within which to pursue the measure of freedom allotted to us on this earth; however, whereas belief in God seems like an all-or-nothing affair, acceptance of some biological notion of necessity seems a bit more amenable to the pragmatist strategy of repairing a sinking ship one plank at a time. In a effort to engage nontheistic moderns, I would like to consider the plank of abortion.

Nowhere is the blurring of freedom and necessity more insidious than in the current practice of abortion in the Western world. Abortion must be seen in terms of the larger assault on nature that began with the rise of modern science in seventeenth-century Europe. Modern man has based his liberation from necessity on the domination of nature, including the domination of his own body through the self-exploitation we euphemistically call the Protestant work ethic; modern woman has followed suit by placing her hopes for emancipation on the domination of that part of nature most specific to her, her body in its capacity to bear children. As the emancipation of the American male depended on the enslavement of Africans and the extermination of Native Americans, so the emancipation of the American female seems to depend on the abortion of her children.

Presented as liberation, the infanticidal hygiene of abortion best embodies the contradictions that Michel Foucault has identified with the modern regime of "power over life." What Foucault has written of nuclear weapons can be said of abortion: "The power to expose a whole population to death is the underside of the power to guarantee an individual's continued existence." Abortion, more so than nuclear holocaust if only by its routine practice, epitomizes what Foucault calls the *"anatomo-politics of the human body"* and the *"bio-politics of the population."* Premodern infanticide belongs to that world in which power manifests itself in what Foucault calls the "power of life and death," the power to take life or let live; modern abortion manifests a qualitatively different power over life "bent on generating forces, making them grow, and ordering them, rather than one dedicated to impeding them, making them submit, or destroying them." [18] As the number of abortions grow, so do the number of abortion narratives. Increasingly, therapists encourage women to tell the story of their abortion(s). Abortion comes to be figured as yet another opportunity for personal growth—by no means pleasant, of course, but redeemable as an act of autonomy and control over one' life course.

In the face of this infanticidal absurdity, the most vocal opponents of abortion have only been able to offer the notion of a "right to life." This merely invests the unborn child with the rights-constituted individuality that the mother invokes in demanding safe and legal abortion. Asserting an absolute right to life seems as misguided as asserting an absolute right to choose. As Arendt has observed, the injunction against murder is only one among ten commandments; it is not the first, and it possesses no privileged standing with respect to the others.[19] The sterility of the language of rights with respect to abortion points not only to the sterility of the modern divorce between natural right and natural law but also to the futility of extending the language of rights—the language of freedom—to every aspect of life. In these matters, the bourgeois moralist cuts the baby in two and claims for himself the wisdom of Solomon. Solomon knew better.

The recovery of necessity suggested by the rejection of abortion must be accompanied by a recovery of the freedom that Arendt associates with the category of "action." Arendt defines action as the "activity that goes on directly between men without the intermediary of things or matter." Action "corresponds to the human condition of plurality, to the fact that men, not Man, live on the earth and inhabit the world."[20] The realm of action is the realm of equality, and as such is unpredictable, irreversible, anonymous. Its characteristic forms are the living deed and the spoken word, which pursue no end, exhaust their full meaning in their performance, and leave nothing behind. Arendt locates the life of action in the public sphere of politics, a sphere which in ancient times was restricted to the aristocratic few. Modern democracy has of course officially rejected this "elitism" and dedicated itself to opening the public sphere to as many people as possible; in pursuing this goal, it has not only produced its own form of elitism but it has lost sight of all possible boundaries for the public and the political. Most of what passes for politics today is actually economics; as such, it fosters the instrumentalization of every aspect of life in the service of "society." As a symptom, the tradition of conspicuous criticism points to the deficiencies of a single-minded pursuit of "participation" apart from consideration of the process being participated in. The pressing political question today is not "How can we increase participation?" but "What is politics?" Short of diplomacy and war, I have difficulty imagining the kind of "political" activities appropriate to the tropes of "action," but I feel that those tropes themselves may provide some guidance in defining the formal realm of politics.

Finally, the recovery of the formal spheres of freedom and necessity should bring with it a respect for the informal realm that exists to some degree in both of these spheres. This informal world I take to be the ordinary life of work and love. Respect for this world entails a rejection of the modern "affirmation" that rationalized ordinary life into a locus of meaning; it entails a much humbler "acceptance" of ordinary life in all its ordinariness and informality. The world of friendship—of drinking and talking, working and playing, loving and hating—may bring happiness, or it may not; in neither case does it bring "meaning." It is no less important for being, in a sense, meaningless. Our modern spiritual efficiency experts, including many social historians, tremble at the prospect of some ordinary experience failing to produce meaning. Acceptance of ordinary life requires an acceptance of waste still anathema to most people in our work-obsessed culture. All things do not exist to be read. Experience does not have to be written to be valid. The informal must be left informal.

Of course, distinctions between the formal and the informal, or freedom and necessity, only make sense within specific traditions. The modern revolt against God and nature has all but incapacitated the Western world's ability to think within a tradition. The only hope for addressing the issues I have raised in this conclusion lies in the great surviving traditions of the premodern West: orthodox Judaism, Roman Catholicism, the Orthodox churches, and Islam. For those outside of these traditions, I can only offer the words of C. Wright Mills to his liberal critics: "I feel no need for, and perhaps am incapable of arranging for you, a lyric upsurge, a cheerful little pat on the moral back."[21] The bourgeois attempt to construct a rational alternative to tradition has failed.

Notes

■

Introduction

1. The attempt to establish a convincing causal relation between text and context has proven to be an intellectual dead end. The "intellectual" history of ideas always seems abstract and disembodied from social reality, whereas the "social" history of ideas always threatens to reduce ideas to the conditions (usually material) that "produce" them. If the best kind of intellectual history has sought to avoid these extremes by insisting on the "dialectical" interrelation of text and context, then the limitations of this approach are suggested by Roberto Unger's damning rhetorical question, "What is it that the dialectic will not show?" On this issue, see Roberto Mangabeira Unger, *Knowledge and Politics* (1975), 15. My understanding of social science in general is deeply indebted to Unger's reading of modern liberal thought.

2. Richard J. Bernstein, *Beyond Objectivism and Relativism* (1985), 16, 17.

3. Here again I follow the general account of modern rationality found in Unger, *Knowledge and Politics*.

4. *Alan Swingewood, A Short History of Sociological Thought* (1991), 10, 79. On the priority of the instrumental relation between humans and things to substantive social relations between people in modern thought, see Louis Dumont, *From Mandeville to Marx* (1977), 5.

5. Swingewood, *Sociological Thought*, 11–13.

6. Ibid., 25, 27.

7. Unger, *Knowledge and Politics*, 153.

8. Henry F. May, *The Enlightenment in America* (1976), 337.

9. Thorstein Veblen, *The Theory of the Leisure Class* [1899, 1912] (1953), 111, 26.

10. For the best short account of the destabilization of received meanings within consumer capitalism, see Jean-Christophe Agnew, "The Consuming Vision of Henry James" (1983), 68–74.

11. See, for example, Daniel Bell, *The Cultural Contradictions of Capitalism* (1976).

12. My understanding of the place of the work ethic in Reformation thought draws on Charles Taylor, *Sources of the Self* (1989), 13, 14, 224.

13. On this conception of tradition, see Alasdair MacIntyre, *Three Rival Versions of Moral Enquiry* (1990), 63, 69.

Chapter 1. The Perspective of Workmanship

1. For these characterizations, see Dorothy Ross, *The Origins of American Social Science* (1991), 204; Daniel Aaron, *Men of Good Hope* (1951), 211–13; and David Riesman, *Thorstein Veblen* (1953), 44, 106.

2. Peter Dobkin Hall, *The Organization of American Culture, 1700–1900* (1984), 90.

3. For these characterizations, see in general Ross, *Origins of American Social Science;* Thomas Haskell, *The Emergence of Professional Social Science* (1977); Mary O. Furner, *Advocacy and Objectivity* (1975); Morton Gabriel White, *Social Thought in America* (1949).

4. John F. Kasson, *Civilizing the Machine* (1976), 4; James B. Gilbert, *Work without Salvation* (1977), vii. On the middle-class "crisis of work," see also Daniel T. Rodgers, *The Work Ethic in Industrial America, 1850–1920* (1978).

5. For this characterization of Veblen, see Ross, *Origins of American Social Science*, 213, 372. For Veblen's praise of technicians, see his *Engineers and the Price System* [1921]) 1965, 52.

6. This phrase comes from T. J. Jackson Lears, "Beyond Veblen: Rethinking Consumer Culture in America" (1989), 73–96.

7. Thorstein Veblen, *The Instinct of Workmanship and the State of the Industrial Arts* [1914] (1964), vii; henceforth *IW.*

8. Dumont, *From Mandeville to Marx,* 150, 100, 153, 99. On the opposition of the industrial and the pecuniary, see Ross, *Origins of American Social Science,* 210. On the significance of "production" to modern thought, see Jean Baudrillard, *The Mirror of Production* (1975).

9. On the priority of instrumentality to hierarchy in modern thought, see Dumont, *From Mandeville to Marx,,* 20.

10. John P. Diggins, *The Bard of Savagery* (1978).

11. Again, on the significance of this distinction, see Dumont, *From Mandeville to Marx,* 5.

12. See Thorstein Veblen, *The Theory of Business Enterprise* [1904] (1965); henceforth *TBE.*

13. See, for example, Martha Banta, "At Odds/In League" (1989), 203–72.

14. For a reading of the Arts and Crafts Movement as therapy, see T. J. Jackson Lears, *No Place of Grace* (1981), chap. 2.

15. Thorstein Veblen, "The Intellectual Pre-Eminence of Jews in Modern Europe" [1934] (1954), 223, henceforth "IPJE."

16. Thorstein Veblen, *The Higher Learning in America* [1918] 1954, 181; henceforth *HL.*

Chapter 2. *Middletown* as Transition

1. Dwight Hoover, "Middletown Again" (1990), 448.

2. John Madge, *The Origins of Scientific Sociology* (1962), 128.

3. Dwight Hoover, *Middletown Again*, 445, 446. On the events leading up to the Lynds' involvement with the Institute for Social and Religious Research, see in general Richard Wightman Fox, "Epitaph for Middletown" (1983), 101–42. On the centrality of ethnicity to the dominant schools of sociology in the 1920s, see Ross, *Origins of American Social Science*, 352, 321, 473.

4. Madge, *Origins of Scientific Sociology*, 126, 133. Dwight Hoover, "Middletown Again," 447. Maurice R. Stein, *The Eclipse of Community* (1960). On the rise of the small town in literature, see Christopher Lasch, *The True and Only Heaven* (1991), 85–103.

5. Robert S. Lynd and Helen Merrell Lynd, *Middletown* (1929), vi; subsequent page number citations are enclosed in parentheses.

6. On this, see Unger, *Knowledge and Politics*, 46, 47.

7. On medieval guild organization, see Anthony Black, *Guilds and Civil Society in European Political Thought from the Twelfth Century to the Present* (1984), 7–15.

8. On the rise of the notion of "solidarity" as the root of the social bond, see in general Jacques Donzelot, *L'Invention du social* (1984).

9. For an example of this characterization, see Fox, "Epitaph for Middletown."

10. On advice manuals, see Anthony Giddens, *Modernity and Self-Identity* (1991), 2.

11. Here we see the beginnings of the notion of "quality time."

12. In the case of movies, the social relation of technocracy manifests itself in the entire industry of commentary and criticism that has grown up alongside film during the twentieth century—from highbrow academic film studies departments, to mid-cult *New York Times* film criticism, to the mass-cult capsule movie reviews of *People Magazine*. In a world where reading is valued more than any particular thing read, movies tend to take on value the degree to which they are occasions for interpretation. The popularity of review shows such as *At the Movies* and *Siskel and Ebert* suggests how, in a technocracy, the act of criticizing a movie can actually take precedence over viewing the movie itself. People do not watch these shows simply as consumer guides to various movies, but as forms of entertainment in their own right.

Chapter 3. A New Individualism

1. John Dewey, *Individualism Old and New* (1930), 121; subsequent page number citations are enclosed in parentheses.

2. Tocqueville quoted in Steven Lukes, *Individualism* (1973), 3–4, 8, 11–13, 26.

3. Ibid.

4. On the idea of "possessive" individualism, see C. B. Macpherson, *The Political Theory of Possessive Individualism* (1962).

5. Henry David Thoreau, *Walden*, chap. 1, "Economy."

6. Ibid., 286.

7. Ibid.

8. Ibid., 287–88.

9. On the nineteenth-century opposition of "culture" and "society," see in general Raymond Williams, *Culture and Society, 1780–1950* (1958).

10. For a survey of social-democratic thought at the turn of the century, see James T. Kloppenberg, *Uncertain Victory* (1986).

11. See Ellis Hawley's untitled essay in *Herbert Hoover and the Crisis of American Capitalism*, edited by J. Joseph Huthmacher and Warren I. Susman (1973), 6.

12. On this formulation, see Herbert Croly, *The Promise of American Life* [1909] 1964, chap. 2.

13. Hawley, in *Herbert Hoover*, edited by Huthmacher and Susman 6, 8, 10, 16.

14. Herbert Hoover, *American Individualism* (1922), 45–46.

15. Ibid., 46, 47.

16. Ibid., 47.

17. Ibid., 10, 20–22, 37.

18. Ibid., 44, 64.

19. Ibid., 66, 70–71.

20. Robert B. Westbrook, *John Dewey and American Democracy* (1991), 557–58.

21. See in general Kloppenberg, *Uncertain Victory;* Cornel West, *The American Evasion of Philosophy* (1989); and Westbrook, *John Dewey and American Democracy.*

Chapter 4. Patterns of Control

1. See, for example, Warren I. Susman, "The Culture of the Thirties," in his *Culture as History* (1984), 153.

2. Ibid.

3. Williams, *Culture and Society,* xiv.

4. Ibid., 30.

5. Ibid., 130.

6. Ibid., xvi.

7. Ibid., 30.

8. George W. Stocking, Jr., "Matthew Arnold, E. B. Tylor, and the Uses of Invention," in his *Race, Culture, and Evolution* (1968), 89.

9. Williams, *Culture and Society,* 115.

10. Stocking, "Matthew Arnold, E. B. Taylor," in *Race, Culture, and Evolution,* 89.

11. Ibid.

12. Ibid., 80.

13. Stocking, "Franz Boas and the Culture Concept in Historical Perspective," in *Race, Culture, and Evolution,* 201.

14. Ibid., 225.

15. Ibid., 226.

16. Ibid., 227.

17. Richard Handler, "Boasian Anthropology and the Critique of American Culture" (1990), 252.

18. Susman, "The Culture of the Thirties," in *Culture as History,* 164.

19. Ruth Benedict, *Patterns of Culture* [1934] 1959, 48; subsequent page number citations are enclosed in parentheses.

20. Susman, "The Culture of the Thirties," in *Culture as History,* 168. For a critique of the culture concept as an ideology of "conformity," see Herbert Marcuse, *Eros and Civilization* (1955), Epilogue; and Christopher Lasch, *Haven in a Heartless World* (1977), chap. 4.

21. On the linking of freedom to culture, see Philip Gleason, "World War II and the Development of American Studies" (1984), 343–58.

22. For these characterizations, see Warren Susman's influential essay, " 'Personality' and the Making of Twentieth-Century Culture," in *Culture as History,* 271–85.

Chapter 5. Culture for What?

1. For this reading of *Knowledge for What?* see Richard Pells, *Radical Visions and American Dreams* (1973), 118.

2. Robert S. Lynd, *Knowledge for What?* (1940), 1; henceforth *KW.*

3. On this theme, see David B. Davis, "Some Themes of Counter-Subversion" (1960), 205–22; and Neil Harris, *Humbug* (1973), chap. 3. On the notion of "no secrets" with particular respect to social science, see William Leach, *True Love and Perfect Union* (1980), chap. 2.

4. See Fox, "Epitaph for Middletown."

5. On the ideology of separate spheres, see Nancy F. Cott, *The Bonds of Womanhood* (1977).

6. Robert S. Lynd and Helen Merrell Lynd, *Middletown in Transition: A Study in Cultural Conflicts* (1937), "Acknowledgments"; henceforth *MT.*

7. On being caught between two worlds as the American literary narrative of self, see Werner Sollors, *Beyond Ethnicity* (1986).

8. Susman, "The Culture of the Thirties," in *Culture as History*, 168.

9. Handler, "Boasian Anthropology," 253, 268. Handler focuses his study on Margaret Mead, but he sees her as representative of Boasian anthropology in general, so his assessment can be taken to include implicitly the work of Benedict as well.

10. For this argument, see William Stott, *Documentary Expression and Thirties America* (1973).

11. Peter Burke, *Popular Culture in Early Modern Europe* (1978), 286, 190.

12. Take, for example, the following quotation from Benedict: "None of the peoples we have discussed in this volume were studied in the field with any preconception of a consistent type of behaviour which that culture illustrated. The ethnology was set down as it came, with no attempt to make it self-consistent" (*Patterns of Culture*, 229).

13. For this characterization of the carnivalesque, see Lawrence W. Levine, *Highbrow/Lowbrow* (1988), 68.

14. Gleason, "Development of American Studies," 351.

15. Handler, "Boasian Anthropology," 261–64.

16. Margaret Mead, *And Keep Your Powder Dry* (1942), 255.

17. Hofstadter quoted in John Patrick Diggins, *The Proud Decades* (1988), 255. Robert F. Berkhofer, "Clio and the Culture Concept" (1973), 78.

18. See in general Louis Hartz, *The Liberal Tradition in America* (1955).

19. Berkhofer, "Clio and the Culture Concept," 89.

20. Richard Hofstadter, *The Age of Reform* (1955).

Chapter 6. The Sociological Imagination

1. Terance Ball, "The Politics of Social Science in Postwar America" (1989), 80–81.

2. Richard Gillam, "C. Wright Mills and the Politics of Truth" (1975), 460.

3. Ibid., 461.

4. For this interpretation, see in general Ball, "Politics of Social Science," 76–92.

5. The paradigm being what Richard Gillam has called the "Critical Ideal." See, in general, Richard Gillam, "Richard Hofstadter, C. Wright Mills, and 'the Critical Ideal' " (1977–78), 69–86.

6. C. Wright Mills, *The Sociological Imagination* (1959), 194; subsequent page number citations are enclosed in parentheses.

7. Mills, "The Conservative Mood," in *Power* (1963), 208.

8. Ibid.

9. Ibid. For the classic "consensus" dismissal of the prospect for true conservatism in America, see Hartz, *Liberal Tradition in America*.

10. Mills, "Liberal Values in the Modern World," in *Power*, 191.

11. Mills, "On Knowledge and Power," in *Power*, 599.

12. Mills, "Liberal Values," in *Power*, 191–94.

13. Walter Lippmann, *Drift and Mastery* [1914] 1961.

14. Mills, "Culture and Politics," in *Power*, 237–38.

15. Mills, "The Social Role of the Intellectual," in *Power*, 293.

16. Mills, "Culture and Politics," in *Power*, 244.

17. Irving Louis Horowitz, *C. Wright Mills* (1983), 316.

18. Ibid., 88.

19. Mills, "The Professional Ideology of Social Pathologists," in *Power*, 538.

20. Ibid., 536.

21. Ibid., 538–39.

22. See, for example, Horowitz, *C. Wright Mills*, 325.

23. Mills, "Professional Ideology," in *Power*, 536–37.

24. Mills, "Two Styles of Social Science Research," in *Power*, 563.

25. Mills, "Mass Media and Public Opinion," in *Power*, 586.

26. Edward A. Purcell, Jr., *The Crisis of Democratic Theory* (1973), 237.

27. Mills, "Mass Media," in *Power*, 579.

28. Mills, "Mass Society and Liberal Education," in *Power*, 358–59, Mills; "Mass Media," in *Power*, 580–81.

29. Mills, "Mass Media," in *Power*, 579.

30. See, for example, Horowitz, *C. Wright Mills*, 216.

31. Mills, "Mass Media," in *Power*, 587.

32. Ibid.

33. Richard Gillam, "*White Collar* from Start to Finish" (1981), 6.

34. Ibid., 7.

35. Ibid.

36. Mills, "Mass Media," in *Power*, 588.

37. Ibid., 586.

38. Ibid., 594.

39. Ibid., 590.

40. On this floating point as the essence of "the social," see again Donzelot, "L'Invention du social."

41. Mills, "The Cultural Apparatus," in *Power*, 405.

42. Ibid.

43. Ibid., 406.

44. For an example of Mills's relentless, self-consuming contextualizing, see his "Situated Actions and Vocabularies of Motive," in *Power*, 439–52.

45. Though not quite so reductive, for this kind of interpretation, see West, *American Evasion of Philosophy*, 131–32.

46. Lasch, *True and Only Heaven*, chap. 10.

47. Mills, "Liberal Values," in *Power,* 194.

48. Mills, "Mass Society," in *Power,* 367.

49. Mills, "The Structure of Power in American Society," in *Power,* 23.

50. On the "ethics of inarticulacy," see Taylor, *Sources of the Self,* chap. 3.

51. Horowitz, *C. Wright Mills,* 94–95.

52. See Taylor, part 3, "The Affirmation of Ordinary Life," in *Sources of the Self.*

53. See in general Max Weber, *The Protestant Ethic and the Spirit of Capitalism* (1958).

54. C. Wright Mills, *White Collar* (1951), 189.

55. Gillam, *"White Collar,"* 7.

56. See Ian Watt, *The Rise of the Novel* (1957), chap. 1.

57. Delmore Schwartz, "John Dos Passos and the Whole Truth" (1938), 365–66.

58. Mills, "Two Styles," in *Power,* 556–57.

59. Ibid.

Conclusion

1. Horowitz, *C. Wright Mills,* 106.

2. Gillam, "Richard Hofstadter," 84.

3. Ibid., 70, 73.

4. I base this characterization of Rorty on a series of articles he wrote in the mid-1980s: "The Contingency of Community" (1986), 10–14; "The Contingency of Language" (1986), 3–6; "The Contingency of Selfhood" (1986), 11–15; "Postmodernist Bourgeois Liberalism" (1983), 583–89; and "Solidarity or Objectivity?" (1984), 1–19. Rorty uses the phrase "aestheticized culture" in "The Contingency of Community," 11. These essays have since been revised and published in his *Contingency, Irony, and Solidarity* (1989).

5. Unger, *Knowledge and Politics,* 109, 111–13. In contrasting ambiguity to irony, let me be clear: Premodern ambiguity is not a deep, authentic use value to be played off against a superficial, bogus exchange value of modern irony. It is not a more complex kind of irony, nor is it a kind of "irony with a heart." Ambiguity is not simpler or more complex than irony; it stands for an incommensurably different form of simplicity and complexity.

6. Ibid.

7. Ibid.

8. MacIntyre, *Three Rival Versions,* 59–60.

9. Ibid., 60–61, 63, 69.

10. Lasch, *True and Only Heaven,* 27, 25, 29, 30, 27.

11. See in general Paul Boyer, *Urban Masses and Moral Order in America, 1820–1920* (1978).

12. See in general Joseph Haroutunian, *Piety versus Moralism* (1932).
13. Lasch uses this phrase in *True and Only Heaven*, 26.
14. Hannah Arendt, *The Human Condition* (1958), 16, 17, 134, 205, 265.
15. Ibid., 33, 288.
16. Ibid., 9.
17. Ibid., 62–63.
18. Michel Foucault, *The History of Sexuality* (1978), 1:136, 137, 139.
19. Arendt, *Human Condition*, 288.
20. Ibid., 9, 10.
21. C. Wright Mills, "Culture and Politics," in *Power*, 243.

Bibliography

■

Aaron, Daniel. *Men of Good Hope: A Story of American Progressives.* New York: Oxford University Press, 1951.

Agnew, Jean-Christophe. "The Consuming Vision of Henry James." In *The Culture of Consumption: Critical Essays in American History, 1880–1980*, edited by Richard Wightman Fox and T. J. Jackson Lears. New York: Pantheon Books, 1983.

Arendt, Hannah. *The Human Condition: A Study of the Central Dilemmas Facing Modern Man.* Chicago: University of Chicago Press, 1958.

Ball, Terence. "The Politics of Social Science in Postwar America." In *Recasting America: Culture and Politics in the Age of Cold War*, edited by Lary May. Chicago: University of Chicago Press, 1989.

Banta, Martha. "At Odds/In League: Brutality and Betterment in the Age of Taylor, Veblen, and Ford." *Prospects* 14 (1989): 203–72.

Baudrillard, Jean. *The Mirror of Production.* Translated and with an introduction by Mark Poster. St. Louis: Telos Press, 1975.

Bell, Daniel. *The Cultural Contradictions of Capitalism.* New York: Basic Books, 1976.

Benedict, Ruth. *Patterns of Culture.* Preface by Margaret Mead. Boston: Houghton Mifflin Co., [1934] 1959.

Bercovitch, Sacvan. *The American Jeremiad.* Madison: University of Wisconsin Press, 1978.

Berkhofer, Robert F. "Clio and the Culture Concept: Some Impressions of a Changing Relationship in American Historiography." In *The Idea of Culture in the Social Sciences*, edited by Louis Schneider and Charles Bonjean. Cambridge: Cambridge University Press, 1973.

Bernstein, Richard J. *Beyond Objectivism and Relativism: Science, Hermeneutics, and Praxis.* Philadelphia: University of Pennsylvania Press, 1985.

Black, Antony. *Guilds and Civil Society in European Political Thought from the Twelfth Century to the Present.* London: Methueun & Co., 1984.

Boyer, Paul. *Urban Masses and Moral Order in America, 1820–1920.* Cambridge: Harvard University Press, 1978.

Burke, Peter. *Popular Culture in Early Modern Europe.* New York: Harper & Row, 1978.

Bushman, Richard L. *From Puritan to Yankee: Character and Social Order in Connecticut, 1690–1765.* Cambridge: Harvard University Press, 1967.

Coser, Lewis A. *Men of Ideas.* New York: Free Press, 1970.

Cott, Nancy F. *The Bonds of Womanhood: "Women's Sphere" in New England, 1780–1835.* New Haven: Yale University Press, 1977.

Croly, Herbert. *The Promise of American Life.* Introduction by Cushing Strout. New York: Capricorn Books, [1909] 1964.

Davis, David B. "Some Themes of Counter-Subversion: An Analysis of Anti-Masonic, Anti-Catholic, and Anti-Mormon Literature." *Mississippi Valley Historical Review* 47 (September 1960): 205–22.

Dewey, John. *Individualism Old and New.* New York: Minton, Balch & Co., 1930.

Diggins, John P. *The Bard of Savagery: Thorstein Veblen and Modern Social Theory.* New York: Seabury Press, 1978.

———. *The Proud Decades: America in War and Peace, 1941–1960.* New York: W. W. Norton & Co., 1988.

Donzelot, Jacques. *L'Invention du social: Une essaie sur le passion politique.* Paris: Fayard, 1984.

Dumont, Louis. *From Mandeville to Marx: The Genesis and Triumph of Economic Ideology.* Chicago: University of Chicago Press, 1977.

Ellis, Joseph J. *After the Revolution: Profiles of Early American Culture.* New York: W. W. Norton & Co., 1979.

Foucault, Michel. *The History of Sexuality.* Vol. 1, *An Introduction.* Translated by Robert Hurley. New York: Random House, 1978.

Fox, Richard Wightman. "Epitaph for Middletown: Robert S. Lynd and the Analysis of Consumer Culture." In *The Culture of Consumption: Critical Essays in American History, 1880–1980,* edited by Richard Wightman Fox and T. J. Jackson Lears. New York: Pantheon Books, 1983.

Frederickson, George M. *The Inner Civil War: Northern Intellectuals and the Crisis of the Union.* New York: Harper & Row, 1965.

Furner, Mary O. *Advocacy and Objectivity: A Crisis in the Professionalization of American Social Science, 1865–1905.* Lexington: University of Kentucky Press, 1975.

Giddens, Anthony. *Modernity and Self-Identity: Self and Society in the Late Modern Age.* Stanford: Stanford University Press, 1991.

Gilbert, James B. *Work without Salvation: America's Intellectuals and Industrial Alienation, 1880–1910.* Baltimore: Johns Hopkins University Press, 1977.

Gillam, Richard. "C. Wright Mills and the Politics of Truth: *The Power Elite* Revisited." *American Quarterly* 27 (October 1975): 461–75.

———. "Richard Hofstadter, C. Wright Mills, and 'the Critical Ideal.' " *American Scholar* 47 (winter 1977–78): 69–86.

———. "*White Collar* from Start to Finish: C. Wright Mills in Transition." *Theory and Society* 10 (January 1981): 1–30.

Gleason, Philip. "World War II and the Development of American Studies." *American Quarterly* 36 (Bibliography, 1984): 343–58.

Hall, Peter Dobkin. *The Organization of American Culture, 1700–1900: Private Institutions, Elites, and the Origins of American Nationality.* New York: New York University Press, 1984.

Handler, Richard. "Boasian Anthropology and the Critique of American Culture." *American Quarterly* 42 (June 1990): 252–73.

Haroutunian, Joseph. *Piety versus Moralism: The Passing of the New England Theology.* New York: Henry Holt, 1932.

Harris, Neil. *Humbug: The Art of P. T. Barnum.* Chicago: University of Chicago Press, 1973.

Hartz, Louis. *The Liberal Tradition in America: An Interpretation of American Political Thought since the Revolution.* New York: Harcourt, Brace & Co., 1955.

Haskell, Thomas. *The Emergence of Professional Social Science: The American Social Science Association and the Nineteenth-Century Crisis of Authority.* Urbana: University of Illinois Press, 1977.

Hatch, Nathan O. *The Sacred Cause of Liberty: Republican Thought and the Millennium in Revolutionary New England.* New Haven: Yale University Press, 1977.

Henretta, James A. *The Evolution of American Society, 1700–1815: An Interdisciplinary Analysis.* Lexington: D. C. Heath and Co., 1973.

Hofstadter, Richard. *The Age of Reform: From Bryan to F.D.R.* New York: Alfred A. Knopf, 1955.

Hoover, Dwight. "Middletown Again." *Prospects* 15 (1990): 445–85.

Hoover, Herbert. *American Individualism.* New York: Doubleday, Page & Co., 1922.

Horowitz, Irving Louis. *C. Wright Mills: An American Utopian.* New York: Free Press, 1983.

Huthmacher, J. Joseph, and Warren I. Susman, eds. *Herbert Hoover and the Crisis of American Capitalism.* Cambridge: Schenkman Publishing Co., 1973.

Kasson, John F. *Civilizing the Machine: Technology and Republican Values in America, 1776–1900.* New York: Penguin Books, 1976.

King, John Owen, III. *The Iron of Melancholy: Structures of Spiritual Conversion in America from the Puritan Conscience to Victorian Neurosis.* Middletown: Wesleyan University Press, 1983.

Kloppenberg, James T. *Uncertain Victory: Social Democracy and Progressives in*

European and American Thought, 1870–1920. New York: Oxford University Press, 1986.

Kolko, Gabriel. *The Triumph of Conservatism: A Reinterpretation of American History, 1900–1916.* New York: Free Press, 1963.

Lasch, Christopher. *Haven in a Heartless World: The Family Besieged.* New York: Basic Books, 1977.

———. *The True and Only Heaven: Progress and Its Critics.* New York: W. W. Norton & Co., 1991.

Leach, William. *True Love and Perfect Union: The Feminist Reform of Sex and Society.* New York: Basic Books, 1980.

Lears, T. J. Jackson. *No Place of Grace: Antimodernism and the Transformation of American Culture, 1880–1920.* New York: Pantheon Books, 1981.

———. "Beyond Veblen: Rethinking Consumer Culture in America." In *Consuming Visions: Accumulation and Display of Goods in America, 1880–1920,* edited by Simon J. Bronner. New York: W. W. Norton & Co., 1989.

Levine, Lawrence W. *Highbrow/Lowbrow: The Emergence of Cultural Hierarchy in America.* Cambridge: Harvard University Press, 1988.

Lippmann, Walter. *Drift and Mastery: An Attempt to Diagnose the Current Unrest.* Englewood Cliffs: Prentice Hall, [1914] 1961.

Lukes, Steven. *Individualism.* New York: Harper & Row, 1973.

Lynd, Robert S. *Knowledge for What? The Place of Social Science in American Culture.* Princeton: Princeton University Press, 1940.

Lynd, Robert S., and Helen Merrell Lynd. *Middletown: A Study in American Culture.* New York: Harcourt Brace & Co., 1929.

———. *Middletown in Transition: A Study in Cultural Conflicts.* New York: Harcourt, Brace & World, 1937.

MacIntyre, Alasdair. *Three Rival Versions of Moral Enquiry: Encyclopedia, Genealogy, and Tradition.* Notre Dame: University of Notre Dame Press, 1990.

———. *After Virtue: A Study in Moral Theory.* Notre Dame: University of Notre Dame Press, 1981.

Macpherson, C. B. *The Political Theory of Possessive Individualism.* London: Oxford University Press, 1962.

Madge, John. *The Origins of Scientific Sociology.* New York: Free Press of Glencoe, 1962.

Marcuse, Herbert. *Eros and Civilization.* Boston: Beacon Press, 1955.

May, Henry F. *The Enlightenment in America.* New York: Oxford University Press, 1976.

Mead, Margaret. *And Keep Your Powder Dry: An Anthropologist Looks at America.* New York: William Morrow and Co., 1942.

Mills, C. Wright. *White Collar: The American Middle Classes.* New York: Oxford University Press, 1951.

———. *The Sociological Imagination.* New York: Oxford University Press, 1959.

———. *Power, Politics, and People: The Collected Essays of C. Wright Mills.* Edited with an introduction by Irving Louis Horowitz. New York: Oxford University Press, 1963.

Pells, Richard. *Radical Visions and American Dreams: Culture and Social Thought in the Depression Years.* Middletown: Wesleyan University Press, 1973.

Polanyi, Karl. *The Great Transformation.* Boston: Beacon Press, 1957.

Purcell, Edward A., Jr. *The Crisis of Democratic Theory: Scientific Naturalism and the Problem of Value.* Lexington: University of Kentucky Press, 1973.

Riesman, David. *Thorstein Veblen: A Critical Interpretation.* New York: Charles Scribner's Sons, 1953.

Rodgers, Daniel T. *The Work Ethic in Industrial America, 1850–1920.* Chicago: University of Chicago Press, 1978.

Rorty, Richard. "Postmodernist Bourgeois Liberalism." *Journal of Philosophy* 80, no. 10 (1983): 583–89.

———. "Solidarity or Objectivity?" *Nanzan Review of American Studies* 6 (1984): 1–19.

———. "The Contingency of Language." *London Review of Books* (17 April 1986): 3–6.

———. "The Contingency of Selfhood." *London Review of Books* (8 May 1986): 11–15.

———. "The Contingency of Community." *London Review of Books* (4 July 1986): 10–14.

———. *Contingency, Irony, and Solidarity.* Cambridge: Cambridge University Press, 1989.

Ross, Dorothy. *The Origins of American Social Science.* Cambridge: Cambridge University Press, 1991.

Schwartz, Delmore. "John Dos Passos and the Whole Truth." *Southern Review* 4 (October 1938): 351–81.

Sollors, Werner. *Beyond Ethnicity: Consent and Descent in American Culture.* New York: Oxford University Press, 1986.

Stein, Maurice R. *The Eclipse of Community: An Interpretation of American Studies.* New York: Harper & Row, 1960.

Stocking, George W., Jr. *Race, Culture, and Evolution.* New York: Free Press, 1968.

Stott, William. *Documentary Expression and Thirties America.* Chicago: University of Chicago Press, 1973.

Susman, Warren I. *Culture as History: The Transformation of American Society in the Twentieth Century.* New York: Pantheon Books, 1984.

Swingewood, Alan. *A Short History of Sociological Thought.* London: Macmillan, 1991.

Taylor, Charles. *Sources of the Self: The Making of Modern Identity.* Cambridge: Harvard University Press, 1989.

Thoreau, Henry David. *Walden and Other Writings.* Edited by William Howarth. Modern Library. New York: Random House, 1981.

Turner, James. *Without God, Without Creed: The Origins of Unbelief in America.* Baltimore: Johns Hopkins University Press, 1985.

Unger, Roberto Mangabeira. *Knowledge and Politics.* New York: Free Press, 1975.

Veblen, Thorstein. *The Theory of the Leisure Class: An Economic Study of Institutions.* Introduction by C. Wright Mills. New American Library. New York: Macmillan Co., 1899, 1912. Reprint, New York: Mentor Books, 1953.

———. *The Theory of Business Enterprise.* New York: A. M. Kelly, [1904] 1965.

———. "The Place of Science in Modern Civilization." *American Journal of Sociology* 11 (March 1906): 585–609.

———. *The Instinct of Workmanship and the State of the Industrial Arts.* Introduction by Joseph Dorfman. New York: Macmillan Co., [1914] 1964.

———. *The Higher Learning in America: A Memorandum on the Conduct of Universities by Business Men.* Introduction by David Riesman. Stanford: Academic Reprints, [1918] 1954.

———. *Engineers and the Price System.* New York: Viking Press, [1921] 1965.

———. "The Intellectual Pre-Eminence of Jews in Modern Europe." In *Essays in Our Changing Order,* edited by Leon Ardrooni. New York: Viking Press, [1934] 1954.

Vidich, Arthur J., and Stanford M. Lyman. *American Sociology: Worldly Rejections of Religion and Their Directions.* New Haven: Yale University Press, 1985.

Watt, Ian. *The Rise of the Novel: Studies in Defoe, Richardson, and Fielding.* Berkeley: University of California Press, 1957.

Weber, Max. *The Protestant Ethic and the Spirit of Capitalism.* Translated by Talcott Parsons, with a foreword by R. H. Tawney. New York: Charles Scribner's Sons, 1958.

Weinstein, James. *The Corporate Ideal in the Liberal State, 1900–1918.* Boston: Beacon Press, 1968.

West, Cornel. *The American Evasion of Philosophy: A Genealogy of Pragmatism.* Madison: University of Wisconsin Press, 1989.

Westbrook, Robert B. *John Dewey and American Democracy.* Ithaca: Cornell University Press, 1991.

White, Morton Gabriel. *Social Thought in America: The Revolt against Formalism.* New York: Viking Press, 1949.

Williams, Raymond. *Culture and Society, 1780–1950.* New York: Harper & Row, 1958.

Index

∎

critical thought, xv, 18, 22, 24–25,
96
Croly, Herbert, 68
"Cultural Apparatus, The" (Mills),
155
culture, xi, 91–104; and critical consciousness, ix, 90, 96, 103–104,
124–27; Dewey's definition of, 64,
86; history of the idea of, 87–90;
and lag, 7, 44, 60, 64, 97; Mills on,
145–46; progressivism and, 62; society and, 67; teleology and, 106,
128; Veblen's conception of, xiv, 3,
6–9, 19, 21
"Culture and Politics" (Mills), 175,
188

democracy, ix, 22, 63, 108, 113–14,
135, 159, 163–66, 187
depth, psychological, 37–38, 67, 109–
10, 152
Descartes, René, xi–xii
desire, 111–13
determinism, 95
Dewey, John, ix, xv, 22, 31, 62–64,
87, 91, 101, 106, 145, 156, 162,
177
Diggins, John Patrick, 7
divorce, 50–51, 63
documentary, social, 125–27
Drift and Mastery (Lippmann), 137
Durkheim, Emile, 171, 179

economics: classical, xii–xiii, 44–45,
62, 86, 111, 115, 130; and culture
concept, 97–101; and professionalization, 1; and science, 83
Edwards, Jonathan, 182–83
egalitarianism, 63, 84, 86
Emerson, Ralph Waldo, 124, 154
emotions, and social life, 83–84, 114
Enlightenment, xi–xiii, xv, 176, 177,
182; and antinomies of bourgeois
thought, 21; and culture concept,
88; place in Mills's thought, 158–
59, 161; Veblen's account of, 13

Enormous Room, The (cummings),
168
ethics, 111, 166
everyday life, 60, 125, 152
evolution, 2, 4–5, 7, 85, 88, 91, 94–
95
experts, 112–13, 124

Gemeinschaft and Gesellschaft, 128
Gestalt psychology, 92
Gilbreth, Frank, 38
Gillam, Richard, 133, 152, 176
grand theory, 135, 147, 148, 168, 174
Great Depression, 105, 125
guilds, 9–12, 40–42

handicraft, era of, 9–16
Hartz, Louis, 129
hierarchy, 84
Higher Learning in America, The (Veblen), 25
history, ix, 5, 21; and culture, 94–95;
and narrative, 7, 21, 22; Mills's conception of, 138, 164–65; Veblen's
conception of, 5–7, 10, 11, 18–19
Hobbes, Thomas, xii, 45
Hofstadter, Richard, 129–31, 176
Hoover, Herbert, 68–70, 101, 103
Horowitz, Irving Louis, 166, 176
human nature, 96
human variety, the, 149
humanism, ix, 3, 38, 77, 96, 123, 136,
139, 144, 147, 160, 169, 178
hybridization: definition of, 6–7; ideal
of selfhood, 23–25

identity, and culture, 93
independence, as a social relation, 42–
43, 53–54, 57–58, 102
individual, the, xiv, 11, 23–24, 29,
44–45, 48–49, 58–59
individualism: and culture, 87; history
of, 64–70; and planning, 45; possessive, 65, 131
Individualism Old and New (Dewey):
advertising, 75; business, 63–64,

Books in the Series

■

Without God, Without Creed: The Origins of Unbelief in America
James Turner

From Colonies to Commonwealth: Familial Ideology and the Beginnings of the American Republic
Melvin Yazawa

The Morality of Spending: Attitudes toward the Consumer Society in America, 1875–1940
Daniel Horowitz

Masters and Statesmen: The Political Culture of American Slavery
Kenneth S. Greenberg

Scholarly Means to Evangelical Ends: The New Haven Scholars and the Transformation of Higher Learning in America, 1830–1890
Louise L. Stevenson

The New Urban Landscape: The Redefinition of City Form in Nineteenth-Century America
David Schuyler

Intimacy and Power in the Old South: Ritual in the Lives of the Planters
Steven Stowe

The Republic Reborn: War and the Making of Liberal America, 1790–1820
Steven Watts

Consciousness in New England: From Puritanism and Ideas to Psychoanalysis and Semiotic
James Hoopes

William James, Public Philosopher
George Cotkin

A Consuming Faith: The Social Gospel and Modern American Culture
Susan Curtis

Paradox Lost: Free Will and Political Liberty in American Culture, 1630–1760
Jon Pahl

Sublime Thoughts/Penny Wisdom: Situating Emerson and Thoreau in the American Market
Richard F. Teichgraeber III

Conspicuous Criticism: Tradition, the Individual, and Culture in American Social Thought, from Veblen to Mills
Christopher Shannon

Library of Congress Cataloging-in-Publication Data

Shannon, Christopher, 1962–
  Conspicuous criticism : tradition, the individual, and culture in American
social thought, from Veblen to Mills / Christopher Shannon.
      p.   cm.—(New studies in American intellectual and cultural history)
Includes bibliographical references and index.
ISBN 0-8018-5151-3 (hc : alk. paper)
  1. Social sciences—United States—History—20th century.   2. Social
scientists—United States—History—20th century.   3. United States—Study
and teaching—History—20th century.   4. Americanists—History—
20th century.   5. Intellectuals—United States—History—20th
century.   6. Individualism—United States—History—20th
century.   7. Culture—Study and teaching—United States—History—
20th century.   8. United States—Social conditions.
I. Title.   II. Series.
H53.U5S5   1996
303.3'72'0973—dc20   95-18525